MATRIX STRUCTURED
IMAGE PROCESSING

EDWARD R. DOUGHERTY, Ph.D.

Fairleigh Dickinson University

CHARLES R. GIARDINA, Ph.D.

Stevens Institute of Technology

Prentice-Hall, Inc., Englewood Cliffs, New Jersey 07632

Library of Congress Cataloging-in-Publication Data

Dougherty, Edward R.   (date)
    Matrix structured image processing.

    Includes index.
    1. Image processing—Digital techniques.
2. Computer vision.   I. Giardina, Charles Robert.
II. Title.
TA1632.G53   1987   006.3'7   86-12374
ISBN   0-13-565623-0

Editorial/production supervision and
   interior design: Gloria Jordan
Cover design: George Cornell
Manufacturing buyer: Ed O'Dougherty

Printed in the United States of America

10   9   8   7   6   5   4   3   2   1

ISBN   0-13-565623-0   025

Prentice-Hall International (UK) Limited, *London*
Prentice-Hall of Australia Pty. Limited, *Sydney*
Prentice-Hall Canada Inc., *Toronto*
Prentice-Hall Hispanoamericana, S.A., *Mexico*
Prentice-Hall of India Private Limited, *New Delhi*
Prentice-Hall of Japan, Inc., *Tokyo*
Prentice-Hall of Southeast Asia Pte. Ltd., *Singapore*
Editora Prentice-Hall do Brasil, Ltda., *Rio de Janeiro*

To our wives, Terry and Betty

CONTENTS

PREFACE

Because of the necessity to provide computers with the ability to make "intelligent" decisions concerning visual data, the relatively new field of digital image processing has undergone a substantial growth spurt during the past twenty years. As is often the case in the scientific quest for new knowledge, the organization of that knowledge and its concomitant accessibility to investigators in related fields receives insufficient attention. It is our hope that this book will help rectify the situation.

It is easy to put into succinct terms the rationale behind our approach: to embed existing digital imaging techniques into a consistent and unified mathematical framework, and to accomplish this task at a level accessible to upper division undergraduates and beginning graduate students in computer science, engineering, the physical sciences, and those other areas of contemporary technology where computer-assisted analysis of digital images plays a central role.

To reach this goal, we introduce at the outset a mathematical structure, to be employed throughout the text, for the representation of digital images. This structure, the "bound matrix," is used in conjunction with block diagrams to serve as a vehicle for the concise expression of digital image processing operators. While we do not present rigorous mathematical proofs, the definitions are precise and the properties given are exactly expressed so that implementation and application can be accomplished in a systematic fashion.

Throughout the text there is an abundance of illustrative examples to help students "walk through" the imaging algorithms. We believe that methodology must always remain in a "how to" mode, allowing students to gain a working knowledge of fundamental image processing procedures. Our desire was not to write an encyclopedia of imaging operations; rather, we wanted to give a representative selection of techniques at an implementable level.

The concept of a digital image, together with its bound matrix representation, is given in Chapter 1. That chapter also includes primitive mathematical operations on bound matrices from which digital image processing algorithms are composed. Fundamental gray-level processing procedures are discussed in Chapter 2.

Edge detection is introduced in Chapter 3. The emphasis is on the Prewitt, Sobel, Roberts and other gradient-type detectors. Compass gradient techniques such as the Kirsh are also presented.

In Chapter 4, the elements of morphology are presented. Because of its intuitive geometric character and the relatively fast processing speed of its underlying operators, morphology is becoming evermore important in digital image processing. This chapter also details basic Minkowski algebra as well as its essential properties. It also introduces size distributions, morphological covariance, and the skeleton.

Versions of the well-known tracking, region growing, curve filling, and template matching methodologies are given in Chapter 5. These are presented in terms of precise specifications within the bound matrix structure. Detailed walk-throughs are provided.

A major topic in any discussion of image processing is transforms. The concept of a matrix image transform is introduced in Chapter 6 for a systematic presentation. Among the topics covered are the DFT, cyclic convolutions, the Hadamard transform, and the singular value decomposition transform.

The last chapter presents novel computer architectures well-suited to the natural structure of digital images and to operations on those images. Data flow, systolic and wavefront array systems are explained. Matrix multiplication, which plays a crucial role in image transform methodology, is implemented using both a systolic system and a wavefront array.

Insofar as prerequisites for the text are concerned, they are minimal. Except for some knowledge of matrix theory, no specific mathematical, engineering, or computer science background is required. Nonetheless, some sophistication with regard to algorithm development and computer implementation would be helpful.

Edward R. Dougherty
Fairleigh Dickinson University

Charles R. Giardina
Stevens Institute of Technology

INTRODUCTION

What Does It Mean to Form an Image?

Perhaps the best way to understand the problems and goals that constitute the subject of image processing is to reflect on our own human vision system. Although visual sensation, object recognition, and the decision for action seem almost instantaneous, the complexity of the process is to this day beyond full comprehension. Imagine a batter awaiting the pitch that will momentarily arrive from the mound. In a fraction of a second, a stringent real-time constraint, the following must be accomplished:

1) Visual sensors, the batter's eyes, must *sense* the reflected light coming from the ball.

2) This purely physical sensory data must be organized into an *image*; the image must be *created*.

3) The image must be *cleaned up*; it must be preprocessed so as to yield an image that is not distorted by the act of sensation. The image must be *restored* to some "perfect" image that, by experience, the batter believes it to be. For example, he expects a ball to be coming toward him, and he must restore the image so that *noisy* interference such as light or fog do not result in something other than a ball.

4) The image is *enhanced* so that the ball stands out more starkly from the background.

5) The enhanced image is *segmented*; the ball is cut from the rest of the image except insofar as the background is necessary to determine the speed and trajectory of the ball.

6) Fundamental *features* of the image are *selected* and perhaps computed. *Compression* takes place in that extraneous information, that which is not required for the task at hand (hitting the ball), is filtered out and removed from further processing by the brain.

7) The position and internal data of the batter himself are *registered* and *linked* to the image. The complexity of this step is extreme in that the new knowledge concerning the image must be combined with the batter's self-knowledge of himself, including his own inertial system.

8) The total image must be *classified*; for example, the type of pitch, such as a curve ball, fast ball, or slider, must be determined.

9) A *decision*, or a complex of decisions, must be made, for example, to swing or not to swing, where to swing, and how hard to swing.

To fully appreciate the enormity of the task faced by any vision system, one should recognize that each of these stages consists of numerous substages, all to be accomplished in less than a second!

The purpose and overall logical structure of a computer vision system are essentially the same as for the human vision system; indeed, our approach to the problem of artificial vision systems naturally follows the conception we have of our own vision system. It could not be otherwise, for the manner in which we frame our understanding of optical intelligence can only arise from reflection on and investigation of that unique system in which vision and human intelligence are linked, the human vision system. Image understanding, as it applies to artificial systems, must utilize the notions of shape, texture, edge, and position, among others, that are common to human comprehension. It is precisely these categories to which we refer when we make decisions based on optical data. Not only must incoming data be represented digitally in a computer vision system, but they must also be organized into configurations and categories that model those arising naturally in the human being.

At one time it was thought that the human vision system was essentially passive. Sensation was not clearly distinguished from perception. The role of the brain in the constitution of the image was overlooked, and the perceived image was thought to be a faithful copy of the "actual" image. Today we realize that the "actual" image is not a subject of scientific investigation. All systems create images from the data of sensation. While it is true that we naturally hold out our Euclidean imaging system as the standard, it is important to keep in mind that ours is only one model among many. All scientific endeavor is anthropocentric in that it takes place relative to the sense data received by human beings; nevertheless, an artificial system is artificial only insofar as it is not human. It too must be equipped with sensors, it too must process the initial image, and it too must classify and decide based on heuristic criteria established independently of any particular bundle of sensations.

Four Levels of Image Processing

To begin, we would like to identify four macrolevels of image processing:

0) Image representation
1) Image-to-image transformations
2) Image-to-parameter (image-to-real number) transformations
3) Parameter-to-decision transformations

At level 0, we encounter the problem of digital representation. The sensed data must be organized into a data structure compatible with the digital nature of the computer. Even if we are to work only with black and white pictures, an assumption that will be made throughout this text, human perception seemingly involves a continuously changing level of gray, whereas the computer can hold only discrete gray levels. Moreover, if we look at a two-dimensional photograph, it appears as though the space upon which the gray-level values are defined is a Euclidean plane. In other words, it appears that a two-dimensional black and white image should be represented by a function $I = f(x, y)$, where the position in the plane is given by the coordinate pair (x, y) and the gray-level intensity I is a real number.

At once two difficulties arise. First, there is the problem of *quantization*; what discrete values of I should be allowed? Second, there is the problem of *digitization*; how should we choose some finite number of coordinate pairs (x, y) at which to specify the intensities of the image? In simple terms, how should the image be created from the data so that it still maintains the optical properties necessary for an acceptable modeling of the human image? Later we shall give an account of digital image representation; however, the *sampling problem*, that is, how to choose quantization and digitization levels, is essentially beyond the level of this book.

Level 1 involves image-to-image operations, for instance, those that occur in restoration, enhancement, and segmentation. At level 1, most processing takes place, and it is with this level that most of this text is concerned. Fundamental to the implementation of the algorithms involved in image-to-image transformations is a precise, rigorously defined mathematical structure. This structure must allow the specification of unambiguous image operations, and it should be designed to facilitate the development of both imaging languages and imaging architectures. For this purpose the notion of *bound matrices* is introduced in Section 1.3, and the corresponding definitions of low-level imaging operations are developed throughout the remainder of Chapter 1.

Once an image has been prepared for the extraction of information, processing must occur that results in the establishment of parameters that give quantitative specification of the information. There may be several different parameters, or sets of parameters, each related to a particular feature of the image. We refer to an array of such parameters as a *feature vector*. In a sense, our scientific understanding of the image is encoded in the feature parameters we have extracted from the image. Operations that result in feature parameters are the level 2 transformations. Examples of such transformations are the textural descriptors of mathematical morphology, which are described in Chapter 4.

Once quantitative knowledge has been extracted from the image in the form of parameters, logical decisions can be implemented. The chain is now complete. The image, which was originally constituted from incoming sensory data, is now classified, and a decision is made as a result of this classification. Such logical transformations belong to level 3. What is desired is identification of the image as a member of a predetermined finite class of candidates; for example, the image is a square and not a triangle or circle. Based on this classification, a knowledge-based decision to choose one of a number of actions is taken. The transformations at this level are problematic in that they require a goodly amount of preprogrammed heuristics. They always involve some degree of uncertainty owing to the earlier quantization and digitization modeling and to the multiple levels of processing that have already occurred. However, keep in mind that this uncertainty is no different from the uncertainty faced by any human attempting to decide between several alternatives. That decision, too, is affected by the accuracy of the visual model, the completeness of the knowledge base, and the quality of the optical processing.

Computer Vision

Our thrust has been in the direction of recognition and decision. The goal of the text is to introduce fundamental digital techniques that lead to the formation of quantitative knowledge parameters and to quantitative decision techniques, the latter being central to the development of artificially intelligent systems. The nine stages of processing introduced metaphorically for the baseball batter constitute the stages of a *recognizer* system. An image of a three-dimensional set of objects is obtained, and the recognizer must decide whether or not some prespecified object is a member of the set. Moreover, all the processing must be accomplished in real time; that is, the absolute difference in time from when the object is sensed to when a decision is made must be less than some prespecified amount. This prespecified amount of time may change from application to application, but whatever it might be, the predetermined time line cannot be exceeded.

Whether or not a given object can be detected in real time by only processing imaging information is problematic; detection capability is a function of numerous factors. Among them are the overall set of objects that might be viewed, their similarity to the object one wishes to detect, the different possible aspect angles used in viewing the object (the more angles, the greater the difficulty of identification), the type of sensors involved, the amount of distortion and noise, the algorithms and procedures employed, the architecture of the computer being utilized, the specific real-time constraint, and the confidence level required for making a final decision.

An ideal recognizer system is depicted in Figure I.1. In an ideal system, we suppose that a set of objects is observed by a perfect imaging sensor. This sensor might utilize an optical technique such as a camera, or it might sense the heat as in an infrared (IR) sensor, or it might sense the illumination as in a synthetic aperture radar (SAR). In any event, the sensor is assumed to be perfect in that it results in an image without noise or distortion. In fact, such assumptions are not realistic. No sensor is perfect.

A more realistic scenario is depicted in Figure I.2, where one can recognize the nine stages given earlier for the batter. Usually the image is *created* by a mathematical

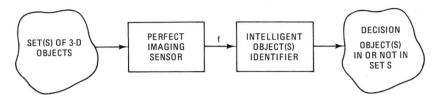

Figure I.1 Object Recognizer Using Imaging

procedure applied to the incoming sense data. It may be cleaned up, or *restored*, by processing it so as to produce an estimate of the perfect image. It may be *enhanced* to make more definitive those features of the image that are key for future processing. Once enhanced, the image is often *segmented* into mutually exclusive pieces that are easier to process and recognize in subsequent object identification procedures. Features are *selected* that are useful for classification. Since the sensor itself does not represent an absolute frame of reference, its relevant aspects, such as velocity and attitude, must be *registered*. These sensory data must be coordinated with the image data. Finally, before decision procedures can be implemented, *classification* operations must take place. For instance, the segmented objects in the image may be checked against a predetermined class of objects to see if a desired object is present, or an estimate of the location and velocity of an object within the image may be computed. In any case, a large number of steps is involved from integration of the object by the sensors to making the actual *detection decision*.

A digital computer that performs the preceding steps in real time must usually have an architecture that is custom-made or developed in accordance with the algorithms that perform the functions associated with each of these blocks. An in-depth account of relevant architectures is given in Chapter 7. For the interim, however, consider Figure I.3. In this diagram the digital processor is a multiple-instruction, multiple-data (MIMD) or a combined single-instruction, multiple-data (SIMD) and multiple-instruction, single-data (MISD) type of processor. These processors may make use of pipelining and array processing. In addition, they are configured to increase the throughput and thereby possibly meet the real-time constraints of the image-processing system.

In the succeeding chapters, we shall develop a precise structure for image representation and utilize certain fundamental imaging operations to implement higher-level procedures that accomplish many of the tasks outlined. It is not our purpose to give an encyclopedia of imaging operations, but rather to illustrate a representative collection of transformations that lead to artificially intelligent image analysis. As noted earlier, the roles of humanly understood concepts, such as shape and texture, are central, as are the procedures that result in the implementation of the stages in Figure I.2.

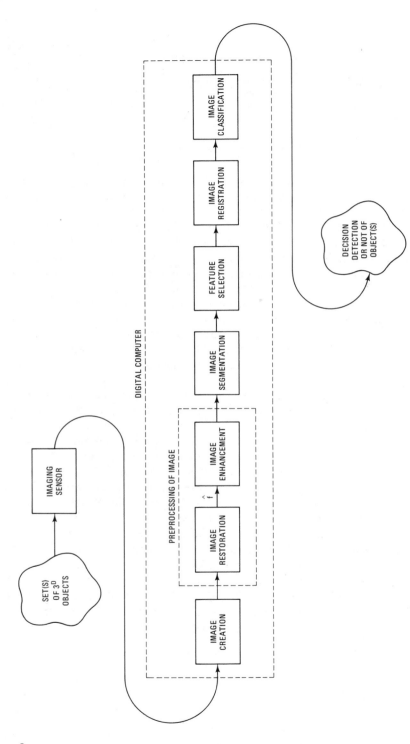

Figure I.2 Imaging Operations for Recognizer

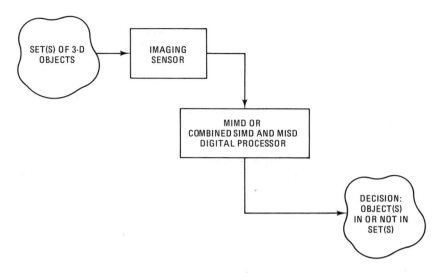

Figure I.3 Digital Object Recognizer

1

IMAGE-PROCESSING
OPERATIONS

In this chapter the notion of a digital image is introduced. It is presented together with a representation structure called a *bound matrix*. The operations which are fundamental to the processing of images are defined and illustrated. These operations are the building blocks from which important image-processing transformations are formed.

1.1 Digital Images

A digital image is similar to a matrix or array of numbers. It is a useful vehicle for representing pictures and is well suited for digital machines. Before the actual definition is given, an example will be presented to furnish motivation.[1]

Consider a television set with a fixed, nonchanging square picture. A digital image representing this picture is desired. A sensor, in the form of a light meter, is provided to help in the determination of this image. The meter has integral readings from 0 to $2^n - 1$, where 0 denotes white and $2^n - 1$ denotes black. The intermediate numbers constitute a scale running from light to dark, with the light values near 0 and the dark values near $2^n - 1$. To obtain the digital image, partition the television screen into 2^n smaller squares. This might be accomplished by drawing equidistant vertical and horizontal lines on the screen. Next, on a large piece of opaque material such as cardboard, cut a square hole equal in size to a single small square on the screen. Then place the opaque material and the light meter at a fixed distance from the screen. Finally, take 2^n

---

[1]From G. T. Herman, *Image Reconstruction from Projection*, Academic Press, Inc., New York, 1980.

readings from the light meter by moving the opaque material 2^n times, once for each time a small square area on the screen and the hole coincide.

In our example, each small square is called a *pixel*, which is an abbreviation for *picture element*. The collection of readings taken with the light meter is a mapping performed on the set of 2^n pixels. The set of all pixels, each with a number between 0 and $2^n - 1$ attached, is an example of a digital image.

To make the preceding notions more precise, consider the xy plane as being partitioned into square regions, much like graph paper, with each square *centered* at a lattice point (i, j), i and j in the set Z of integers. As in the previous example, each square centered at a lattice point is called a pixel, with the square centered at (i, j) being called the (i, j)th pixel. The set of all lattice points is denoted by $Z \times Z$. A digital image is obtained by assigning to each pixel a value, called a *gray value*, between 0 and $2^n - 1$. Depending on the application, the number of gray values may be as small as 2 ($n = 1$) or 4 ($n = 2$), or as large as 256 ($n = 8$). Sometimes negative or noninteger values are used to denote levels of gray. Consequently, it will often be convenient to denote gray levels using values in the set of real numbers. In any event, it is always assumed that larger gray values denote darker shades of gray.

Finally, a digital image is almost always obtained by assigning values of gray to some but not all pixels. The television example is a case in point. Only 2^n pixels were assigned gray values, while all the rest (an infinite number outside the TV screen) were ignored. As a result, a digital image f, or *image* for short, is defined as a function $f:D \to R$, where D is a subset of the set of all lattice points $Z \times Z$ and R is the set of real numbers. D is the *domain* of the image f, and R is the *codomain*. Sometimes the notation D_f will be employed to denote the domain of f.

Notice the subtle change near the end of the previous paragraph. Whereas previously we spoke as if the small squares carried the gray values, suddenly an image was defined as a function on the lattice points. Mathematically, this change was necessary, since the lattice points are addresses of the small squares. Therefore, even though the small squares are technically the pixels, the lattice points will frequently be referred to as pixels. This slight abuse of terminology is of no consequence since it is unlikely to lead to any confusion.

1.2 Representation of Digital Images

Usually the domain D of a digital image f will be rectangular in shape and contain a finite number of elements. In such a case, a digital image will be represented in a manner similar to a matrix or a two-dimensional array. The image will have a gray value for each position (specified by a row number and column number) within the array. However, unlike a conventional matrix, the matrix representation of an image must have a location within the set of lattice points $Z \times Z$. Some of these concepts will now be illustrated in Example 1.1.

Example 1.1

Consider the digital image f illustrated in Figure 1.1. The domain consists of the six pixels darkly outlined. Rigorously, the image $f:D \rightarrow R$, where $D = \{(i, j): i = 0, 1 \text{ and } j = -1, 0, 1\}$. The gray value at (i, j) in D [denoted $(i, j) \in D$] is $f((i, j))$ or, more conveniently, $f(i, j)$. Thus $f(0, 0) = 2, f(0, -1) = 0, f(1, -1) = -3, f(1, 0) = 4, f(0, 1) = 3$, and $f(1, 1) = 5$.

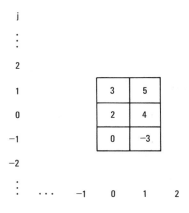

Figure 1.1 Image with Six Pixels in Domain

It will be convenient to use matrix notation to represent finite digital images with *rectangular domains*. For the image f of Example 1.1, the matrix representation is

$$f = \begin{pmatrix} 3 & 5 \\ ② & 4 \\ 0 & -3 \end{pmatrix} \quad \text{or equivalently} \quad f = \begin{pmatrix} 3 & 5 \\ 2 & 4 \\ 0 & -3 \end{pmatrix}_{0,\,1}$$

Both representations of f are examples of bound matrices, a topic to be more formally introduced in Section 1.3. In the first representation, the element of the matrix corresponding to the $(0, 0)$ lattice point of the xy coordinate system is circled. This means that the gray level denoted by 2, which occurs in the second row, first column, is the number indicating the gray value assigned to pixel $(0, 0)$, the origin. The values for other pixels in D are determined by positioning the matrix at the specified $(0, 0)$ location and reading off the corresponding matrix values.

In the second matrix representation for f, the two subscripted integers outside the lower-right part of the matrix specify the absolute location in the xy lattice of the uppermost, leftmost entry in the matrix. In other words, the first row, first column entry of the matrix is positioned at $(0, 1)$: $f(0, 1) = 3$. It is as if the matrix were to be "hung" on the $(0, 1)$ "peg" of the lattice, with the "slot" for hanging being through the first row, first column entry of the matrix.

A matrix representation can be constructed for any finite digital image with rectangular type domain D. The matrix involved will be called a *bound matrix* since it has a fixed location on graph paper. The situation is analogous to that of bound vectors in mechanics, where the vectors are not free to translate or slide. If the image f has an $(m \times n)$ rectangular domain given by $D = \{(i, j): r \le i \le r + n - 1 \text{ and } s \le j \le s + m - 1 = t\}$, then f can be represented as

$$\begin{pmatrix} a_{11} & a_{12} & \cdots & a_{1n} \\ a_{21} & a_{22} & \cdots & a_{2n} \\ \vdots & \vdots & & \vdots \\ a_{m1} & a_{m2} & \cdots & a_{mn} \end{pmatrix}_{r,\, t}$$

The values of gray for the image are given as a_{pq} in the bound matrix $(a_{pq})_{rt}$. Here p denotes the matrix row and q the matrix column for the location of the value a_{pq}. The integers r and t specify the leftmost and uppermost pixel (r, t) in D, the domain of the image f. The gray value at this pixel is a_{11}; that is, $f(r, t) = a_{11}$. For any other pixel (i, j) in D, it can be seen that

$$f(i, j) = a_{m + s - j,\, i + 1 - r} = a_{t + 1 - j,\, i + 1 - r}$$

or, equivalently,

$$a_{pq} = f(q + r - 1, m + s - p) = f(q + r - 1, t + 1 - p)$$

The preceding relationships can best be seen by overlaying the matrix representation on the pixel grid structure ("hanging" the matrix), as in Figure 1.2.

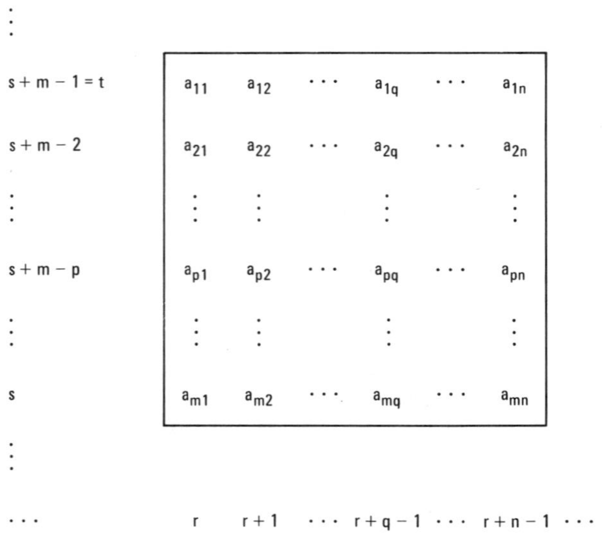

Figure 1.2 Overlay of Matrix and Grid Structures

Example 1.2

Let f be the image given in Example 1.1. Then employing the notation of bound matrices, one obtains

$$f = \begin{pmatrix} a_{11} & a_{12} \\ a_{21} & a_{22} \\ a_{31} & a_{32} \end{pmatrix}_{0,\,1} = \begin{pmatrix} 3 & 5 \\ 2 & 4 \\ 0 & -3 \end{pmatrix}_{0,\,1}$$

This is the gray value at location $(0, 1)$. Thus, by definition, $a_{11} = f(0, 1) = 3$.

This is the gray value for the pixel located one unit to the right and two units down from $(0, 1)$. Thus $a_{32} = f(1, -1) = -3$.

While it can be seen from the positioning that $a_{32} = f(1, -1)$, this relationship can be directly computed from $f(i, j) = a_{t+1-j,\,i+1-r}$. The algorithm for obtaining the values of f from the values in the bound matrix, and vice versa, is important for computer implementation and for mechanization purposes. However, in this text it will generally suffice to have a good understanding of the geometric explanation for identifying the appropriate pixel locations.

1.3 Bound Matrices

Consider the array-type structure consisting of m by n entities:

$$\begin{pmatrix} a_{11} & a_{12} & \cdots & a_{1n} \\ a_{21} & a_{22} & \cdots & a_{2n} \\ \vdots & \vdots & & \vdots \\ a_{m1} & a_{m2} & \cdots & a_{mn} \end{pmatrix}_{r,\,t}$$

where

1) each a_{pq} is a real number or a $*$ (star)
2) $1 \le p \le m,\ 1 \le q \le n$
3) r and t are integers

Such a data structure is called a *bound matrix*, or an $(m \times n)$ bound matrix, and the stars denote values that are not known. The location in $Z \times Z$ of the a_{11} entry, which may be a $*$, is (r, t). The location of the entry a_{pq} in $Z \times Z$ is $(q + r - 1, t + 1 - p)$. Examples of bound matrices without stars were given in Section 1.2. The star will be utilized to allow nonrectangular images to be represented by bound matrices. It is helpful to visualize all values *outside* a bound matrix to be stars.

Example 1.3

Consider the image $f : D \to R$, where $D = \{(1, 1), (1, 2), (2, 2)\}$ and $f(1, 1) = 8$, $f(1, 2) = 4$, and $f(2, 2) = 6$. Then a bound matrix representing f is given by

$$\begin{pmatrix} 4 & 6 \\ 8 & * \end{pmatrix}_{1,\,2}$$

Two other bound matrices representing the image f are

$$\begin{pmatrix} * & 4 & 6 \\ * & 8 & * \\ * & * & * \end{pmatrix}_{0,\,2} \quad \text{and} \quad \begin{pmatrix} * & 4 & 6 \\ * & 8 & * \\ \circledast & * & * \end{pmatrix}$$

Note that in the origin specification the circle is always around the gray value for the $(0, 0)$ pixel. In this example that pixel happens not to be part of the image; nevertheless, the notation must be used in a consistent fashion.

When we say that an $(m \times n)$ bound matrix $(a_{pq})_{rt}$ *represents* a (necessarily finite) image $f: D \to R$, we mean that the gray values of f lie in $(a_{pq})_{rt}$ in the proper position and that all other values (if any) of a_{pq} are $*$. Rigorously, $(a_{pq})_{rt}$ represents the finite image $f: D \to R$ if for every (i, j) in D there corresponds the element $a_{t+1-j,\,i+1-r}$ in $(a_{pq})_{rt}$, where $a_{t+1-j,\,i+1-r} = f(i, j)$. Furthermore, all other a_{pq} in $(a_{pq})_{rt}$ must have the entry $*$.

It is important to know how to go from a picture representation of an image to a bound matrix representation, and vice versa. This is most simply done geometrically by overlaying one structure on the other. There is no need to memorize the formula for relating gray values using matrix notation a_{pq} with the function notation $f(i, j)$. The complexity of the relation arises from the somewhat backwardly rotated notation used in representing tuples in matrices relative to the xy coordinate labeling.

For any digital image with finite, nonempty domain, a *minimal bound matrix*, denoted f^*, can be found to represent f. If $(a_{pq})_{rt}$ is an $(m \times n)$ bound matrix representing f, then the new matrix f^* is an $(m^* \times n^*)$ bound matrix representing f, where $m^* \le m$ and $n^* \le n$. The minimal bound matrix for f is simply that representation for which m and n are as small as possible. In Example 1.3, the first bound matrix given is the minimal one. It is simply the representation that contains no extraneous rows or columns of stars.

Using bound matrices to represent images is convenient and often space saving. It is an illustration of a data-compression technique. This is particularly true when there are few stars in the bound matrix.

1.4 Information Density of a Bound Matrix

In general, for an image $f: D \to R$ with nonempty, finite domain D containing d elements, $3d$ pieces of data must be stored: For each of the d pixels the x and y locations must be registered along with the gray value $f(x, y)$. This same image, when represented by an $(m \times n)$ bound matrix $(a_{pq})_{rt}$, can be specified by using $(m \cdot n + 4)$ pieces of data. The data are the positive integers m and n, followed by the $m \cdot n$ tuples a_{pq} of the matrix, and then by the absolute *location* of the a_{11} tuple, that is, r and t. The gray values of the other pixels are found by either computation or geometry.

It is obvious that the minimal bound matrix f^* associated with f is specified using the least amount of data among all bound matrices representing f. When the image f has a domain that is *nearly rectangular* in shape, a common occurrence, the minimal bound matrix representation provides a data compression close to one-third. Instead of specifying the location of each gray value of f, the location of the a_{11} element of f^* is specified. Then all $m \cdot n$ elements of f^* have locations that are easily found using relative-address-type techniques.

A measure of the amount of information in an $(m \times n)$ bound matrix $(a_{pq})_{rt}$ is given by the *information density u*. The quantity u is defined as the ratio of the number of nonstarred values, say s, divided by $m \cdot n$. Therefore, $u = s/(m \cdot n)$. When $u = 1$, there are no stars and the image occupies the entire matrix. Since a minimal bound matrix represents a finite, nonempty image with a minimal amount of data, it possesses the maximum possible information density.

1.5 Block Diagrams

In many disciplines, such as computer architecture and communications, block diagrams are a useful device. In matrix-structured image processing, their role is much more fundamental. They serve as a language for describing and performing operations with and between images and bound matrices.

Consider the image $f{:}D \rightarrow R$, with D finite and nonempty. As before, let f^* signify the minimal bound matrix associated with f. Let MINBOUND denote the operation of obtaining f^* from f; that is, MINBOUND$(f) = f^*$. A block diagram illustrating the process MINBOUND will be denoted by

$$f \rightarrow \boxed{\text{MINBOUND}} \rightarrow f^*$$

There is only one input in this block diagram, the image f. The output is the minimal bound matrix f^*. The block diagram will sometimes be written with words in the bottom of the block to serve as a reminder of the operation being performed. For instance,

$$f \rightarrow \boxed{\begin{array}{c} \text{MINBOUND} \\ \text{Minimal Bound Matrix Determiner} \end{array}} \rightarrow f^*$$

Given any bound matrix $(a_{pq})_{rt}$, there is an image f naturally associated with it. This image is found by identifying all nonstar values a_{pq} and specifying the absolute location of these gray values. If IMAGE denotes the operator that extracts the image f from a bound matrix $(a_{pq})_{rt}$, then we write IMAGE$[(a_{pq})_{rt}] = f$. In block form,

$$(a_{pq})_{rt} \rightarrow \boxed{\text{IMAGE}} \rightarrow f$$

Example 1.4

A trivial example will be given first. When all the entries a_{pq} in $(a_{pq})_{rt}$ are stars, then IMAGE$[(a_{pq})_{rt}] = \emptyset$, the *empty image*.

Example 1.5

Consider the 4 × 4 bound matrix

Corresponding pixel location is (0, 3)

Corresponding pixel location is (0, 0)

$$(a_{pq})_{0,\,3} = \begin{pmatrix} * & * & * & * \\ 3 & 2 & 0 & * \\ 2 & * & -3 & * \\ 8 & 1 & 5 & * \end{pmatrix}_{0,\,3}$$

Note that the information density is $u = \frac{1}{2}$, which is rather low. The situation can be improved by finding the minimal bound matrix. This can be done by cascading MINBOUND with IMAGE. In other words, apply IMAGE to obtain the corresponding image, and then apply MINBOUND to obtain the minimal bound matrix. In block diagram form,

$$(a_{pq})_{rt} \rightarrow \boxed{\text{IMAGE}} \rightarrow f =$$

4			
3			
2	3	2	0
1	2		−3
0	8	1	5

  0   1   2   ...

and

$$f \rightarrow \boxed{\text{MINBOUND}} \rightarrow f^* = \begin{pmatrix} 3 & 2 & 0 \\ 2 & * & -3 \\ 8 & 1 & 5 \end{pmatrix}_{0,\,2}$$

Notice the much improved information density: $u^* = \frac{8}{9}$.

Because of the correspondence between a finite, nonempty image f and its minimal bound matrix representation f^*, that is, since

$$\text{MINBOUND}[\text{IMAGE}(f^*)] = f^*$$

and

$$\text{IMAGE}[\text{MINBOUND}(f)] = f$$

no distinction will be made between the two structures. In particular, a minimal bound matrix for a finite, nonempty image f will also be denoted by f, and not by f^*. Abuse of notation will also occur in that any bound matrix will often be called an image and be denoted by f.

1.6 Arithmetic-type Binary Operations for Images

Binary operations can be performed on images just as they can be performed on real numbers, vectors, and matrices. Two images can be added together to form another image, the *sum* of the two input images.

The *addition* of images is performed *pointwise* (or, more appropriately, *pixelwise*). The gray values of corresponding pixels are added numerically. To be precise, ADD is a binary (two input) operation defined by

$$[ADD(f, g)](i, j) = \begin{cases} f(i, j) + g(i, j), & \text{if } f \text{ and } g \text{ are both defined at } (i, j) \\ *, & \text{if either } f \text{ or } g \text{ is undefined at } (i, j) \end{cases}$$

where f and g are the input images. Saying that the sum is $*$ simply means $ADD(f, g)$ is undefined whenever either f or g is undefined. Hence the domain of $ADD(f, g)$ is the intersection of the domains of f and g. The block diagram for ADD is

$$f \rightarrow \boxed{\quad ADD \quad} \rightarrow ADD(f, g)$$
$$g \rightarrow$$

Example 1.6

Consider the images f and g in Figure 1.3. The image f has the domain $D_f = \{(0, 0), (0, 1), (1, 1), (2, 1)\}$ and g has the domain $D_g = \{(0, 0), (0, 1), (0, 2), (1, 1)\}$. Furthermore,

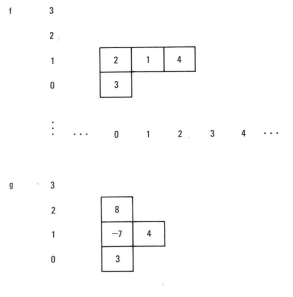

Figure 1.3 Images with Different Domains

$f(0, 0) = 3$, $f(0, 1) = 2$, $f(1, 1) = 1$, and $f(2, 1) = 4$. Also, $g(0, 0) = 3$, $g(0, 1) = -7$, $g(0, 2) = 8$, and $g(1, 1) = 4$. Operating by ADD yields

$$\text{ADD}(f, g) = \begin{pmatrix} -5 & 5 \\ 6 & * \end{pmatrix}_{0, 1} = \begin{pmatrix} -5 & 5 \\ \textcircled{6} & * \end{pmatrix}$$

That is,

$$[\text{ADD}(f, g)](0, 0) = 3 + 3 = 6$$

$$[\text{ADD}(f, g)](0, 1) = -5$$

$$[\text{ADD}(f, g)](1, 1) = 5$$

Moreover, $[\text{ADD}(f, g)](1, 0) = *$, since both f and g are undefined at $(1, 0)$. Equivalently, $f(1, 0) = g(1, 0) = *$. It should be recognized that, if just one of the images were undefined at $(1, 0)$, then ADD would still be $*$ (undefined) there. Also note that $[\text{ADD}(f, g)](0, 2) = *$, since $f(0, 2) = *$. This is implicit in the bound-matrix representation of the image f, since all values outside the bound matrix are assumed to be $*$.

Similar to the addition of images are the operations of multiplying images and finding the maximum and minimum of two images. These operations are also defined pointwise. Moreover, like addition, whenever one of the inputs is undefined, so is the output. *Multiplication* of two images f and g, denoted MULT(f, g), is defined by

$$[\text{MULT}(f, g)](i, j) = \begin{cases} f(i, j) \cdot g(i, j), & \text{if both inputs are defined at } (i, j) \\ *, & \text{if either input is undefined at } (i, j) \end{cases}$$

The block diagram corresponding to multiplication is

$$f \rightarrow \boxed{\text{MULT}} \rightarrow \text{MULT}(f, g)$$
$$g \rightarrow$$

Example 1.7

Let f and g be the images given in Figure 1.3. Then

$$f = \begin{pmatrix} 2 & 1 & 4 \\ 3 & * & * \end{pmatrix}_{0, 1} \longrightarrow$$

$$g = \begin{pmatrix} 8 & * \\ -7 & 4 \\ 3 & * \end{pmatrix}_{0, 2} \longrightarrow \boxed{\text{MULT}} \rightarrow \begin{pmatrix} -14 & 4 \\ 9 & * \end{pmatrix}_{0, 1}$$

$$= \quad \begin{array}{c} 2 \\ 1 \\ 0 \\ \vdots \end{array} \quad \begin{array}{|c|c|} \hline -14 & 4 \\ \hline 9 & \\ \hline \end{array}$$
$$\quad\quad\quad\quad 0 \quad 1 \quad 2$$

The *maximum* operator, MAX(f, g), compares two images in a pointwise manner and returns the maximum, or highest, value at each pixel. If either f or g is undefined at a particular pixel, then MAX(f, g) is likewise undefined there. Functionally,

$$[\text{MAX}(f, g)](i, j) = \max[f(i, j), g(i, j)]$$

unless either $f(i, j) = *$ or $g(i, j) = *$, in which case $[\text{MAX}(f, g)](i, j) = *$. MAX has the block diagram

$$f \rightarrow \boxed{\quad \text{MAX} \quad} \longrightarrow \text{MAX}(f, g)$$
$$g \rightarrow$$

Example 1.8

Using the same inputs as in Example 1.7 gives

$$f = \begin{pmatrix} 2 & 1 & 4 \\ 3 & * & * \end{pmatrix}_{0, 1} \rightarrow \boxed{\quad \text{MAX} \quad} \rightarrow \begin{pmatrix} 2 & 4 \\ 3 & * \end{pmatrix}_{0, 1}$$

$$g = \begin{pmatrix} & 8 & * \\ -7 & 4 & \\ 3 & * & \end{pmatrix}_{0, 2} \rightarrow$$

Note that

$$[\text{MAX}(f, g)](0, 1) = \max(2, -7) = 2$$

and

$$[\text{MAX}(f, g)](0, 2) = *, \quad \text{since } f(0, 2) = *$$

Similar to MAX is the *minimum* operator MIN defined by

$$[\text{MIN}(f, g)](i, j) = \min[f(i, j), g(i, j)]$$

unless either $f(i, j) = *$ or $g(i, j) = *$, in which case the value of MIN(f, g) at (i, j) is $*$ ($[\text{MIN}(f, g)](i, j)$ is undefined). The block diagram for MIN is defined in the customary manner:

$$f \rightarrow \boxed{\quad \text{MIN} \quad} \rightarrow \text{MIN}(f, g)$$
$$g \rightarrow$$

Example 1.9

Once again using the inputs of Example 1.7,

$$\begin{pmatrix} 2 & 1 & 4 \\ 3 & * & * \end{pmatrix}_{0,1} \longrightarrow \boxed{\text{MIN}} \rightarrow \begin{pmatrix} -7 & 1 \\ 3 & * \end{pmatrix}_{0,1}$$

$$\begin{pmatrix} 8 & * \\ -7 & 4 \\ 3 & * \end{pmatrix}_{0,2} \longrightarrow$$

The operator MULT is binary in that it takes two inputs. Like ADD, MAX, and MIN, it takes inputs that are of the same type or *sort*. Both inputs are images. Not all multi-input operations take operands of the same sort. The next operation to be introduced is also a form of multiplication; however, although it is still binary, its inputs are of different types. SCALAR is an image operator that takes an image as one input and a real number as another. The *scalar multiplication* of an image f by a real number r is an image denoted by $\text{SCALAR}(r; f)$ and defined by

$$[\text{SCALAR}(r; f)](i, j) = r \cdot f(i, j)$$

unless $f(i, j) = *$, in which case $\text{SCALAR}(r; f)$ is also undefined ($*$). To put it simply, to find $\text{SCALAR}(r; f)$, multiply each gray value of f by r. Scalar multiplication in image processing is analogous to the same-named operation in vector algebra, and it has the block diagram

$$\begin{array}{c} r \rightarrow \\ f \rightarrow \end{array} \boxed{\text{SCALAR}} \rightarrow \text{SCALAR}(r; f)$$

Note the semicolon between r and f in the notation for scalar multiplication, which indicates that r and f are different sorts of entities.

Example 1.10

Letting f be as in Example 1.7,

$$\begin{array}{c} 3 \rightarrow \\ f \rightarrow \end{array} \boxed{\text{SCALAR}} \rightarrow \begin{pmatrix} 6 & 3 & 12 \\ 9 & * & * \end{pmatrix}_{0,1}$$

1.7 Unary Arithmetic Operators for Images

A unary operator is one that requires one input. The simplest image to image unary transformation is *subtraction*, or *negation*. It is defined pointwise by

$$[\text{SUB}(f)](i, j) = -f(i, j)$$

for every (i, j) in the domain of f. SUB has the block diagram

$$f \to \boxed{\text{SUB}} \to \text{SUB}(f)$$

Example 1.11

$$\begin{pmatrix} * & 3 \\ 4 & 0 \\ -7 & 1 \end{pmatrix}_{0,0} \to \boxed{\text{SUB}} \to \begin{pmatrix} * & -3 \\ -4 & 0 \\ 7 & -1 \end{pmatrix}_{0,0} = \begin{pmatrix} \circledast & -3 \\ -4 & 0 \\ 7 & -1 \end{pmatrix}$$

The subtraction of f is nothing more than scalar multiplication of f by -1.

Unary *division*, or *reciprocation*, is also defined on an image f. It is defined by

$$[\text{DIV}(f)](i, j) = \begin{cases} \dfrac{1}{f(i, j)}, & \text{if } f(i, j) \text{ is real and not } 0 \\ *, & \text{if } f(i, j) = 0 \text{ or } f(i, j) = * \end{cases}$$

In other words, one divided by zero is, as usual, undefined. The block diagram for reciprocation is

$$f \to \boxed{\text{DIV}} \to \text{DIV}(f)$$

Example 1.12

$$\begin{pmatrix} 1 & * \\ 0 & 2 \end{pmatrix}_{0,0} \to \boxed{\text{DIV}} \to \begin{pmatrix} 1 & * \\ * & \frac{1}{2} \end{pmatrix}_{0,0}$$

1.8 Translation Operation

Among the most useful operators involving images is the *translation* operator TRAN. This operator is trinary with three inputs, an image and two integers. Given an image f and two integer inputs i and j, $\text{TRAN}(f; i, j)$ is an image that is the same as f, but moved over i pixels to the right and up j pixels. In terms of bound matrices, if $f = (a_{pq})_{rt}$, then

$$\text{TRAN}(f; i, j) = (a_{pq})_{r + i, t + j}$$

In full bound matrix format, if

$$f = \begin{pmatrix} a_{11} & a_{12} & \dots & a_{1n} \\ \vdots & \vdots & & \vdots \\ a_{m1} & a_{m2} & \dots & a_{mn} \end{pmatrix}_{r, t}$$

then

$$\text{TRAN}(f; i, j) = \begin{pmatrix} a_{11} & a_{12} & \cdots & a_{1n} \\ \vdots & \vdots & & \vdots \\ a_{m1} & a_{m2} & \cdots & a_{mn} \end{pmatrix}_{r + i, t + j}$$

Notice that no values a_{pq} change; only the location of the gray values change by a translate. The block diagram for TRAN is given by

$$f = (a_{pq})_{rt} \rightarrow$$
$$i \quad \rightarrow \quad \boxed{\text{TRAN}} \rightarrow \text{TRAN}(f; i, j) = (a_{pq})_{r + i, t + j}$$
$$j \quad \rightarrow$$

Translation can also be defined pointwise. In reading the pointwise description of TRAN, keep in mind that i and j represent inputs, and u and v correspond to the coordinates of the pixel under consideration. Pointwise,

$$[\text{TRAN}(f; i, j)](u, v) = f(u - i, v - j)$$

Pay particular attention to the minus signs in the argument for f. The somewhat confusing situation of a minus sign on the variable for a right translation is similar to that for real-valued functions in calculus.

Example 1.13

Let

$$f = \begin{pmatrix} 3 & 4 \\ 1 & * \end{pmatrix}_{0, 0}$$

The domain of f is given by $D_f = \{(0, 0), (1, 0), (0, -1)\}$. Applying translation with integer inputs 4 and 1 gives

$$f \rightarrow$$
$$4 \rightarrow \quad \boxed{\text{TRAN}} \rightarrow h = \begin{pmatrix} 3 & 4 \\ 1 & * \end{pmatrix}_{4, 1}$$
$$1 \rightarrow$$

The domain of $h = \text{TRAN}(f; i, j)$ is $D_h = \{(4, 1), (5, 1), (4, 0)\}$, with $h(4, 1) = 3$, $h(5, 1) = 4$, and $h(4, 0) = 1$. With inputs 4 and 1, the domain of the image has been shifted four pixels to the right and one pixel up. The gray values have remained unchanged in their relative positions. This might best be seen by writing h in the origin specification form:

$$h = \begin{pmatrix} * & * & * & * & 3 & 4 \\ \circledast & * & * & * & 1 & * \end{pmatrix}$$

1.9 Rotation and Flip Operations

Images can be rotated 90°, 180°, 270°, and 360° = 0°. A counterclockwise 90° *rotation* of f is denoted by NINETY(f). It is given in pointwise form by

$$[\text{NINETY}(f)](i, j) = f(j, -i)$$

This means that if $f(3, 1) = 4$ then $[\text{NINETY}(f)](-1, 3) = 4$. A 180° rotation of f is found by applying two 90° rotations in succession. To simplify notation, a composition of two 90° rotations is denoted by NINETY^2. In other words,

$$\text{NINETY}^2(f) = \text{NINETY}[\text{NINETY}(f)]$$

Similarly, a 270° rotation is equal to NINETY^3, NINETY applied three times in succession. The respective block diagrams for NINETY, NINETY^2, and NINETY^3 are

$$f \to \boxed{\qquad \text{NINETY} \qquad} \to \text{NINETY}(f)$$

$$f \to \boxed{\qquad \text{NINETY}^2 \qquad} \to \text{NINETY}^2(f)$$

$$f \to \boxed{\qquad \text{NINETY}^3 \qquad} \to \text{NINETY}^3(f)$$

Example 1.14

Let

$$f = \begin{pmatrix} 3 & 2 \\ 1 & * \\ 5 & 2 \end{pmatrix}_{3, 4} = \begin{pmatrix} * & * & * & 3 & 2 \\ * & * & * & 1 & * \\ * & * & * & 5 & 2 \\ * & * & * & * & * \\ \circledast & * & * & * & * \end{pmatrix} \begin{matrix} \text{Rotate } f\ 90° \\ \text{with origin} \\ \text{as pivot} \end{matrix}$$

origin

Then

$$f \longrightarrow \boxed{\quad \text{NINETY} \quad} \longrightarrow \begin{pmatrix} 2 & * & 2 \\ 3 & 1 & 5 \end{pmatrix}_{-4, 4} = \begin{pmatrix} 2 & * & 2 & * & * \\ 3 & 1 & 5 & * & * \\ * & * & * & * & * \\ * & * & * & * & * \\ * & * & * & * & \circledast \end{pmatrix}$$

This can be seen from a pointwise perspective by letting $h = \text{NINETY}(f)$. Then

$$h(-4, 4) = f(4, 4) = 2$$
$$h(-3, 4) = f(4, 3) = *$$
$$h(-2, 4) = f(4, 2) = 2$$
$$h(-4, 3) = f(3, 4) = 3$$
$$h(-3, 3) = f(3, 3) = 1$$
$$h(-2, 3) = f(3, 2) = 5$$

and

$$h(i, j) = *, \quad \text{for all other } (i, j)$$

In general, if f is given by the m by n minimal bound matrix $(a_{pq})_{rt}$, then NINETY(f) will be given by an n by m bound matrix with first row, first column gray value located at $(-t, r + n - 1)$.

The rotation operator NINETY^2 is of particular importance. In terms of the domain D of an image f, NINETY^2 rotates D 180° around the origin. In precise terms, this means that (i, j) is an element of D if and only if $(-i, -j)$ is an element in the domain of NINETY$^2(f)$ (see Figure 1.4).

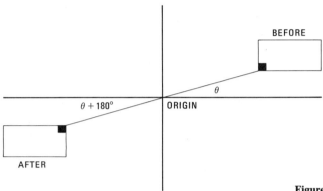

Figure 1.4 180° Rotation about Origin

Images can also be *flipped*. There is a horizontal, a vertical, and two distinct diagonal flips (a 45° and a 135°). Only the 135° flip, denoted FLIP, will be discussed in detail. The others are obtained by using FLIP in conjunction with the rotation operation defined previously. Pointwise, FLIP is given by

$$[\text{FLIP}(f)](i, j) = f(-j, -i)$$

The block diagram for FLIP is

$$f \longrightarrow \boxed{\qquad \text{FLIP} \qquad} \longrightarrow \text{FLIP}(f)$$

Example 1.15

Using the image f of Example 1.14,

$$\begin{pmatrix} 3 & 2 \\ 1 & * \\ 5 & 2 \end{pmatrix}_{3,\,4} \longrightarrow \boxed{\qquad \text{FLIP} \qquad} \longrightarrow \begin{pmatrix} 3 & 1 & 5 \\ 2 & * & 2 \end{pmatrix}_{-4,\,-3}$$

There are two salient points. First, notice how the coordinates of the upper-left pixel have flipped both position and sign. Second, notice that in matrix terms the output of FLIP is the transpose of the input. (The rows and columns have reversed roles, the rows becoming the columns and the columns becoming the rows.) Using these two facts, we can easily generate the outcome of FLIP if given a bound matrix input.

Geometrically, the result of the preceding can be explained with the help of the 9 by 9 bound matrix in Figure 1.5. In that representation, the image is thought to be rigidly fastened to the 135° line. This line is then twisted 180° on its own axis. This causes the upper-right elements to come out of the page and then occupy the lower-left position, the desired result being obtained in the process.

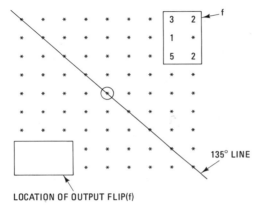

LOCATION OF OUTPUT FLIP(f)

Figure 1.5 Reflection about 135° Line

1.10 Data-base-type Image Operations

The two image-processing operations introduced in this section are similar to operators found in data-base algebras. The first operator is the *selection* operator SELECT. It is used for extracting part of an image from a given image $f = (a_{pq})_{rt}$. Intuitively, SELECT leaves entries within a specified *window* unchanged, and it *stars out* all entries outside this window. To use the selection operator, the size and locaton of the window must be given. More precisely, five inputs must be specified. The first type of input to be specified is the image f; the next two inputs give the *size m* by *n, m, n* ≥ 1, of the desired image $h = (b_{pq})_{r't'}$; and the final two inputs determine the location (r', t') in $Z \times Z$ of the first row, first column element b_{11} in the resulting image h. By definition, $h(i, j) = f(i, j)$ for all points inside the window, for all (i, j) such that $r' \leq i < r' + n$ and $t' - m < j \leq t'$. For all other (i, j) in $Z \times Z$, $h(i, j) = *$. The block diagram illustrating the operation SELECT($f; m, n, r', t'$) = h is given by

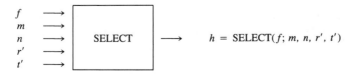

Example 1.16

Let

$$f = \begin{pmatrix} 3 & 7 & 5 & * \\ -2 & \boxed{4 \;\; 1} & 3 \\ 0 & \boxed{* \;\; 8} & 2 \end{pmatrix}_{1,\,1}$$

SELECT selects this portion of f.

Then

Input image $\quad f \longrightarrow$

Output image
is 4 by 2 $\qquad 4 \longrightarrow$
$\qquad\qquad\qquad 2 \longrightarrow$ SELECT $\longrightarrow h = \begin{pmatrix} 4 & 1 \\ * & 8 \\ * & * \\ * & * \end{pmatrix}_{2,\,0}$

b_{11} element of $\quad 2 \longrightarrow$
output image is $\quad 0 \longrightarrow$
located at (2, 0)

The bound matrix resulting from the application of SELECT is 4 by 2 and has its b_{11} entry located at (2, 0).

Another important data-base-type operator for image processing is the *extension* operator EXTEND. Whereas the selection operator extracts a smaller piece of an image from a given image, the extension operator takes two images and renders a larger image. Rigorously, given images f and g, the extension operator is defined by

$$[\text{EXTEND}(f,\, g)](i,\, j) = \begin{cases} f(i,\, j), & \text{if } f \text{ is defined at } (i,\, j) \\ g(i,\, j), & \text{elsewhere} \end{cases}$$

EXTEND(f, g) is obtained by *adjoining* to f that part of g which does not overlay f. The image f is called *dominant* since it is extended by using a *piece* of the *subordinate* image g. The block diagram for the extension operator is

f (dominant image) $\quad\longrightarrow$
g (subordinate image) $\quad\longrightarrow$ EXTEND $\longrightarrow$ EXTEND(f, g)

It must be recognized that the extension operator is not commutative. In general, we do not have EXTEND(f, g) = EXTEND(g, f). Therefore, when using the block diagram, it is important to write the dominant input above the subordinate input.

Example 1.17

The following block diagram illustrates extension.

$$f = \begin{pmatrix} 4 & 5 & * \\ 3 & 7 & 8 \\ -2 & * & 5 \\ * & * & 3 \end{pmatrix}_{0,\,-3}$$

$$g = \begin{pmatrix} * & * & * & * \\ * & * & * & 3 \\ 4 & 5 & 8 & 9 \\ 2 & * & 1 & 3 \\ 5 & 0 & 1 & 1 \end{pmatrix}_{0,\,-3}$$

EXTEND

$$h = \begin{pmatrix} 4 & 5 & * & * \\ 3 & 7 & 8 & 3 \\ -2 & 5 & 5 & 9 \\ 2 & * & 3 & 3 \\ 5 & 0 & 1 & 1 \end{pmatrix}_{0,\,-3}$$

Notice that $h(0, -6) = 2$ since $f(0, -6) = *$ and $g(0, -6) = 2$. Additionally, $h(2, -6) = 3$ since $f(2, -6) = 3$, even though $g(2, -6) = 1$. Furthermore, $h(0, -7) = 5$ since $f(0, -7) = *$ and $g(0, -7) = 5$.

It is now appropriate to demonstrate the power of the operators thus far introduced. By using them in combination, a host of higher-level operators can be obtained. This is accomplished by composing the given operators to generate desired outputs.

As an illustration, consider the following block diagram:

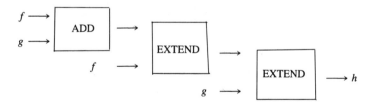

What is the output h? The ADD operator outputs an image that is the sum of f and g on their common domain $D_f \cap D_g$ and is undefined ($*$) elsewhere. This output is then used as the dominant input into an EXTEND, while f is used as the subordinate input. Hence ADD(f, g) is extended so that it equals f on the part of the domain of f that does not intersect the domain of g ($D_f - D_g$ in set theoretic notation). This new output is then input into EXTEND as the dominant input, while g is used as the subordinate input. Hence the image is extended so that it equals g on $D_g - D_f$. The final output can be written as

$$h = \text{EXTEND [EXTEND (ADD } (f, g), f), g]}$$

This new higher-level operator sums f and g on the intersection of their domains and leaves them unaltered elsewhere. In fact, it is a common image-processing operator and is given the name *extended addition* and denoted by EXTADD(f, g). It has the usual block diagram:

$$f \quad \longrightarrow \quad \boxed{\text{EXTADD}} \quad \longrightarrow \quad \text{EXTADD}(f, g)$$
$$g \quad \longrightarrow$$

Example 1.18

Consider the images

$$f = \begin{pmatrix} 2 & 1 & 0 & 4 & * & * \\ 4 & 0 & 3 & -1 & * & * \\ 3 & 1 & -3 & 3 & * & * \\ \textcircled{1} & 2 & 5 & 2 & * & * \end{pmatrix}$$

and

$$g = \begin{pmatrix} * & * & * & * & * & * \\ * & * & 2 & 1 & 7 & 9 \\ * & * & 5 & -2 & 8 & 7 \\ \textcircled{*} & * & 2 & 0 & 8 & 9 \end{pmatrix}$$

Then

$$\text{EXTADD}(f, g) = \begin{pmatrix} 2 & 1 & 0 & 4 & * & * \\ 4 & 0 & 5 & 0 & 7 & 9 \\ 3 & 1 & 2 & 1 & 8 & 7 \\ \textcircled{1} & 2 & 7 & 2 & 8 & 9 \end{pmatrix}$$

whereas

$$\text{ADD}(f, g) = \begin{pmatrix} * & * & * & * & * & * \\ * & * & 5 & 0 & * & * \\ * & * & 2 & 1 & * & * \\ \textcircled{*} & * & 7 & 2 & * & * \end{pmatrix}$$

Many other useful operations will be derived throughout the text utilizing more primitive transformations. For example, in addition to EXTADD, there are extended arithmetic binary operations for multiplication, maximum, and minimum. These are EXTMULT, EXTMAX, and EXTMIN, respectively (see the exercises). Like EXTADD, each performs the appropriate arithmetic operation on the intersection of the two input domains and leaves the inputs as they were elsewhere.

1.11 Structural Transformations

To this point, all the image-processing transformations introduced have been of a certain kind. Each has had at least one image for an input, and each has had a single image for its output. It is true that an operator may have had some auxiliary inputs of a different sort; nevertheless, it would not be inappropriate to characterize the operators thus far introduced as being *image-to-image operators*. Recalling our introductory comments, these operators belong properly to the class of level 1 type transformations. Excluding the auxiliary inputs, which have thus far been either integers or real numbers, the input image data structure has been matched by the output data structure. In this section, three operators that are not image-to-image are discussed. One has two nonimage inputs and an image output, and the other two have single image inputs and single nonimage outputs.

An image, or more precisely a bound matrix, is a data structure consisting of a two-dimensional array together with four integers. By relative-address-type techniques, it can be changed to a three-dimensional array or, equivalently, a two-dimensioinal array consisting of absolute locations (i, j) together with a one-dimensional array consisting of real-valued gray levels $f(i, j)$. Throughout the remainder of this section the latter approach will be assumed, since from an intuitive standpoint it fits best with the structural operators to be defined.

Imagine two stacks called DOMAIN and RANGE. Each stack contains the same number of entries, the first containing ordered pairs (i, j) and the second containing real numbers (see Figure 1.6). Together the stacks implicitly contain an image, for if they were popped simultaneously, the corresponding words would form a location together with its gray value. One could logically go so far as to say that an image is a *pair of stacks* (DOMAIN, RANGE). It simply depends on one's point of view. Yet when the stacks are separated, each can be treated as an individual data structure, and its contents can be operated on independently of the other. Once such operations are completed, the stacks can once again be considered as a pair and a new image created, or the results of the independent operations can be output.

With the preceding in mind, the *creation* operator is defined. CREATE, as it will be called, takes an array consisting of real numbers or stars and an array of integer-ordered pairs (or, equivalently, a two-dimensional array of integers) and outputs an image (or bound matrix). For each (i, j) in the array of ordered pairs, pixel (i, j) is given the corresponding value, be it a real number or a star, in the other array. All remaining pixels are given the value $*$. Except for the addressing techniques required to change a three-dimensional array to a bound matrix, the operation CREATE is purely *structural* in that it simply alters structure. Nevertheless, for logical reasons it needs to be specifically

DOMAIN STACK

| (i_1, j_1) |
| (i_2, j_2) |
| (i_3, j_3) |
| $\vdots$ |
| (i_n, j_n) |

RANGE STACK

| a_1 |
| a_2 |
| a_3 |
| $\vdots$ |
| a_n |

Figure 1.6 Decomposition of an Image into Stacks

articulated. Moreover, from a low-level programming point of view or from an architectural perspective, it does involve an actual operation. The block diagram for CREATE is given by

$$D \xrightarrow{\quad} \boxed{\text{CREATE}} \xrightarrow{\quad} \text{CREATE}(D, R)$$
$$R \xrightarrow{\quad}$$

where D is an array of ordered integer pairs, R is an array of real numbers or stars, and each array contains the same number of entries. A schematic is given in Figure 1.7. Keep in mind that the two input stacks are not considered an image until *joined* by CREATE. This point is crucial since the image results not only from the contents of the stacks but also from the ordering within the stacks. As long as the stacks remain independent, each can have its ordering permuted by some nonimage-type operation. The output of CREATE depends on those orderings.

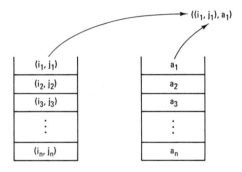

Figure 1.7 Creating Image by Popping Stacks

Example 1.19

Consider the two arrays

$$A = [(0, 0), (0, 1), (1, 0), (2, 0), (2, 1)]$$
$$B = [1, *, 0, 2, 6]$$

Then

$$\text{CREATE}(A, B) = \begin{pmatrix} * & * & 6 \\ 1 & 0 & 2 \end{pmatrix}_{0, 1}$$

Just as two arrays of the appropriate types can be joined to form an image, an image can be *disjoined* to form two arrays, each of which is not an image. These operations, called DOMAIN and RANGE, collectively invert CREATE. DOMAIN takes an image input and yields an array of ordered pairs that make up the domain of the image.

RANGE takes an image and yields an array consisting of the gray values of the input image. If f is the input image, their respective block diagrams are given by

$$f \quad \longrightarrow \quad \boxed{\text{DOMAIN}} \quad \longrightarrow \quad \text{DOMAIN}(f)$$

and

$$f \quad \longrightarrow \quad \boxed{\text{RANGE}} \quad \longrightarrow \quad \text{RANGE}(f)$$

It will be assumed that the data are taken from the image f and put into DOMAIN(f) and RANGE(f) in a compatible manner. In other words, the image is *read* in both instances from top down and from left to right. This uniformity of approach allows the exact image to be reconstructed by CREATE as long as the arrays DOMAIN(f) and RANGE(f) have not been transformed in any manner:

$$\text{CREATE} \ [\ \text{DOMAIN}(f), \ \text{RANGE}(f) \ ] \ = f$$

Example 1.20

Let

$$f = \begin{pmatrix} 2 & 4 & 0 \\ * & 2 & 1 \end{pmatrix}_{1, \ 1}$$

Then

$$\text{DOMAIN}(f) \ = \ [(1, \ 1), \ (2, \ 1), \ (2, \ 0), \ (3, \ 1), \ (3, \ 0)]$$

and

$$\text{RANGE}(f) \ = \ [2, \ 4, \ 2, \ 0, \ 1]$$

In Example 1.20, note that composing CREATE with the outputs DOMAIN(f) and RANGE(f) returns f. But this is not usually what occurs in practice. First, there might be a permutation of the elements in DOMAIN(f) or there might be an arithmetic operation performed on the gray levels in RANGE(f). Second, a new stack might be popped simultaneously with DOMAIN(f) to form a new image. Whatever the case might be, the intention is to utilize these operators to go from the image world to the number or set world (RANGE and DOMAIN), and to go from the number world and set world back to the image world (CREATE).

As an illustration, suppose one wishes to *insert* a gray value r into the (i, j) location of a bound matrix f. This is to be done whether or not a gray value is there already. Whatever the given value of f at (i, j), its new value is to become r. The operator INSERT is used to acccomplish this end. Therefore, INSERT is defined by

$$[\text{INSERT}(f;\ r;\ i,\ j\ )](u,\ v) = \begin{cases} r, & \text{if } u = i \text{ and } v = j \\ f(u,\ v), & \text{otherwise} \end{cases}$$

INSERT is a four-input operator. It requires an image, a real number, and two integers. Its block diagram is given by

$$
\begin{array}{l}
f \longrightarrow \\
r \longrightarrow \\
i \longrightarrow \\
j \longrightarrow
\end{array}
\boxed{\quad \text{INSERT} \quad} \longrightarrow \text{INSERT}(f;\ r;\ i,\ j)
$$

Let us now implement INSERT employing only the operators thus far introduced. The key is to utilize the image g, where

$$g = (r)_{i,j}$$

is the image with singleton domain $\{(i,\ j)\}$ and gray value r at $(i,\ j)$. The image g needs to be created. INSERT can be implemented by the following block diagram:

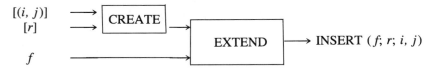

DOMAIN and RANGE are both level 2 operators, to use the classification scheme presented in the introduction. They take images to arrays (and hence to sets). However, RANGE can also be utilized to take an image to a real number. It does so, in the most trivial case, by taking a 1 by 1 image to an array of length 1 (which is logically equivalent to a real number). However, it can achieve much more than that.

Suppose we wish to find the total of all the gray levels in an image. This might be done for a number of reasons, one being to gauge the overall darkness of the image. Two methods to accomplish this operation, called PIXSUM, will be demonstrated.

Figure 1.8 gives the first method. It involves the 180° rotation of the input image f, followed by the DOMAIN operator and a collection of parallel translations of f, one for each element in the output of DOMAIN. (Whenever a pair output from DOMAIN is input into TRAN, the pair is being treated as two integer inputs to TRAN.) The net effect is to have one translated copy of f for each pixel in its domain, each copy having a unique gray value of f at the origin $(0, 0)$. SELECT picks out those origin pixels for 1 by 1 images, and ADD gets the desired sum as the gray value of a 1 by 1 image located at the origin. RANGE produces a real number. The tricky thing to note is the manner in which NINETY[2] provides a movement *back* to the origin when employed as an input to TRAN.

In Figure 1.9, a different approach is taken. One simply *dumps* the gray values of f into an array and then sends the contents of that array through a high-speed adder. This second diagram appears simpler; however, two points should be noted. First, it utilizes an add operation that is outside the image world. This can require the introduction of

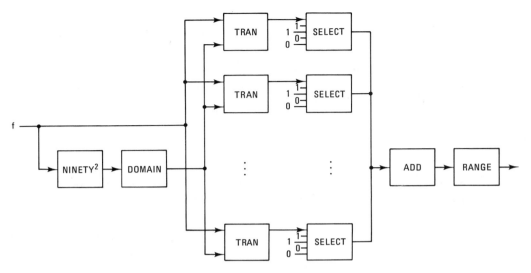

Figure 1.8 Block Diagram of PIXSUM

nonimage operators even when such operators are not necessary. Second, the amount of processing required may not turn out to be much less. Speed is a function of architecture, among other things, and a highly parallel architecture can take full advantage of the inherently parallel nature of the first method. In that method, TRAN and SELECT are each applied in parallel. Moreover, each is a very simple operation. TRAN merely changes the subscripts of a bound matrix, and SELECT, as it is applied in Figure 1.8, merely pulls out one pixel. In fact, by making full use of VLSI technology, the entire implementation of PIXSUM may be hardwired, with each ordered pair of the output array of DOMAIN being sent directly to one of the TRAN processors. This would avoid a delay due to unnecessary pushing and popping.

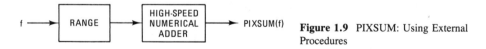

Figure 1.9 PIXSUM: Using External Procedures

1.12 Matrix Multiplication

It is convenient to define a matrix-type multiplication of images that is very similar to the usual multiplication of matrices. Let f be given by an m by n bound matrix $(a_{pq})_{rt}$, and let g be given by an n by k bound matrix $(b_{pq})_{r,t}$,. Bound matrices f and g are said to be *compatible* (for matrix multiplication) if f is of size m by n and g is of size n by k. The *matrix multiplication* operator, denoted simply by X, is defined by $X(f, g) = h$, where h is the m by k bound matrix $(c_{pq})_{rt}$, with

$$c_{pq} = \sum_{i=1}^{n} a_{pi} b_{iq}$$

where $1 \leq p \leq m$ and $1 \leq q \leq k$. As usual, if either $a_{pi} = *$ or $b_{iq} = *$, then the product is $*$; moreover, if any term in the sum is $*$, then the result is $*$. The block diagram for bound matrix multiplication is given by

f (leftmost image) $\longrightarrow$

g (rightmost image) $\longrightarrow$ $\boxed{\text{X}}$ $\longrightarrow$ $h = X(f, g)$

It is crucial to recognize that the output of the operation X depends upon the particular bound matrix representations of the inputs.

Example 1.21

Let

$$f = \begin{pmatrix} 3 & 4 \\ 7 & * \\ 5 & 1 \end{pmatrix}_{8,\,3} \quad \text{and } g = \begin{pmatrix} 1 & 5 & 8 & 4 \\ * & 3 & 5 & 8 \end{pmatrix}_{2,\,5}$$

Since the bound matrices are compatible, the operator X can be employed.

$f \longrightarrow \boxed{\text{X}} \longrightarrow \begin{pmatrix} * & 27 & 44 & 44 \\ * & * & * & * \\ * & 28 & 45 & 28 \end{pmatrix}_{8,\,3} = X(f, g)$

$g \longrightarrow$

In studying Example 1.21, note two things. First, the formal method of arriving at the terms of the product is exactly similar to that utilized in normal matrix algebra, except here there is the stipulation regarding the manner in which stars are to be handled. Second, the position of the output matrix (the absolute location of c_{11}) is determined solely by the position of the first bound matrix in the product.

EXERCISES

1.1 Let

$$f = \begin{pmatrix} * & * & * \\ ③ & 2 & * \\ * & 1 & * \end{pmatrix}$$

(a) Find the minimal bound matrix $f*$ associated with the image f.
(b) What are the information densities for f and $f*$?

1.2. For the images f and g

$$f = \begin{pmatrix} 2 & * \\ 3 & 1 \\ 4 & 0 \end{pmatrix}_{1,\,2}, \qquad g = \begin{pmatrix} 3 & 5 & 1 \\ * & * & * \\ 2 & 2 & 1 \\ 3 & 1 & 4 \end{pmatrix}_{0,\,4}$$

determine the image resulting from the following operations:
- **(a)** ADD(f, g)
- **(b)** MULT(f,g)
- **(c)** MAX(f, g)
- **(d)** MIN(f, g)
- **(e)** SCALAR($3;f$)
- **(f)** SUB(g)
- **(g)** DIV(f)
- **(h)** TRAN(f; -1, -2)
- **(i)** NINETY(f)
- **(j)** NINETY^2(f)
- **(k)** NINETY^3(f)
- **(l)** FLIP(f)
- **(m)** SELECT(f; 2, 2, 1, 1)
- **(n)** EXTEND(g, f)
- **(o)** X(g, f)

1.3. Using the images f and g defined in Exercise 1.2, find:
- **(a)** EXTADD(f, g)
- **(b)** EXTMULT(f, g)
- **(c)** EXTMAX(f, g)
- **(d)** EXTMIN(f, g)
- **(e)** DOMAIN(f)
- **(f)** RANGE(f)

1.4. Using block diagrams involving the operators previously described, express the operation $h = $ DOMULT(f, g), where

$$h(i, j) = \begin{cases} f(i, j) \times g(i, j), & f(i, j) \neq * \text{ and } g(i, j) \neq * \\ f(i, j), & f(i, j) \neq * \text{ and } g(i, j) = * \\ *, & \text{otherwise} \end{cases}$$

1.5. For any n by m bound matrix $f = (a_{pq})_{uv}$, give the sequence of operations using block diagrams that yields the n by $2m$ bound matrix g, where

$$g = \begin{pmatrix} a_{11} & a_{12} & \cdots & a_{1m} & a_{11} & a_{12} & \cdots & a_{1m} \\ \vdots & & & & \vdots & & & \\ a_{n1} & a_{n2} & \cdots & a_{nm} & a_{n1} & a_{n2} & \cdots & a_{nm} \end{pmatrix}_{u,\,v}$$

Here the first m columns of the bound matrix g are the same as those of f, and the last m columns are also the same as those of f.

1.6. Describe the following reflection operations in terms of block diagrams involving operators described in this chapter.

(a) $g = \text{HORREFLCT}(f)$, where $g(i, j) = f(i, -j)$

(b) $g = \text{VERTREFLCT}(f)$, where $g(i, j) = f(-i, j)$

(c) $g = \text{DIFLIP}(f)$, where $g(i, j) = f(j, i)$

2

GRAY-LEVEL PROCESSING

2.1 Thresholding

One of the most useful methods for extracting a figure or a feature of particular interest from an image is to apply the method of thresholding. The *threshold* operator produces a black and white image in which the object of interest is black and the background is white. It does so by producing a *binary* image, one where there are only two gray values, 0 (white) and 1 (black). (There might also be stars but these are not affected by thresholding.) Numerous variants of the operator are in use; nevertheless, the essential methodology can be demonstrated with one underlying definition.

Consider the image f given by the bound matrix in Figure 2.1 and sketched in Figure 2.2. In both figures the gray-level quantization runs from 0 through 8, where 0 represents white and 8 represents black. To *threshold* the image f at the value 7 is to *white out* (set the value equal to 0) all pixels with a gray value less than 7 and to *blacken* (set the value equal to 1) all pixels with a gray value greater than or equal to 7. The resulting image (Figure 2.3) has only two gray values, 0 and 1, where a dash (−) has been used in place of the numeral 0 to make the resulting image more distinguishable to the human eye. The letter H is clearly discernible in the thresholded image. It is important to note that, whereas the dashes are part of the image and denote the gray value 0, the stars (∗) are not in the domain of the image and starred pixels are not involved in the thresholding operation. They are invariant.

The fundamental thresholding operation is a binary operation. The inputs are an image f and a real number t. The output is a pure black and white image without intermediate gray values. Notationally, the thresholded image is denoted by THRESH(f; t). It is a binary image and is defined by

$$[\text{THRESH}(f; t)](i, j) = \begin{cases} 1, & \text{if } f(i, j) \geq t \\ 0, & \text{if } f(i, j) < t \\ *, & \text{if } f(i, j) = * \end{cases}$$

The block diagram is given by

$$\begin{pmatrix}
\circledast & 0 & 0 & 0 & 0 & * & 0 & 0 & 0 & 0 & 1 & 2 & 3 & * & 3 & 3 \\
0 & 0 & 0 & 0 & 0 & 1 & 1 & 6 & 0 & 0 & 2 & 3 & 3 & 3 & 3 & 4 \\
0 & 0 & 0 & 2 & 1 & 1 & 0 & 0 & * & 4 & 4 & 6 & 5 & 5 & 5 & 4 \\
0 & 0 & 2 & 7 & 7 & 7 & 5 & 0 & 2 & 5 & 8 & 8 & 8 & 6 & 5 & 5 \\
0 & 0 & 2 & 6 & 7 & 7 & 2 & 0 & 4 & 6 & 8 & 8 & 8 & 6 & 5 & 3 \\
0 & 0 & 2 & 6 & 7 & 8 & 2 & 0 & 3 & 5 & 8 & 8 & 8 & 7 & 6 & 5 \\
0 & 1 & 2 & 7 & 8 & 7 & 7 & 7 & 8 & 8 & 8 & 8 & 8 & 6 & 6 & 4 \\
0 & 0 & 4 & 7 & 7 & 7 & 7 & 7 & 7 & 8 & 8 & 8 & 8 & 7 & 5 & 6 \\
0 & 2 & 2 & 7 & 7 & 7 & 3 & 4 & 4 & 7 & 8 & 8 & 8 & 6 & 4 & 3 \\
1 & 1 & 4 & 7 & 8 & 8 & 2 & 0 & 1 & * & 8 & 8 & 8 & 5 & 6 & 7 \\
1 & 0 & 2 & 7 & 7 & 8 & 2 & 2 & 1 & 5 & 8 & 8 & 8 & 6 & 6 & 5 \\
0 & 1 & 3 & 3 & 4 & 2 & 2 & 0 & 1 & 4 & 6 & 8 & 7 & 5 & 4 & 3 \\
0 & 0 & 2 & 1 & 1 & 2 & 0 & 0 & 0 & 3 & 4 & 4 & 6 & 6 & 5 & 3 \\
* & 0 & 0 & 0 & 0 & 0 & 0 & 0 & 2 & 2 & 3 & 2 & 3 & 5 & 3 & 3
\end{pmatrix}$$

Figure 2.1 Letter H Hidden in Image

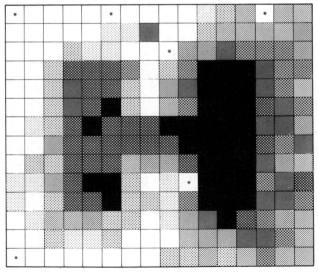

Figure 2.2 Picture of Letter H in Image

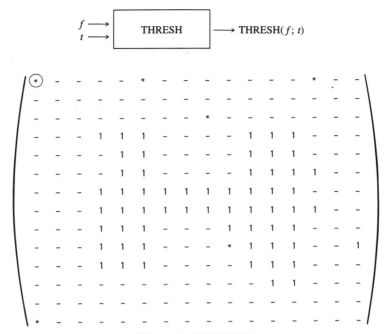

Figure 2.3 THRESH(f;7)

Much can be learned about thresholding in particular, and image processing in general, by studying THRESH(f; 7) as it has been applied to the image f in Figure 2.3. First note the stars. These occur at pixels where the sensor has yielded no information. Starred pixels are not in the domain of the image any more than pixels that are outside the representing bound matrix.

Second, note the two white (zero-valued) pixels at the upper left of the letter H in the thresholded image of Figure 2.3. These originally had the gray value 6, a fairly dark value, but were whitened due to the choice of 7 as the threshold input. Overall it can be seen that the right side of the image f is darker than the left side. This seeming distortion might be due to sensor bias, reflected light, or garbled data transmission, to name a few possibilities.

Analogous to the loss of two pixels in the letter H on the left, there are six extra black pixels on the right. Whereas the lost pixels on the left could be recovered by thresholding at $t = 6$, all but one on the right could be removed by thresholding at $t = 8$. However, the input $t = 7$ appears to be best. Figures 2.4 and 2.5 give the results of thresholding by 6 and 8, respectively. The lower figure creates excess distortion by the inclusion of too many pixels on the right, while the higher figure results in too few pixels on the left.

In the preceding example, it certainly appears that $t = 7$ is the best choice for the threshold. In Section 2.5, where the gray-scale histogram is discussed, an elementary method for choosing the threshold value is introduced.

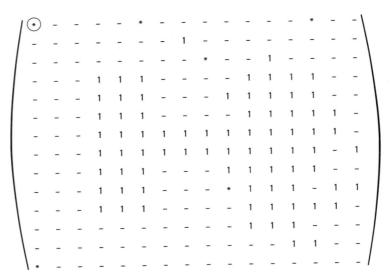

Figure 2.4 THRESH(f;6)

Even for the apparent best choice of threshold input, the letter H is not output in perfect form. While there are many reasons for such inexactness, some of which have been pointed out, the phenomenon of fuzzy demarcation is inherent to image processing. Very often gray values appear extreme, in the sense that an intelligent observer would likely conclude that they are out of place in the picture. Such gray-value readings are referred to as *noise*, a term borrowed from signal processing. Noise is a fact of life in image analysis, and its removal is a central problem.

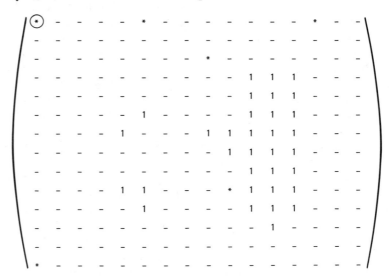

Figure 2.5 THRESH(f;8)

Consider the image *f* of Figure 2.2 and the subsequent thresholded images of Figures 2.3, 2.4, and 2.5. Those pixels of THRESH(*f*; 7) that appear to be missing from the letter H in Figure 2.3 might be termed noisy, since an intelligent observer would likely guess the figure in the image to be H. The excess black values on the right would also be classified as noise. In Figure 2.4, the amount of noise might even result in no identification of the figure. Finally, in Figure 2.5, the choice of too great a threshold could easily lead to the conclusion that the image contains the letter I, and that those blackened pixels toward the left are noise due to sensor distortion, interference, or some other unexplained phenomenon.

To give two of the most important properties of the threshold operator, it is necessary to introduce an order relation regarding images defined on the same domain. One says that image *g* is *less than or equal to* image *h* if *g* and *h* have the same domain and, for any pixel (*i*, *j*) in the common domain, the gray value of *g* is less than or equal to the gray value of *h*, or, in functional notation, $g(i, j) \leq h(i, j)$. The notation for the order relation is $g \leq h$. For example, $g \leq h$ in Figure 2.6. Intuitively, every pixel of *g* is lighter than the corresponding pixel of *h*.

Given this order relation, the threshold operator satisfies the following properties:

a) $g \leq h$ implies THRESH(*g*; *t*) $\leq$ THRESH(*h*; *t*) (increasing monotonicity relative to input image).

b) $t \leq s$ implies THRESH(*g*; *s*) $\leq$ THRESH(*g*; *t*) (decreasing monotonicity relative to input threshold).

Property *a* says that *thresholding* a lighter image *results* in a lighter image. Property *b* states that *thresholding* the same image by a higher threshold *results* in a lighter image.

At this point an implementation of the threshold transformation in terms of the more primitive operations given in Chapter 1 will be provided. As will be the practice throughout the text, this implementation will be given in terms of a block diagram. The representation of higher-level operators in terms of more primitive operators is a fundamental part of image processing. Among other things, it allows for a structured approach to algorithm development and a ready format for programming implementation. The representation for the threshold operator is given in Figure 2.7, where CONST(*g*; *t*) denotes the image that has the same domain as *g* and the gray value *t* at each pixel in the common domain.

Several variants of the fundamental thresholding operation will now be introduced. Each is derivable from THRESH. The symbols employed for these operations are not standard and are introduced solely for explanatory purposes.

It is sometimes useful to be able to identify those pixels on which a given gray value is obtained. This can be done by obtaining a binary image that is 1 where the original image is equal to the given value and 0 on the remaining pixels of the domain

$$g = \begin{pmatrix} 0 & * & 3 & 7 \\ 2 & 2 & 1 & * \\ 1 & 1 & 0 & 3 \end{pmatrix}_{3,2} \qquad h = \begin{pmatrix} 1 & * & 3 & 7 \\ 3 & 5 & 5 & * \\ 1 & 4 & 4 & 4 \end{pmatrix}_{3,2}$$

Figure 2.6 Ordered Images

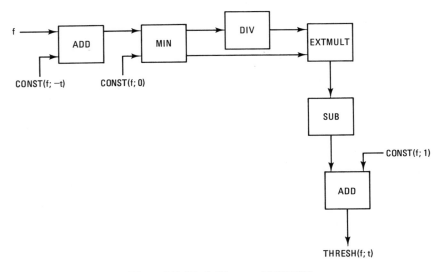

Figure 2.7 Block Diagram of THRESH

of the original image. If f is the image to be processed and t is the gray value of interest, then we are actually solving the equation $f(i, j) = t$ on the domain of f. This *solution* operator will be denoted by EQUAL(f; t) and is defined by

$$[\text{EQUAL}(f; t)](i, j) = \begin{cases} 1, & \text{if } f(i, j) = t \\ 0, & \text{if } f(i, j) \neq t \text{ and } f \text{ is defined at } (i, j) \\ *, & \text{if } f(i, j) = * \end{cases}$$

The operator EQUAL is specified in Figure 2.8. An example is given in Figure 2.9.

While THRESH(f; t) gives the solution set, at least in terms of a binary image, of the inequality $f(i, j) \geq t$, we often need to solve the strict inequality $f(i, j) > t$. The operator that accomplishes this will be called GREATER and is defined by

$$[\text{GREATER}(f; t)](i, j) = \begin{cases} 1, & \text{if } f(i, j) > t \\ 0, & \text{if } f(i, j) \leq t \\ *, & \text{if } f(i, j) = * \end{cases}$$

This operator can also be specified using previously implemented operations. Using the image f of Figure 2.9 and GREATER with $t = 5$, we obtain

$$\text{GREATER}(f; 5) = \begin{pmatrix} - & - & - & - & - & - & - & * \\ - & - & - & 1 & 1 & - & - & - \\ - & - & 1 & 1 & 1 & 1 & - & - \\ - & 1 & 1 & 1 & 1 & 1 & 1 & - \\ - & * & * & 1 & 1 & 1 & - & - \\ - & - & - & 1 & 1 & - & - & - \\ - & - & - & - & 1 & - & - & - \end{pmatrix}_{0,2}$$

The threshold image GREATER(f; 5) reveals a diamond-shaped figure. There appears

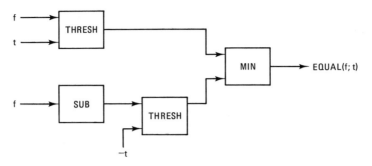

Figure 2.8 Block Diagram of EQUAL

$$f = \begin{pmatrix} 1 & 1 & 2 & 2 & 2 & 2 & 1 & * \\ 0 & 2 & 3 & 6 & 7 & 2 & 1 & 1 \\ 1 & 2 & 6 & 9 & 11 & 7 & 3 & 0 \\ 2 & 7 & 9 & 13 & 14 & 9 & 6 & 3 \\ 3 & * & * & 10 & 9 & 8 & 3 & 1 \\ 1 & 2 & 2 & 8 & 7 & 4 & 4 & 1 \\ 0 & 2 & 1 & 3 & 6 & 2 & 2 & 1 \end{pmatrix}_{0,\,2}$$

$$\text{EQUAL}(f;\,7) = \begin{pmatrix} - & - & - & - & - & - & - & * \\ - & - & - & - & 1 & - & - & - \\ - & - & - & - & - & 1 & - & - \\ - & 1 & - & - & - & - & - & - \\ - & * & * & - & - & - & - & - \\ - & - & - & - & 1 & - & - & - \\ - & - & - & - & - & - & - & - \end{pmatrix}_{0,\,2}$$

Figure 2.9 Use of EQUAL Operation

to be a noisy pixel in the bottom row, and there are two inactivated pixels in the third row from the bottom of the bound matrix. Nevertheless, it is likely that an intelligent observer would identify the figure.

The *less than or equal to* and the *less than* threshold operators are introduced in the exercises. There are also operators of the double inequality type, such as the one that solves the equation

$$s \leq f(i, j) \leq t$$

We shall temporarily call the operator that solves the preceding equation by the name BETWEEN. This operation is defined by

$$[\text{BETWEEN}(f;\, s,\, t)](i, j) = \begin{cases} 1, & \text{if } s \leq f(i, j) \leq t \\ *, & \text{if } f(i, j) = * \\ 0, & \text{otherwise} \end{cases}$$

Notice that BETWEEN is a trinary operator with three inputs, an image and two real numbers. Applying BETWEEN to the image f in Figure 2.9, with the inputs $s = 6$ and $t = 8$, yields

$$
\text{BETWEEN}(f; 6, 8) = \begin{pmatrix}
- & - & - & - & - & - & - & * \\
- & - & - & 1 & 1 & - & - & - \\
- & - & 1 & - & - & 1 & - & - \\
- & 1 & - & - & - & - & 1 & - \\
- & * & * & - & - & 1 & - & - \\
- & - & - & 1 & 1 & - & - & - \\
- & - & - & - & 1 & - & - & -
\end{pmatrix}_{0,2}
$$

Except for the nonactivated pixels (* valued) and one apparent noise pixel, BETWEEN has given the boundary of the diamond.

Rather than threshold to a binary black and white image, it might be desirable to threshold in such a manner as to leave the part of the image above the threshold value intact and to whiten the remaining part of the image. This can easily be accomplished by simply finding THRESH(f; t) and then applying the multiplication operator MULT to THRESH(f; t) and f. In other words, find MULT[f, THRESH(f; t)]. Applied to the image f of Figure 2.9 with the threshold value $t = 6$, this *truncation* operator TRUNC yields

$$
\text{TRUNC}(f; 6) = \begin{pmatrix}
- & - & - & - & - & - & - & * \\
- & - & - & 6 & 7 & - & - & - \\
- & - & 6 & 9 & 11 & 7 & - & - \\
- & 7 & 9 & 13 & 14 & 9 & 6 & - \\
- & * & * & 10 & 9 & 8 & - & - \\
- & - & - & 8 & 7 & - & - & - \\
- & - & - & - & 6 & - & - & -
\end{pmatrix}_{0,2}
$$

It should be apparent that there are many ways of employing thresholding. Unfortunately, there may be *textural* patterns that are actually created by high-frequency gray-value oscillations (rapid and large gray-value variations). In such cases, as in others, it is necessary to preprocess an image before thresholding. The preprocessing consists of the application of other operations prior to taking a threshold. Consequently, the threshold operator will be utilized frequently in the sequel.

2.2 Smoothing

Intuitively, *smoothing* refers to any image-to-image operation that tends to flatten the input image by leveling off rapidly fluctuating gray values. In this text, the term will apply to a particular type of averaging operation that is often used to improve the image by reducing the level of noise in the image.

We must now introduce the concept of a *neighborhood*. In general, a neighborhood of a pixel (i, j) is simply a collection of pixels containing (i, j). However, whenever the term is employed, reference will invariably be being made to some predetermined collection of pixel elements. For example, the *square neighborhood* of (i, j), denoted by SQUARE(i, j), refers to (i, j) together with the pixels immediately above, immediately below, at the sides, and at the corners. In coordinate notation,

$$\text{SQUARE}(i, j) = \{(i, j), (i + 1, j), (i - 1, j), (i, j + 1),$$
$$(i, j - 1), (i + 1, j + 1), (i - 1, j - 1),$$
$$(i + 1, j - 1), (i - 1, j + 1)\}$$

Pictorially, SQUARE(i, j) is given by

$(i - 1, j + 1)$	$(i, j + 1)$	$(i + 1, j + 1)$
$(i - 1, j)$	(i, j)	$(i + 1, j)$
$(i - 1, j - 1)$	$(i, j - 1)$	$(i + 1, j - 1)$

While many other neighborhoods are utilized, only SQUARE will be specifically named.

Associated with the notion of neighborhood is the concept of a *mask*. A mask is a two-dimensional array of real numbers, one of which will be referred to as the *center*. In Figure 2.10, M is a mask with value $\frac{1}{2}$ at the center.

In fact, a mask is nothing but a bound matrix containing the origin within its domain. Hence it is an image! The reason for introducing the new terminology is the special use to which these particular images will be put. Given a neighborhood, a mask of the same shape can be placed over the neighborhood to *weight* the pixels within it. For example, the preceding mask can be associated with SQUARE(i, j) in such a manner. The intent here is to create a weighting schema that will be utilized in the definition of certain image operations.

The operator SMOOTH will assign to each pixel in an image a weighted average of the gray values in some predefined neighborhood containing the pixel. By doing this, each resulting gray value will tend to be less differentiated from its neighbors than it was originally. The net effect will be an image that is flattened. Rapidly oscillating highs and lows will be mediated. As a result, high-frequency salt-and-pepper noise, a type composed of isolated high-intensity gray-value fluctuations, will be attenuated. However, an unwanted side result will be the blurring of contrast within the image. The distinguishability of features that result from substantial differences in the gray values of surrounding pixels will be reduced.

The operator SMOOTH is a binary operator in that it has two inputs: (1) an image f and (2) a mask M. However, the mask is of a particular type in that its entries must be nonnegative and they must sum to 1. Such a mask will be called an *averaging mask* since

$$M = \begin{pmatrix} \frac{1}{32} & \frac{3}{32} & \frac{1}{32} \\ \frac{3}{32} & \boxed{\frac{1}{2}} & \frac{3}{32} \\ \frac{1}{32} & \frac{3}{32} & \frac{1}{32} \end{pmatrix}$$

Figure 2.10 Image Used as a Mask

its role is to define a weighted average. The mask M of Figure 2.10 is such a mask. SMOOTH is defined by

$$[\text{SMOOTH}(f; M)](i, j) = \sum_{(u, v) \in N} M_{ij}(u, v) \times f(u, v)$$

where N is the neighborhood corresponding to the mask M when the center of M is placed over the pixel (i, j), $M_{ij}(u, v)$ is the mask value at the pixel (u, v) after M has been centered at (i, j), and $f(u, v)$ is the gray value of the image f at (u, v). Intuitively, the value of SMOOTH$(f; M)$ at the pixel (i, j) is the weighted average, the weights given by M, over the M-shaped neighborhood of (i, j), the neighborhood center. The stipulation is made that, if any of the terms of the sum defining SMOOTH$(f; M)$ at (i, j) have a term $f(u, v)$ that is undefined $[f(u, v) = *]$, then SMOOTH will be star valued (undefined) at (i, j).

Example 2.1

Let M be the mask of Figure 2.10 and f be the image given by the bound matrix

$$f = \begin{pmatrix} 0 & 0 & 0 & 0 & 0 & 0 & 0 \\ * & 0 & 0 & 0 & 0 & 0 & 0 \\ 0 & 0 & 8 & 8 & 8 & 0 & 0 \\ 0 & 0 & 8 & 8 & 8 & 0 & 0 \\ 0 & 0 & 8 & 8 & 8 & 0 & 6 \\ 0 & 0 & 0 & 6 & 0 & 6 & 0 \\ 0 & 0 & 6 & 0 & 6 & 0 & 6 \end{pmatrix}_{-3, 3}$$

Assuming a gray-scale quantization of 0 through 8, it can clearly be seen that there is a black square in the middle of the image. It can also be seen that there is some high-frequency noise (the 6's) in the lower-right corner of the image. To compute SMOOTH$(f; M)$, the mask is successively placed over the pixels in the domain of f. (The value of SMOOTH must be $*$ at every pixel for which f is undefined, since a $*$ appears in the sum defining SMOOTH in such a situation.) For instance, recalling that the upper-left entry of the bound matrix is situated at $(-3, 3)$ we can see that $f(1, -1) = 8$ and that, when f is restricted to SQUARE$(1, -1)$, the square neighborhood about $(1, -1)$, the restricted portion of f takes the form

$$f' = \begin{pmatrix} 8 & 8 & 0 \\ 8 & 8 & 0 \\ 6 & 0 & 6 \end{pmatrix}_{0, 0}$$

According to the definition of SMOOTH, the gray values of f' are multiplied times the corresponding values of M and the sum is taken. As a result,

$$[\text{SMOOTH}(f; M)](1, -1) = (\tfrac{1}{32} \times 8) + (\tfrac{3}{32} \times 8) + (\tfrac{1}{32} \times 0)$$

$$+ (\tfrac{3}{32} \times 8) + (\tfrac{1}{2} \times 8) + (\tfrac{3}{32} \times 0)$$

$$+ (\tfrac{1}{32} \times 6) + (\tfrac{3}{32} \times 0) + (\tfrac{1}{32} \times 6)$$

$$= 6\tfrac{1}{8}$$

Pictorially, we can view the mask M over f as in Figure 2.11.

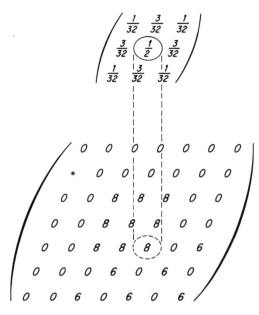

Figure 2.11 Use of Mask in Smooth

Proceeding with the calculation for the remaining pixels in the domain of f, we obtain the following bound matrix for SMOOTH(f; M):

$$
\begin{pmatrix}
* & * & * & * & * & * & * \\
* & * & 1 & 1\frac{1}{4} & 1 & \frac{1}{4} & * \\
* & * & 5\frac{3}{4} & 6\frac{3}{4} & 5\frac{3}{4} & 1 & * \\
* & 1\frac{1}{4} & 6\frac{3}{4} & 8 & 6\frac{3}{4} & 1\frac{7}{16} & * \\
* & 1 & 5\frac{15}{16} & 7\frac{5}{16} & 6\frac{1}{8} & 2\frac{1}{8} & * \\
* & \frac{7}{16} & 2\frac{1}{8} & 4\frac{5}{8} & 2\frac{11}{16} & 3\frac{13}{16} & * \\
* & * & * & * & * & * & *
\end{pmatrix}_{-3,3}
$$

There are two points to notice. First, the outer columns and rows of the image have been lost because the mask centered at these pixels must contain star-valued pixels. There is also a loss of gray values at $(-2, 1)$ and $(-2, 2)$ resulting from the intrusion of a $*$ value at $(-3, 2)$ of the original image. Although in this instance the loss of information does not seem crucial, a repeated use of SMOOTH would eventually decimate the square figure.

The second point concerns the behavior of SMOOTH in terms of flattening. The noisy pixels have had their gray values substantially reduced, but at the cost of a less clear demarcation between the square in the center of the image and its background. The problem can perhaps best be illustrated by applying THRESH to both f and SMOOTH(f; M). If THRESH is applied to f with threshold $t = 7$, then the square is extracted perfectly. However, with the threshold value lowered only to $t = 6$, THRESH applied to the smoothed image yields

$$
\text{THRESH[SMOOTH}(f; M); 6] =
\begin{pmatrix}
* & - & - & - & - \\
* & - & 1 & - & - \\
- & 1 & 1 & 1 & - \\
- & - & 1 & 1 & - \\
- & - & - & - & -
\end{pmatrix}_{-2,2}
$$

where the bound matrix has been put in minimal form. While the smoothing operation has eliminated noise, it has also altered the content of the image beyond recognition. One might argue that there is no need to smooth since the square is clearly delineated with a threshold value of 7. However, suppose the original threshold value had been 6. In other words, suppose we did not know the figure to begin with (the actual situation confronted in practice). Then an original threshold at 6 would have yielded a noisy binary image:

$$\text{THRESH}(f; 6) = \begin{pmatrix} - & - & - & - & - & - & - \\ * & - & - & - & - & - & - \\ - & - & 1 & 1 & 1 & - & - \\ - & - & 1 & 1 & 1 & - & - \\ - & - & 1 & 1 & 1 & - & 1 \\ - & - & - & 1 & - & 1 & - \\ - & - & 1 & - & 1 & - & 1 \end{pmatrix}_{-3,3}$$

In other words, thresholding at $t = 6$ would have made recognition impossible, but so would have smoothing by M and then thresholding at $t = 6$.

Example 2.1 illustrates the hurdle one faces when attempting to apply SMOOTH. In return for a flattening of high-frequency noise, there is a loss of sharpness within the image. However, the problem goes well beyond the specific operator being discussed. SMOOTH is an example of a general class of operators known as *space-invariant moving-average filters*. These operators are defined in Section 2.3. In particular, SMOOTH is a *low-pass filter*, a filter that attenuates high-frequency fluctuations. These operators tend to filter out high frequencies while simultaneously blurring the original contrast of the image. The dilemma is characteristic of low-pass filters. It will be discussed again in Section 2.3.

To facilitate the implementation of SMOOTH in terms of more primary operators, two new operators will be introduced. The first operator, DOT, is binary in that it takes two images for its input. However, its output is not another image, but instead either a real number or a star ($*$). The name DOT is used since the new operator is a generalization of the classic dot product in vector algebra. DOT is defined as follows:

1) If f and g have a common domain D, then

$$\text{DOT}(f, g) = \sum_{(u, v) \in D} f(u, v) \times g(u, v)$$

2) If f and g do not have the same domain, then

$$\text{DOT}(f, g) = * \quad \text{(is undefined)}$$

Example 2.2

Consider images f, g, and h defined, respectively, by

$$f = \begin{pmatrix} 1 & 3 & 4 \\ 2 & 1 & 0 \end{pmatrix}_{2, 0}, \qquad g = \begin{pmatrix} 1 & * & 2 \\ 5 & 3 & 1 \end{pmatrix}_{2, 0}, \qquad h = \begin{pmatrix} 2 & 1 & 0 \\ 5 & 1 & 6 \end{pmatrix}_{2, 0}$$

Then $\text{DOT}(f, g) = *$ since $(3, 0)$ is in the domain of f but not in the domain of g. On the other hand,

$$\text{DOT}(f, h) = (1 \times 2) + (3 \times 1) + (4 \times 0)$$
$$+ (2 \times 5) + (1 \times 1) + (0 \times 6) = 16$$

Some basic properties of DOT are the following:

a) $\text{DOT}(f, g) = \text{DOT}(g, f)$ (commutativity)
b) $\text{DOT}[f, \text{ADD}(g, h)] = \text{ADD}[\text{DOT}(f, g), \text{DOT}(f, h)]$ (distributivity)
c) $\text{DOT}[\text{SCALAR}(t; f), g] = t \times \text{DOT}(f, g)$ (associativity)

where f, g, and h are images, t is a scalar (real number), and in property c the convention is made that the multiplication of a $*$ by either a real number or a $*$ is again a $*$. The last somewhat strange comment means only that, whenever a term that is called for in an arithmetic operation is undefined, the output of the expression is undefined. Those familiar with the dot product in vector algebra should immediately recognize the preceding properties. Intuitively, property a states that DOT commutes, property b states that DOT distributes over ADD, and property c states that a scalar can be pulled out of one of the inputs of DOT and then arithmetically multiplied after DOT has been completed. The block diagram for DOT is given by

$$f \longrightarrow \boxed{\quad \text{DOT} \quad} \longrightarrow \text{DOT}(f, g)$$
$$g \longrightarrow$$

The specification of DOT is given in Figure 2.12. Because the output of DOT is to be $*$ if the domains of the inputs do not coincide, the diagram is a bit complicated. To help see it, consider two cases. First, suppose that f and g have the same domain. Then the sequence EXTEND, NINETY^2, and DOMAIN simply gives their common domain rotated by 180°. The parallel translations of f and g by that rotated domain result in two sets of images, one set having each gray value of f situated at the origin and the other set having each gray value of g situated at the origin. SELECT then picks out those origin gray values, MULT multiplies common pairs, ADD sums the products, and RANGE outputs the resulting real number.

Now suppose the domains of f and g in Figure 2.12 do not coincide. In this case, the sequence EXTEND, NINETY^2, and DOMAIN gives the union of the domains rotated 180°, and this union is strictly larger than at least one of the original domains. Hence the parallel translations and selections yield at least one 1 by 1 image at the origin that is $*$ valued. As a result, at least one of the MULT operations yields an empty image, and the ADD does likewise. The output of RANGE is then $*$.

The second new operator is the *restriction* operator REST. This operator is closely related to the selection operator in that it alters one of its inputs by giving it a smaller domain. REST is a binary operator with two input images. If f and g are the inputs, in that order, then REST(f, g) *restricts* f to the domain of g; it is an image whose domain is the intersection of the domains of f and g and whose gray values are those of f on that domain. Its block diagram is

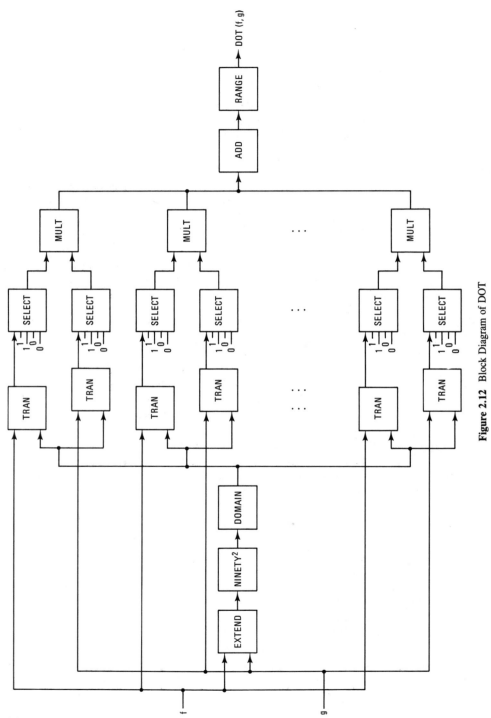

Figure 2.12 Block Diagram of DOT

The order of f and g is important since in general it is not true that REST(f, g) = REST(g, f). The specification of REST is quite simple:

Note that multiplication of f by a constant image that is 1 on the domain of g merely eliminates f everywhere except on the domain of g. Also note that we are letting CONST denote an operator whose output, when given inputs g and t, is CONST$(g; t)$.

The operator REST can be used to define the notion of a *subimage*. Image h is a subimage of image f if h = REST(f, h). In other words, on the domain of h, f and h are identical.

Example 2.3

Let

$$f = \begin{pmatrix} 1 & * & 4 & 5 & 1 \\ * & 2 & * & 1 & 0 \\ 2 & 1 & -1 & 0 & * \end{pmatrix}_{0,\,2}$$

and

$$g = \begin{pmatrix} 4 & 2 & 6 & 1 \\ 2 & * & 1 & 3 \end{pmatrix}_{2,\,1}$$

Then

$$\text{REST}(f, g) = \begin{pmatrix} * & 1 & 0 \\ -1 & * & * \end{pmatrix}_{2,\,1}$$

Employing DOT and REST, Figure 2.13 gives the implementation of the transformation SMOOTH. In the definition of SMOOTH, it can be seen that the summation is a dot-type operation between the mask M translated so that its center is at (i, j) and the portion of the image f that is situated on the same pixels as the translated mask. But this means that the restriction operator has been applied to f to form a subimage of f concentric to the translated mask. Applying DOT followed by CREATE implements the summation of products, as in the definition of SMOOTH, and leaves that value, a real number or a $*$, in the appropriate pixel location. EXTADD then outputs the smoothed image.

The opportunity for parallel design is evident in the specifications of both DOT and SMOOTH. Although architectural questions as such will be addressed in Chapter 7,

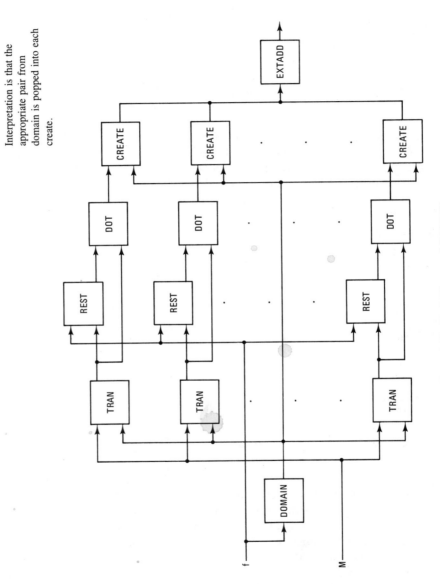

Interpretation is that the appropriate pair from domain is popped into each create.

Figure 2.13 Block Diagram of SMOOTH

52

it is worthwhile to note the extensive parallelism that the block diagram implementations reveal. Often a problem with image processing is the real-time constraint; processing must be accomplished within given time limitations. While bound matrix representations of images might introduce some notational intricacies, they also expose the structural parallelism inherent in the imaging algorithms.

2.3 Moving-average Filters

SMOOTH is an example of a class of operators known as space-invariant moving-average filters. The output image generated by SMOOTH is constructed by taking weighted averages over varying portions of the input image. Hence the term *average* is most appropriate. However, even when a similar procedure is used without employing an averaging mask, the same terminology is applied. Regarding the *space-invariant* phraseology, this relates to the constancy of the mask. The same mask is used for each gray-level computation. To be precise, a space-invariant moving-average filter is an operator of the following form:

$$[\text{FILTER}(f; M)](i, j) = \sum_{(u,\, v)\, \in\, N} [\text{TRAN}(M; i, j)](u, v) \times f(u, v)$$

where $\text{TRAN}(M; i, j)$ is the mask M translated so that its center lies at (i, j), and N is the domain of the translated mask. As with SMOOTH, the stipulation is made that all terms in the defining sum must be defined or else the output is $*$ (undefined). If M happens to be a 3 by 3 averaging mask, then the preceding definition coincides with the definition of SMOOTH. Since the only difference between an arbitrary space-invariant moving-average filter and the particular operator SMOOTH is the input mask, any such filter can be specified in exactly the same manner as SMOOTH by using the translation operator TRAN together with REST, DOT, CREATE, and EXTADD.

It has been pointed out that SMOOTH can be considered to be a low-pass filter in that it attenuates high frequencies (rapidly fluctuating gray values). To be a bit more precise, a low-pass filter transmits with relatively little alteration an input image that fluctuates slowly with respect to pixel changes, but it levels out an input image that fluctuates rapidly with respect to such changes. On the other hand, a *high-pass filter* has the reverse effect. It alters little a rapidly fluctuating input image but accentuates changes in a slowly changing image. Each type has its advantages and drawbacks. A low-pass filter reduces high-frequency noise at the cost of blurring contrast. While filters play a role in image processing, the theoretical details belong more properly to a course on signal processing.

Example 2.4

Consider the mask M and the image f given, respectively, by

$$M = \begin{pmatrix} 0 & -1 & 0 \\ -1 & \circledR{8} & -1 \\ 0 & -1 & 0 \end{pmatrix}$$

and

$$f = \begin{pmatrix} 0 & 0 & 0 & 0 & 0 & 0 & 0 \\ 0 & 1 & 1 & 1 & 1 & 1 & 0 \\ 0 & 1 & 2 & 2 & 2 & 1 & 0 \\ 0 & 1 & 2 & 2 & 2 & 1 & 0 \\ 0 & 1 & 2 & 2 & 2 & 1 & 0 \\ 0 & 1 & 1 & 1 & 1 & 1 & 0 \\ 0 & 0 & 0 & 0 & 0 & 0 & 0 \end{pmatrix}_{-3,3}$$

Filtering f by using M yields

$$\text{FILTER}(f; M) = \begin{pmatrix} 6 & 4 & 4 & 4 & 6 \\ 4 & 10 & 9 & 10 & 4 \\ 4 & 9 & 8 & 9 & 4 \\ 4 & 10 & 9 & 10 & 4 \\ 6 & 4 & 4 & 4 & 6 \end{pmatrix}_{-2,2}$$

Assuming the gray-scale quantization to run from 0 to 31, it might be difficult to distinguish the square of gray value 2 in the middle of f. Not only would it be difficult for the eye to detect, but a threshold parameter t would have to be chosen in the range $1 < t \leq 2$, a very small range considering the gray range of 0 to 31. Filtering with the mask M has increased the contrast between the 3 by 3 square and its surrounding pixels. Notice, however, the seemingly noisy pixels at the corners of the image and the new gray-level variation introduced into the square. The square has been more markedly revealed at the cost of some loss of intensity uniformity and the introduction of some noise. The full impact of the dilemma is demonstrated by filtering f with the mask N, where

$$N = \begin{pmatrix} 0 & -2 & 0 \\ -2 & \textcircled{10} & -2 \\ 0 & -2 & 0 \end{pmatrix}$$

In this case we obtain

$$\text{FILTER}(f; N) = \begin{pmatrix} 6 & 2 & 2 & 2 & 6 \\ 2 & 8 & 6 & 8 & 2 \\ 2 & 6 & 4 & 6 & 2 \\ 2 & 8 & 6 & 8 & 2 \\ 6 & 2 & 2 & 2 & 6 \end{pmatrix}_{-2,2}$$

Filtering with N has introduced enough noise to destroy the figure of the square. Indeed, thresholding with $t = 6$ gives

$$\text{THRESH}[\text{FILTER}(f; N); 6] = \begin{pmatrix} 1 & - & - & - & 1 \\ - & 1 & 1 & 1 & - \\ - & 1 & - & 1 & - \\ - & 1 & 1 & 1 & - \\ 1 & - & - & - & 1 \end{pmatrix}_{-2,2}$$

while thresholding with $t = 7$ yields

$$\text{THRESH}[\text{FILTER}(f; N); 7] = \begin{pmatrix} - & - & - & - & - \\ - & 1 & - & 1 & - \\ - & - & - & - & - \\ - & 1 & - & 1 & - \\ - & - & - & - & - \end{pmatrix}_{-2,2}$$

Example 2.4 has once again shown the problematic nature of space-invariant moving-average filters. The situation can be improved somewhat by removing the requirement of space invariance. Instead of utilizing a single mask and translating it to the pixel at which it is needed, one can define a collection of masks, each to be used at a specific pixel or set of pixels within the image domain. For example, if the sensor equipment is such that one portion of the image is usually noisy while the rest is not, we need only smooth on the noisy portion while leaving the rest of the image alone.

Example 2.5

Consider the image f of Example 2.1 and the mask M of Figure 2.10. When SMOOTH was applied using input mask M, there was certainly a leveling of the supposed noise pixels, but there was also an undesirable loss of contrast. It appears that in f the noise is constrained to the lower-right corner of the image. Suppose the image engineer has seen this phenomenon occur repeatedly and has decided to smooth only the 12 pixels in the bottom three rows and rightmost four columns. Then he or she might segment the image into two regions, one where the mask $I = (\text{①})$ is to be applied and the other where M is to be applied. (Note that averaging with I is equivalent to leaving the pixel unchanged.) The resulting image, after rounding off all entries to integers, is

$$\begin{pmatrix} 0 & 0 & 0 & 0 & 0 & 0 & 0 \\ * & 0 & 0 & 0 & 0 & 0 & 0 \\ 0 & 0 & 8 & 8 & 8 & 0 & 0 \\ 0 & 0 & 8 & 8 & 8 & 0 & 0 \\ 0 & 0 & 8 & 7 & 6 & 2 & * \\ 0 & 0 & 0 & 5 & 3 & 4 & * \\ 0 & 0 & 6 & * & * & * & * \end{pmatrix}_{-3,3}$$

Whereas thresholding at $t = 6$ after applying SMOOTH gave a figure that was not recognizable as a square, a similar thresholding in this instance would yield a square together with one isolated black pixel not adjacent to the square. Filters that apply different masks, such as the one in this example, are called *space-variant* filters. Although the filter in this example is rather trivial, it nonetheless demonstrates the possible advantage of space-variant filters over space-invariant filters.

2.4 A Local Noise-removal Technique

To improve the design of noise-reducing filters, it is necessary to realize that noise is random. It may be that in some instances it tends to cluster on one region of the image; nevertheless, the exact coordinate positions at which it will occur are usually unknown.

While it is true that some beforehand knowledge concerning the manner in which the noise will distribute itself allows the application of probabilistic filtering techniques, such methodologies are beyond the scope of the present text.

Yet there is a characteristic of noise that allows a simple smoothing-type filter to be designed, one that is not a moving-average filter. The pixels that would likely be classified as noisy in a given image tend to have gray values that appear out of place with regard to the surrounding pixels. A noise pixel tends to have a gray value that differs substantially from the average gray value of some neighborhood containing it. The idea is to replace the gray value of a pixel by a neighborhood average if that pixel appears to be noisy. One of the essential problems with SMOOTH is that it smooths all gray values, rather than just those that are noisy. Even space-variant filters make an a priori decision as to what mask should be applied at each pixel. This new approach is "after the fact." Smoothing is applied according to a predetermined acceptance bound for isolated pixel variation.

This approach, too, has its problems, since the choice of a pixel as a noise pixel depends on the trigger value to decide whether or not it differs too much from the surrounding pixels. It also depends on the size of the comparison neighborhood. Moreover, as with any noise-reduction scheme, we can never be certain that an extreme value at a pixel does not properly belong to the actual noise-free image—that it is not noise at all! For example, the method now to be introduced would likely smooth tiny black spots on a white background. It might make these spots invisible to some thresholding operation and thereby cause their detection to be overlooked. Nonetheless, the method is useful for certain situations where some degree of regularity in the figure to be discovered is expected.

The pixel (i, j) in the domain D of image f will be treated as a noise pixel if it possesses a gray value that differs by at least some trigger value q from the average gray level taken over the neighborhood SQUARE(i, j). In terms of imaging operators, this average, which will be temporarily denoted by AV, is given by

$$AV(f; i, j) = DOT[SELECT(f; 3, 3, i - 1, j + 1), TRAN(C; i, j)],$$

where C is the *constant* averaging mask

$$C = \begin{pmatrix} 1/9 & 1/9 & 1/9 \\ 1/9 & \textcircled{1/9} & 1/9 \\ 1/9 & 1/9 & 1/9 \end{pmatrix}$$

Since the sign of difference between the gray value and the neighborhood average is of no consequence, (i, j) is considered a noise pixel if

$$|f(i, j) - AV(f; i, j)| \geq q$$

Recall that DOT yields a $*$ if the two input images do not have common domains. As a result, $AV(f; i, j)$ is undefined if f possesses a star-valued pixel in SQUARE(i, j). In such an event, the preceding inequality is undefined, and by convention the pixel (i, j) is considered noisy. The situation is somewhat analogous to that encountered with SMOOTH, where the intrusion of $*$ values into the image caused a diminution of the size of the overall image. Such pathologies are referred to as *boundary conditions*.

For any pixel that is considered noisy, the gray value is redefined by smoothing locally at the pixel itself. The smoothing is done by utilizing a predetermined averaging mask M, such as that given in Figure 2.10. The pixels for which the trigger value q is not exceeded are left alone.

It is important to note that this new local noise-reduction operator, LOCSMOOTH, requires three inputs, each of a different type:

1) An image f
2) A mask M
3) A trigger value q

In fact, the use of SQUARE(i, j) as the averaging neighborhood is not required. A more general version of LOCSMOOTH can be obtained by requiring the averaging neighborhood to be a fourth input; however, this generalization will not be pursued here. In any event, LOCSMOOTH is defined precisely by

$$[\text{LOCSMOOTH}(f; M; q)](i, j) = \begin{cases} \text{DOT [SELECT}(f; 3, 3, i - 1, j + 1), \text{TRAN}(M; i, j)], \\ \quad \text{if } (i, j) \text{ is noisy} \\ f(i, j), \quad \text{if } (i, j) \text{ is not noisy} \end{cases}$$

Example 2.6

Let f be the image

$$f = \begin{pmatrix} 0 & 2 & 3 & 3 & 0 & 2 \\ 1 & 3 & 8 & 2 & 0 & 1 \\ 1 & 3 & 1 & 2 & 0 & * \\ 1 & 2 & 0 & 1 & 2 & 3 \\ 1 & 2 & 9 & 2 & 1 & 0 \\ 1 & 0 & 1 & 1 & 0 & 1 \end{pmatrix}_{0,5}$$

Using the trigger value $q = 4$, there are two noise pixels that do not result from boundary conditions. They are $(2, 4)$ and $(2, 1)$, whose respective neighborhood averages are AV$(f; 2, 4)$ $= 3$ and AV$(f; 2, 1) = 2$. Letting $M = C$, the constant mask defined previously, the output of the operation LOCSMOOTH is

$$\text{LOCSMOOTH}(f; C; q) = \begin{pmatrix} 3 & 3 & 2 & * \\ 3 & 1 & 2 & * \\ 2 & 0 & 1 & * \\ 2 & 2 & 2 & 1 \end{pmatrix}_{1,4}$$

Two points concerning Example 2.6 should be recognized. First, the destruction of part of the original image due to the boundary conditions appears especially important because of the small size of the image. In practice, images are often 256 by 256 or larger with very few, if any, $*$ values inside the minimal bound matrix. Hence the stipulation made with respect to $*$ values is usually not of any consequence. Second, if the two pixels that were moderated had represented traces of some hard-to-detect substance, LOCSMOOTH would have been just as inappropriate an operation as SMOOTH. Once again it should be emphasized that heuristic judgments on the part of the image engineer are crucial for the pragmatic employment of noise-reduction techniques.

In general, the application of LOCSMOOTH requires the user to select the trigger value q and the averaging mask M. Insofar as q is concerned, the dilemma faced is similar to that encountered with the choice of a threshold value when applying THRESH. With regard to M, the weighting scheme must depend on the application. Usually it is wise to weight the center pixel more heavily than the surrounding pixels to give more importance to the actual sensor reading. Moreover, the actual size of M can be varied so that a larger pixel neighborhood is used to help determine the new gray value of the noisy pixel.

We can go much further. The entire method for determining whether or not a given pixel should be considered noisy can be altered, and, in so doing, different variants of LOCSMOOTH can be constructed. For instance, (i, j) can be classified as noisy if it differs in absolute value by more than q from more than some fixed number of its neighbors. Or the average used to determine noisiness may be done with a weighted averaging mask instead of a constant mask. Or some other more sophisticated technique can be applied. In a sense, the variations are endless. The appropriateness of any specific choice depends on the image engineer.

A last point to note prior to proceeding to the specification of LOCSMOOTH is that it is not considered to be a moving-average filter. In a moving-average filter, the weighting mask may vary from pixel to pixel (space-variant filter); however, the pixels to which a given mask is applied are determined independently of the input image. In other words, all input images are acted on in the same manner by a moving-average filter. Weighting is decided on prior to the fact. With LOCSMOOTH, it is determined after the fact.

To assist in the implementation of LOCSMOOTH, another important imaging operation will be specified first. That operator, ABS, is the *absolute value* operator. Given an input image, it returns an image having the same domain and having gray values equal to the absolute values of the input gray values. Precisely,

$$[\mathrm{ABS}(f)](i, j) = |f(i, j)|$$

unless $f(i, j)$ is undefined, in which case $\mathrm{ABS}(f)$ is also undefined ($*$) at (i, j). The following block diagram gives an implementation of ABS in terms of more primitive operators.

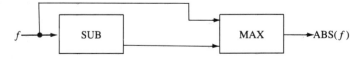

The implementation of LOCSMOOTH will be split into two procedures. First, an image called NOISE$(f; q)$ will be constructed. NOISE$(f; q)$ will have a gray value of

1 at any pixel identified as noisy according to the trigger value q; it will have a $*$ at all other pixels. Then a second block diagram will use NOISE(f; q) as an input to compute LOCSMOOTH(f; M; q).

The operator NOISE is specified in Figure 2.14, where SMOOTH occurs due to the pointwise relation

$$AV(f; i, j) = [SMOOTH(f; C)](i, j)$$

The output of SMOOTH at each pixel is precisely $AV(f; i, j)$. SUB followed by ADD subtracts these averages, and ABS followed by THRESH identifies with a 1 those pixels for which

$$|f(i, j) - AV(f; i, j)| \geq q$$

It assigns the value 0 to those with difference less than q. But this does not complete the picture. Some noise pixels, those for which $AV(f; i, j) = *$, are star-valued after THRESH, whereas they should have gray value 1. An extended multiplication by CONST (f; 1) corrects this. Now all noise pixels have value 1, and all nonnoise pixels in the domain of f have value 0. DIV produces the desired result.

Figure 2.15 provides the specification for LOCSMOOTH. The main body of the diagram is similar to the implementation of SMOOTH in Figure 2.14 except that only the pixels in the domain of NOISE(f; q) are smoothed. The interesting part of the diagram is the path along the bottom. It concerns a boundary condition. Since the output of DOT can be a $*$, we do not simply wish to extend the image of smoothed noise pixels by the entire original image f, but only by the part of f that is not noisy. Some pixels of f under LOCSMOOTH must become star-valued. The bottom part of the diagram accomplishes this end. When the output of DIV is multiplied times f, only the nonnoise pixels of f remain in the domain.

The complications arising in Figures 2.14 and 2.15 due to the occurrence of boundary conditions are not unusual in imaging algorithms. In reading such block diagrams, it is wise to first get a grasp of the structure exclusive of the boundary conditions. They tend to confuse the issue. Once this has been accomplished, then consider the anomalies arising from the occurrence of star-valued pixels.

2.5 Gray-Level Histogram

Consider the image f with discrete gray-value range $\{0, 1, ..., 2^{k-1}\}$, where k is a positive integer. The *gray-level histogram* for f is the discrete graph plotted with the number of pixels, $[HIST(f)](y)$, having gray level y. It gives the distribution of the gray-level intensities over the image without reference to their location, only to the frequency of occurrence.

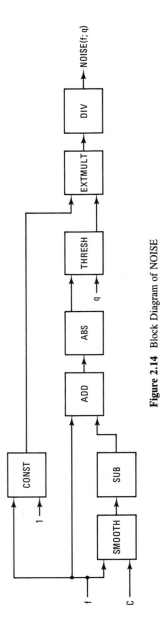

Figure 2.14 Block Diagram of NOISE

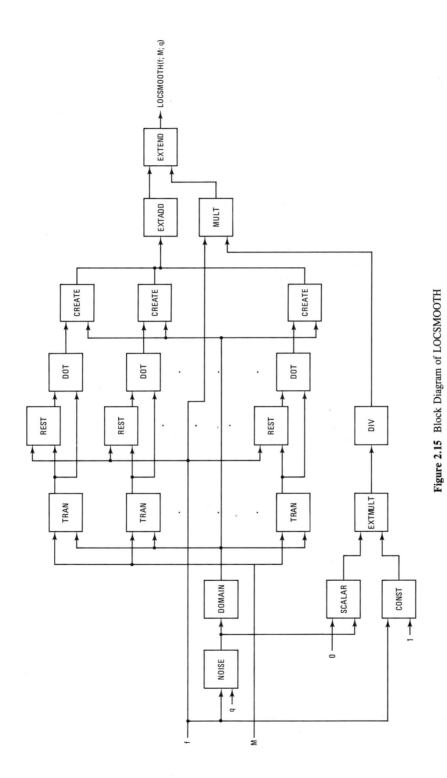

Figure 2.15 Block Diagram of LOCSMOOTH

Example 2.7

Let f be the image

$$f = \begin{pmatrix} 1 & 2 & 1 & 1 & 3 & 2 & 0 & 0 \\ 1 & 2 & 14 & 14 & 15 & 13 & 3 & 2 \\ 3 & 4 & 12 & 3 & 5 & 15 & 1 & 2 \\ 2 & 7 & 13 & 1 & 4 & 15 & 1 & 7 \\ 1 & 6 & 14 & 2 & 3 & 14 & 0 & 1 \\ 3 & 4 & 12 & 4 & 6 & 12 & 9 & 2 \\ 5 & 3 & 15 & 13 & 12 & 11 & 8 & 5 \\ 7 & 6 & 5 & 4 & 8 & 6 & 4 & 3 \end{pmatrix}_{0,\,6}$$

Then f has the histogram HIST(f) given in Figure 2.16. For example, $[\text{HIST}(f)](4) = 6$. It is clear that there are two distinct concentrations of gray levels, the larger consisting of rather light grays and the smaller consisting of darker grays.

[HIST(f)] (y)

```
9   X
8   X  X  X
7   X  X  X
6   X  X  X  X
5   X  X  X  X
4   X  X  X  X  X  X                    X        X  X
3   X  X  X  X  X  X  X  X              X  X  X  X
2   X  X  X  X  X  X  X  X  X           X  X  X  X
1   X  X  X  X  X  X  X  X  X  X     X  X  X  X  X
    0  1  2  3  4  5  6  7  8  9  10 11 12 13 14 15   y
```

Figure 2.16 Illustration of Histogram Operation

Note that HIST is a unary operator with one input, an image, and an output that is an array:

$$[\text{HIST}(f)](0),\ [\text{HIST}(f)](1),\ \ldots,\ [\text{HIST}(f)](n)$$

where $n = 2^k - 1$. Therefore, it can be held in a stack or some similar data structure. A more interesting approach is to consider HIST(f) as the 1 by n image

$$([\text{HIST}(f)](0)\quad [\text{HIST}(f)](1)\quad \cdots \quad [\text{HIST}(f)](n))_{0,\,0}$$

The latter approach makes HIST a unary operator with an image input and an image output. As an image-to-image operator, it is more in line with the majority of the other operators. Moreover, it can be implemented with preexisting operations. This is done in Figure 2.17. First, note that DIV is used, as in the specification of LOCSMOOTH, to eliminate the 0 entries from the domain of a binary image. Second, note the use of the *cardinality* operator CARD. This operator simply counts the elements in the set output by DOMAIN. It is not an image operation. Once the cardinalities of each solution set for the equation $f(i, j) = r$, $r = 0, 1, \ldots, n = 2^{k-1}$, are obtained, they are placed in an array to be input into the creation operator. CREATE forms the desired image HIST(f).

The gray-level histogram can be used for a number of purposes, but as is usually the case in image processing, the techniques must be employed judiciously.

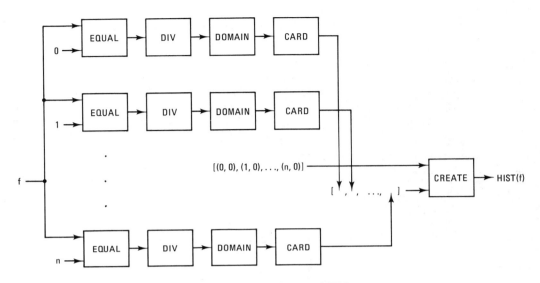

Figure 2.17 Block Diagram of HIST

One potential use of the histogram is to choose a threshold value t when applying THRESH. In Example 2.7, the preponderance of the gray values tends to be split into two concentrations. If there is a shape within the image that is differentiated owing to its darkness or lightness, then thresholding at some t value that separates the two clusters might reveal it. Indeed, applying THRESH to the image f of Example 2.7 with $t = 10$ yields the outline of a rectangle. If $t = 9$ were used, THRESH would have yielded the boundary of a rectangle with one extra black pixel.

The preceding method is certainly not foolproof. HIST(f) gives no information concerning the actual distribution of the gray values over the pixels. Should there be an interpenetration of dark and light pixels throughout the image, the histogram might indeed be bimodal (have two peaks); nevertheless, thresholding at some intermediate value might simply produce a mixed salt and pepper effect.

2.6 Histogram Equalization

One application of the gray-level histogram involves the enhancement of image contrast. Suppose f is an image whose gray values are heavily concentrated toward the light end of the gray scale. It is possible that there are patterns in the image that could be discerned more readily had the entire gray spectrum been utilized. This *skewed* histogram can be equalized to perhaps improve the contrast.

The method is quite straightforward; it involves the rescaling of the gray values in an image. Simply compute the *area* of the image, the area being the number of pixels in the domain, and divide the area by the number of quantization levels in the gray scale. If the gray scale runs from 0 to $(n - 1)$, the desired quantity is given by

$$Q = \frac{\text{AREA}(f)}{n} = \frac{1}{n} \times \text{CARD}[\text{DOMAIN}(f)]$$

The object of equalization is to *spread* the gray values evenly over the gray scale to make uniform use of all quantization levels. If Q is an integer, each gray level is assigned Q pixels. The pixels must be assigned in a monotonic fashion. That is, the darkest original pixels are reassigned to the darkest quantized levels insofar as those levels have the capacity to accept them. The monotonicity must hold right down to the lightest original pixels being reassigned to the lightest levels in the output. No doubt an example can best illustrate the procedure.

Example 2.8

Consider the image

$$f = \begin{pmatrix} 0 & 1 & 2 & 0 & 1 & 2 & 1 & 1 \\ 1 & 1 & 3 & 2 & 3 & 3 & 1 & 0 \\ 2 & 1 & 3 & 3 & 3 & 4 & 2 & 1 \\ 0 & 2 & 4 & 4 & 4 & 4 & 2 & 2 \\ 2 & 3 & 5 & 4 & 5 & 4 & 2 & 2 \\ 1 & 0 & 3 & 2 & 2 & 1 & 2 & 4 \end{pmatrix}_{0,\,5}$$

Assuming a gray scale running from 0 to 7, then $Q = {}^{48}\!/_8 = 6$. The method is to form eight classes, one for each quantization level, call them C_0, C_1, ..., C_7, and assign each of them 6 pixels, C_0 containing the 6 lightest originals and C_7 containing the 6 darkest originals. Since there are only 5 level 0 pixels, all of these must go into class C_0. One more pixel needs to be assigned to C_0. However, there are 11 level 1 pixels. Which one should be put into C_0? Although there are numerous ways of applying prior knowledge to determine the pixel to be chosen, the simplest method is to assign it randomly. Apply a randomization routine to choose one of the 11 pixels with gray value 1. The reason for randomization is that an *error* is introduced by making pixels that were originally the same darkness have varying levels of darkness. The error is hopefully *spread around* by applying a randomization process. This process is external to image processing per se, and is simply applied to the collection of pixels having gray value 1. Suppose pixel (4, 5) is chosen. Then

$$C_0 = \{(0, 2), (0, 5), (1, 0), (3, 5), (4, 5), (7, 4)\}$$

There are 10 remaining level 1 pixels to assign. C_1 can hold 6 of them. Randomly choose the 6. Then C_1 might be

$$C_1 = \{(0, 4), (1, 4), (1, 5), (5, 0), (6, 5), (7, 5)\}$$

The remaining pixels having gray value 1 must be assigned to C_2. There are 14 pixels having gray level 2. Two of them must be chosen to accompany the remaining 4 value 1 pixels in C_2. Suppose randomization yields (3, 0) and (6, 0). Then

$$C_2 = \{(0, 0), (1, 3), (3, 0), (6, 0), (6, 4), (7, 3)\}$$

The process is continued until all classes are filled. For instance, it might be that the last class is

$$C_7 = \{(2, 1), (3, 1), (3, 2), (4, 1), (5, 2), (5, 3)\}$$

A possibility for the equalized image is

$$
h = \begin{pmatrix}
0 & 1 & 4 & 0 & 0 & 4 & 1 & 1 \\
1 & 1 & 6 & 3 & 5 & 5 & 2 & 0 \\
4 & 2 & 5 & 6 & 5 & 7 & 4 & 2 \\
0 & 3 & 6 & 7 & 6 & 7 & 3 & 3 \\
3 & 5 & 7 & 7 & 7 & 6 & 4 & 4 \\
2 & 0 & 5 & 2 & 3 & 1 & 2 & 6
\end{pmatrix}_{0,\,5}
$$

Both f and h reveal a 4 by 4 square (except for one pixel that is lighter) in the middle of the image. However, the overall difference in shade between the square and its background is greater in h than in f. Indeed, if we sum the differences between each pixel on the edge of the square and any background pixel that is horizontally or vertically adjacent, then for f this sum is 32, whereas for g it is 52! Contrast is greater in the figure that has undergone histogram equalization.

Several comments are in order concerning the histogram equalization procedure. First, if Q does not happen to be an integer, the classes $C_0, C_1, \ldots, C_n$ must be chosen so that each contains a number of elements that is less than 1 from Q. No great difficulty is encountered here. Second, if the histogram is strongly bimodal, such as it was in Figure 2.16, the great difference between the figure and its background can be made less stark and the figure will tend to fade out into its background. Consequently, if the figure is quite intricate with respect to its background, that intricacy may become muted and its most fragile characteristics lost. Finally, the operation of histogram equalization, as described herein, is not deterministic. Due to the randomization procedure involved, a given input image f may have any one of a number of outputs. Although such operators can be problematic, the difficulties will not be discussed here, and we will simply write $h = \text{HISTEQUAL}(f)$, a unary operator with single input image.

2.7 Co-occurrence Matrix

Although the gray-level histogram gives information concerning the overall distribution of gray values, it gives no information regarding the manner in which individual gray levels are related to each other. It does not address the question of spatial relationship between gray levels. From an intuitive point of view, it lacks *textural* description.

Consider the images f and g of Figure 2.18. Assuming a quantization scale of {0, 1, 2, 3}, each image has exactly the same gray-level histogram. Indeed, writing the output of HIST as an array,

$$\text{HIST}(f) = \text{HIST}(g) = [10, 10, 10, 10]$$

However, even though the histograms are identical, the images are quite different. This difference might be described as textural. Whereas f contains four vertical strips of varying darkness, each of width 2, g contains eight single-width strips. The gray-scale histogram cannot detect such differences.

$$f = \begin{pmatrix} - & - & 1 & 1 & 2 & 2 & 3 & 3 \\ - & - & 1 & 1 & 2 & 2 & 3 & 3 \\ - & - & 1 & 1 & 2 & 2 & 3 & 3 \\ - & - & 1 & 1 & 2 & 2 & 3 & 3 \\ - & - & 1 & 1 & 2 & 2 & 3 & 3 \end{pmatrix}_{0,\,4}$$

$$g = \begin{pmatrix} - & 1 & 2 & 3 & - & 1 & 2 & 3 \\ - & 1 & 2 & 3 & - & 1 & 2 & 3 \\ - & 1 & 2 & 3 & - & 1 & 2 & 3 \\ - & 1 & 2 & 3 & - & 1 & 2 & 3 \\ - & 1 & 2 & 3 & - & 1 & 2 & 3 \end{pmatrix}_{0,\,4}$$

Figure 2.18 Images Illustrating Texture

To help quantify textural information, we often employ the *co-occurrence matrices*. These focus on the spatial relationships among different gray levels. There are many such matrices for a given image, each determined by some prespecified spatial relationship between pairs of pixels. For instance, we might consider (i, j) related to (u, v) if (u, v) is immediately to the right of (i, j). Another possibility would be (u, v) immediately above (i, j). Once such a relation, call it R, is established, it is used to construct a particular co-occurrence matrix for the image f in the following manner: For any pair of gray levels r and s, the value $Q_R(r, s)$ is the number of pixel pairs (i, j) and (u, v) for which

a) (i, j) -R- (u, v), which means the pixels satisfy the relation R,

b) $f(i, j) = r$ and $f(u, v) = s$.

Assuming the total gray-level range to be $\{0, 1, \cdots, m\}$, the *co-occurrence matrix* $C[f; R]$ is defined by

$$C[f; R] = \begin{pmatrix} Q_R(0, 0) & Q_R(0, 1) & Q_R(0, 2) & \ldots & Q_R(0, m) \\ Q_R(1, 0) & Q_R(1, 1) & Q_R(1, 2) & \ldots & Q_R(1, m) \\ \vdots & \vdots & \vdots & & \vdots \\ Q_R(m, 0) & Q_R(m, 1) & Q_R(m, 2) & \ldots & Q_R(m, m) \end{pmatrix}$$

Each quantity $Q_R(r, s)$ is simply the number of related pixel pairs having gray levels r and s.

Of the set of all possible relations R that might be defined among pixel pairs, the most common are the eight adjacency relations. These are induced by the eight noncentric pixels of SQUARE(i, j). They are as follows:

1) (i, j) -R_1- (u, v) if $u = i + 1$ and $v = j + 1$
2) (i, j) -R_2- (u, v) if $u = i$ and $v = j + 1$
3) (i, j) -R_3- (u, v) if $u = i - 1$ and $v = j + 1$
4) (i, j) -R_4- (u, v) if $u = i - 1$ and $v = j$
5) (i, j) -R_5- (u, v) if $u = i - 1$ and $v = j - 1$
6) (i, j) -R_6- (u, v) if $u = i$ and $v = j - 1$
7) (i, j) -R_7- (u, v) if $u = i + 1$ and $v = j - 1$
8) (i, j) -R_8- (u, v) if $u = i + 1$ and $v = j$

The eight *immediate neighbor* relations merely state that (i, j) -R_k- (u, v) if (u, v) occupies the kth position as one proceeds counterclockwise around the outside pixels of SQUARE(i, j), starting from the upper-right corner. For simplicity of notation, we shall let Q_k denote the entries in the co-occurrence matrix induced by R_k, and we let $C[f; k]$ denote the matrix itself.

Example 2.9

Find $C[f; 6]$ and $C[f; 8]$ for the image f in Figure 2.18. We first find $C[f; 6]$. The way to proceed is to count the pairs of pixels (i, j) and (u, v), where (u, v) is directly beneath (i, j) and where the gray levels of the pair are r and s, respectively. For instance, $Q_6 (0, 0)$ = 8 since there are 8 pairs (i, j) -R_6- (u, v) such that $f(i, j) = 0$ and $f(u, v) = 0$. Put simply, there are 8 pairs of pixels that are vertically adjacent and in which each pixel has gray value 0. Another example is $Q_6 (0, 1) = 0$ since there are no pairs (i, j) -R_6- (u, v) such that $f(i, j) = 0$ and $g(u, v) = 1$(such that the pixel above has gray value 0 while the pixel below has gray value 1). Proceeding through all 16 such calculations, we obtain

$$C[f; 6] = \begin{pmatrix} 8 & 0 & 0 & 0 \\ 0 & 8 & 0 & 0 \\ 0 & 0 & 8 & 0 \\ 0 & 0 & 0 & 8 \end{pmatrix}$$

The relation R_8 is defined by (u, v) immediately to the right of (i, j). In this case, $Q_8 (0, 0) = 5$ since the pixels in the first column of the bound matrix for f have gray value 0, while their right neighbors also have gray value 0. Also, $Q_8 (0, 1) = 5$ since the pixels in the second column of the bound matrix have gray value 0, while their right neighbors have gray value 1. Note that $Q_8 (1, 0) = 0$ since no pixel having gray value 1 has a right neighbor with gray value 0. For the relation right adjacent, we obtain

$$C[f; 8] = \begin{pmatrix} 5 & 5 & 0 & 0 \\ 0 & 5 & 5 & 0 \\ 0 & 0 & 5 & 5 \\ 0 & 0 & 0 & 5 \end{pmatrix}$$

The co-occurrence matrices computed in Example 2.9 contain quite a bit of information concerning the image. As a case in point, $C[f; 6]$ is a diagonal matrix. This reflects the fact that no pixel has a pixel directly beneath it with a different gray level. Moreover, $C[f; 8]$ is an upper triangular matrix. This is because the gray levels are increasing as we traverse the image from left to right. In other words, $Q_8(r, s) = 0$ if $r > s$ since $f(i, j) \leqslant f(i + 1, j)$ for all i and j.

Continuing in this direction, consider the two corresponding co-occurrence matrices for image g in Figure 2.18. The matrix $C[g; 6] = C[f; 6]$. Like f, the image g contains no vertically adjacent pixels with differing gray levels. However, equality does not hold for relation R_8. In fact,

$$C[g; 8] = \begin{pmatrix} 0 & 10 & 0 & 0 \\ 0 & 0 & 10 & 0 \\ 0 & 0 & 0 & 10 \\ 5 & 0 & 0 & 0 \end{pmatrix}$$

While f and g cannot be differentiated by either their gray-level histograms or their co-occurrence matrices generated by the relation R_6 (beneath), they can be differentiated on the basis of their co-occurence matrices generated by the relation R_8 (to the right).

In general, a great deal of information of a textural nature is contained within the co-occurrence matrices. Unfortunately, the computation time for these matrices is quite large, as is the amount of storage. For this reason, we are often restricted to the use of the eight adjacency relations or even some subset of them. However, even in this case further compression may be required. In this direction, we might simply find the co-occurrence matrices for the four *strong neighbor* relations, (u, v) above, to the left, below, and to the right, and then store only that matrix whose entries are found by averaging the respective entries of the four strong neighbor co-occurrence matrices. Other more sophisticated matrix-theoretic compression techniques may also be employed.

No matter how many co-occurrence matrices are computed and stored, interpretation remains problematic. While the preceding examples lead to relatively simple matrix forms, this is not usually the case. For instance, Figure 2.19 gives an image together with its first four adjacency co-occurrence matrices, $C[h; 1]$ through $C[h; 4]$. These are certainly not easy to characterize. Indeed, most realistic images contain complex textural properties. Such properties have not been well defined mathematically and to date remain on the

$$h = \begin{pmatrix} 0 & 1 & 0 & 0 & 1 \\ 1 & 4 & 3 & 4 & 1 \\ 1 & 3 & 4 & 4 & 0 \\ 0 & 4 & 4 & 4 & 0 \\ 1 & 3 & 3 & 4 & 1 \\ 1 & 1 & 0 & 0 & 2 \end{pmatrix}_{2,3}$$

$$C[h; 1] = \begin{pmatrix} 0 & 1 & 0 & 1 & 1 \\ 0 & 1 & 0 & 2 & 2 \\ 0 & 0 & 0 & 0 & 0 \\ 1 & 0 & 0 & 1 & 2 \\ 3 & 2 & 0 & 0 & 3 \end{pmatrix}$$

Figure 2.19 Image with Several Co-Occurence Matrices

Figure 2.19   continued

$$
C[h; 2] = \begin{pmatrix} 1 & 2 & 0 & 1 & 1 \\ 3 & 3 & 0 & 1 & 0 \\ 0 & 1 & 0 & 0 & 0 \\ 1 & 0 & 0 & 0 & 3 \\ 1 & 1 & 0 & 2 & 4 \end{pmatrix}
$$

$$
C[h; 3] = \begin{pmatrix} 0 & 0 & 0 & 2 & 2 \\ 1 & 1 & 0 & 0 & 1 \\ 0 & 0 & 0 & 0 & 1 \\ 1 & 2 & 0 & 0 & 1 \\ 2 & 1 & 0 & 2 & 3 \end{pmatrix}
$$

$$
C[h; 4] = \begin{pmatrix} 2 & 2 & 0 & 0 & 2 \\ 2 & 1 & 0 & 0 & 2 \\ 1 & 0 & 0 & 0 & 0 \\ 0 & 2 & 0 & 1 & 1 \\ 1 & 1 & 0 & 3 & 3 \end{pmatrix}
$$

heuristic level. Nevertheless, co-occurrence matrices have been used rather successfully to classify images according to heuristically defined notions of texture.

EXERCISES

2.1. Consider the image

$$
f = \begin{pmatrix} 0 & 1 & 1 & 0 & 0 & 1 & 0 \\ 0 & 4 & 5 & 1 & 0 & 0 & 0 \\ 1 & 7 & 6 & 1 & 2 & 9 & 0 \\ 2 & 6 & 5 & 3 & 2 & * & 1 \\ 2 & 7 & 8 & 1 & 2 & 0 & 0 \\ 2 & 6 & 5 & 7 & 6 & 3 & 1 \\ 2 & 7 & 8 & 5 & 7 & 1 & 2 \\ 3 & 2 & 2 & 1 & 3 & 0 & 1 \end{pmatrix}_{3,\,2}
$$

Find
  (a) THRESH(f; 5)
  (b) EQUAL(f; 7)
  (c) GREATER(f; 5)
  (d) BETWEEN(f; 5, 8)
  (e) TRUNC(f; 6)
  (f) CONST(f; 4)

2.2. Construct block diagram specifications for the following:
   (a) GREATER
   (b) BETWEEN
   (c) TRUNC
   (d) CONST

2.3. Define a new operator, to be called LESS, by

$$[\text{LESS}(f; t)](i, j) = \begin{cases} 1, & \text{if } f(i, j) < t \\ 0, & \text{if } f(i, j) \geq t \\ *, & \text{if } f(i, j) = * \end{cases}$$

Apply LESS to the image of Exercise 2.1.

2.4. Apply SMOOTH to the image of Exercise 2.1 and the mask

$$M = \begin{pmatrix} 0 & \frac{1}{4} & 0 \\ \frac{1}{4} & \textcircled{0} & \frac{1}{4} \\ 0 & \frac{1}{4} & 0 \end{pmatrix}$$

2.5. Using image f of Exercise 2.1 and the mask M of Exercise 2.4, do a step-by-step walk-through of the block diagram in Figure 2.13.

2.6. Consider the image

$$g = \begin{pmatrix} 1 & 0 & 1 & 0 & 1 & 0 & 1 & 1 \\ 1 & 0 & 1 & 1 & 0 & 0 & 0 & 1 \\ 0 & 0 & 4 & 4 & 4 & 4 & 0 & 1 \\ 1 & 0 & 4 & 4 & 4 & 4 & 0 & 0 \\ 0 & 1 & 4 & 5 & 5 & 4 & 0 & 1 \\ 5 & 1 & 9 & 5 & 4 & 4 & 1 & 1 \\ 1 & 9 & 0 & 4 & 5 & 4 & 0 & 1 \\ 8 & 8 & 0 & 0 & 0 & 0 & 0 & 1 \\ 1 & 1 & 7 & 1 & 0 & 0 & 0 & 1 \end{pmatrix}_{4, 2}$$

Design a space-variant filter to smooth the noise in the lower-left corner of the image, while leaving the rest of the image untouched. Then find a good threshold value to try to locate the 5 by 4 rectangle within the image. Apply THRESH with that value.

2.7. Apply LOCSMOOTH to the image f of Exercise 2.1, the mask M of Exercise 2.4, and the trigger value $q = 3$.

2.8. Define a new operator LOCALSM that requires four inputs: an image f, two averaging masks B and M, and a trigger value q. LOCALSM behaves exactly like LOCSMOOTH except that it uses the input mask B instead of the constant mask C in the computation of AV.
   (a) Construct a block diagram for LOCALSM.
   (b) Let f be the image of Exercise 2.1. Find LOCALSM$(f; B, M; 4)$, where M is the mask of Exercise 2.4 and

$$B = \begin{pmatrix} 0 & 0 & \frac{1}{3} \\ 0 & \textcircled{\frac{1}{3}} & 0 \\ \frac{1}{3} & 0 & 0 \end{pmatrix}$$

2.9. Define a new operator LOCNOISE that requires three inputs: an image f, an integer r, and a trigger value q. LOCNOISE produces an image that has gray value 1 whenever (i, j) has a gray value that differs from the gray value of at least r of its eight adjacent neighbors by more than q, and gray value 0 otherwise. Apply LOCNOISE to the image f of Exercise 2.1 with inputs $r = 6$ and $q = 4$.

2.10. Find HIST(f) for the image f of Exercise 2.1.

2.11. Find HISTEQUAL(g) for the image g of Exercise 2.6.

2.12. For the image h in Figure 2.19, find the co-occurrence matrices $C[h; 5]$, $C[h; 6]$, $C[h; 7]$, and $C[h; 8]$.

3

EDGE DETECTION

3.1 Concept of an Edge

The organization of visual sensory data into patterns is an integral part of human perception. Very often these patterns consist of regions defined by some form of homogeneity with respect to the data. This homogeneity might result from the existence of regions having constant, or essentially constant, gray levels. It might also result from textural properties of regions within the overall image. In either event, it might be possible to segment the image according to a definable homogeneic characteristic. For example, in thresholding, an effort is made to segment the image into *figure and ground* by a judicious choice of threshold value. In doing so, we are considering the degree of darkness, in a bilevel sense, as a measure of homogeneity. If an image happens to contain two figures within it that are both measurably darker than the background, thresholding can detect both of them. However, if one is darker than the background while the other is lighter, then the single application of a simple operator such as THRESH will not detect both. In general, the situation is far more complex than simply the occurrence of two gray-level homogeneous figures.

Figure 3.1 gives an image f together with a pictorial representation. The letter E is discernible to the eye in the picture; however, it would not be discovered by a thresholding operation. The eye is sensitive to the local contrast between dark and light. It discerns the E due to such contrast. On the other hand, an operator such as THRESH takes a global view of the gray-level variation. The image of Figure 3.1 has an *illumination gradient*; it is darker on the top and lighter on the bottom. Hence it is not receptive to a global thresholding. Yet this is precisely the situation often encountered in practice. Although it might be feasible to obtain uniform illumination in a restricted setting such

$$
f = \begin{pmatrix}
7 & 7 & 7 & 6 & 7 & 6 & 7 & 7 & 5 \\
7 & 9 & 9 & 9 & 9 & 9 & 9 & 9 & 6 \\
6 & 9 & 8 & 9 & 8 & 8 & 9 & 8 & 6 \\
6 & 8 & 8 & 8 & 6 & 6 & 6 & 5 & 6 \\
5 & 9 & 8 & 8 & 6 & 6 & 5 & 5 & 6 \\
5 & 7 & 8 & 8 & 5 & 5 & 5 & 5 & 6 \\
5 & 7 & 7 & 8 & 7 & 8 & 7 & 5 & 5 \\
4 & 7 & 7 & 7 & 7 & 7 & 7 & 5 & 4 \\
4 & 7 & 6 & 7 & 4 & 5 & 5 & 4 & 5 \\
4 & 6 & 6 & 6 & 4 & 4 & 4 & 3 & 4 \\
3 & 6 & 5 & 6 & 3 & 3 & 2 & 3 & 3 \\
3 & 5 & 5 & 6 & 6 & 5 & 5 & 5 & 3 \\
2 & 5 & 4 & 5 & 6 & 5 & 4 & 4 & 2 \\
2 & 2 & 1 & 1 & 2 & 2 & 2 & 1 & 2
\end{pmatrix}_{2,\,6}
$$

(a)

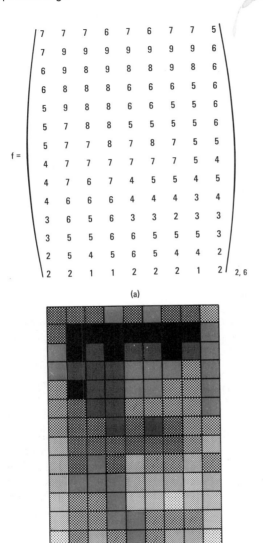

(b)

Figure 3.1 Image with Hidden Letter E

as a laboratory or factory, it is not so feasible in a natural setting. Thresholding might still play a role under the latter circumstances, but it must certainly be preceded by some other type of processing.

It is through the use of *edge-detection* techniques that local contrast differences can be determined. Intuitively, an edge is a zone of demarcation between two regions that differ according to some measure of homogeneity. If one considers local gray-level intensity as such a measure, then the letter E in Figure 3.1 differs from its ground accordingly. If we focus our attention on gray level and ignore texture, then an edge may occur in essentially two ways:

1) As the border between two differing regions, each region being homogeneous with regard to some homogeneity criterion.
2) As a thin, dark *arc* on a light background, or a thin, light arc on a dark background.

This chapter concentrates on the first type of edge; the second type is considered in Chapter 5. The intent here is to input an image and output another image, the latter being a thin figure that represents the edge of whatever object lies within the input image.

The term *thin* must be taken in a relative sense when dealing with edges. While the border between two regions might be representable as a *curve* of single pixels, it might also be a region of transition. Indeed, such a situation is quite common. Imagine a dark figure against a light background where there is some thin region of gray-level gradation between them. Even though this region of gradation might be several pixels wide, it might still be termed an *edge*. Indeed, it would appear so to the human eye. In other words, while the intent in edge detection is the formation of "stick figures" that represent the borders of homogeneous regions, sufficient latitude in terminology must be allowed to include "wide" edges. It is for this reason that the term *curve* is not used interchangeably with the term *edge*. Whereas the former is precisely defined (Chapter 5), the latter is used somewhat loosely.

3.2 Partial Difference Operators

If two adjacent regions exist within an image that differ substantially with respect to gray level at the edge between them, then the computation of a rate of change with respect to gray level can help to determine the edge. What is required is a difference operator that measures the rate of change of gray levels. The value of this operator will be zero on constant domains within the image and vary according to the rate of gray-level fluctuation elsewhere. For those who have had a course in calculus, a *difference operator* is a digital analogue of a differential operator.

The simplest such operators measure the digital rate of gray-level change in either the horizontal or vertical direction. These are the *partial difference operators*. The first measures the rate of gray level change in the x direction, and the second measures the rate of gray change in the y direction. They are the digital analogues of the partial derivative operators from calculus. They are defined respectively by

$$[DX(f)](i, j) = \begin{cases} f(i, j) - f(i - 1, j), & \text{if } f \text{ is defined at} \\ & (i, j) \text{ and } (i - 1, j) \\ *, & \text{otherwise} \end{cases}$$

and

$$[DY(f)](i, j) = \begin{cases} f(i, j) - f(i, j - 1), & \text{if } f \text{ is defined at} \\ & (i, j) \text{ and } (i, j - 1) \\ *, & \text{otherwise} \end{cases}$$

At each pixel, DX yields the difference between the gray level at the pixel and the gray level at the adjacent pixel to the left, while DY yields the difference between the gray level at the pixel and the gray level at the adjacent pixel beneath. DX is useful for the location of vertical edges and DY is useful for the location of horizontal edges. The block diagram for DX is given by

$$f \quad \longrightarrow \quad \boxed{\text{DX}} \quad \longrightarrow \quad \text{DX}(f)$$

DY has a similar block diagram.

Example 3.1

Let

$$f = \begin{pmatrix} * & 4 & 4 & 1 & 0 & 1 \\ 4 & 5 & 4 & 1 & 1 & 2 \\ 5 & 4 & 5 & 2 & 1 & 2 \\ 6 & 6 & 6 & 2 & 3 & 2 \\ 6 & 7 & 6 & 3 & 3 & * \\ 7 & 7 & 7 & 3 & 4 & 4 \\ 8 & 7 & 7 & 4 & 4 & 5 \end{pmatrix}_{0,\ 6}$$

Application of the partial difference operator DX gives the output

$$\text{DX}(f) = \begin{pmatrix} * & * & 0 & -3 & -1 & 1 \\ * & 1 & -1 & -3 & 0 & 1 \\ * & -1 & 1 & -3 & -1 & 1 \\ * & 0 & 0 & -4 & 1 & -1 \\ * & 1 & -1 & -3 & 0 & * \\ * & 0 & 0 & -4 & 1 & 0 \\ * & -1 & 0 & -3 & 0 & 1 \end{pmatrix}_{0,\ 6}$$

Some illustrations of how the gray values of the output have been calculated are

$$[DX(f)](1, 5) = 5 - 4 = 1$$

$$[DX(f)](2, 5) = 4 - 5 = -1$$

$$[DX(f)](3, 5) = 1 - 4 = -3$$

$$[DX(f)](5, 2) = *, \quad \text{since } f(5, 2) = *$$

$$[DX(f)](0, 0) = *, \quad \text{since } f(-1, 0) = *$$

For the same f, DY gives

$$\text{DY}(f) = \begin{pmatrix} * & -1 & 0 & 0 & -1 & -1 \\ -1 & 1 & -1 & -1 & 0 & 0 \\ -1 & -2 & -1 & 0 & -2 & 0 \\ 0 & -1 & 0 & -1 & 0 & * \\ -1 & 0 & -1 & 0 & -1 & * \\ -1 & 0 & 0 & -1 & 0 & -1 \\ * & * & * & * & * & * \end{pmatrix}_{0,\,6}$$

Much can be learned about the use of difference operators in image processing by examining the outputs in Example 3.1. For instance, DX has revealed a vertical edge. In terms of absolute value, the greatest differences show up in the fourth column of the bound matrix representing $\text{DX}(f)$. These differences, which happen to be negative, result from the contrast of dark to light in the original image f that occurs between the third and fourth columns of the bound matrix representing f. The negativity of these extreme values results from the left-to-right shift of dark-to-light intensity.

Since the occurrence of an edge does not depend on the direction of the contrasting intensities, DX should be used in conjunction with the absolute value operator ABS and the thresholding operator THRESH to produce the desired thin figure. The edge is then represented in a black and white image. In other words, the edge-detection operator associated with DX is defined by the block diagram in Figure 3.2. In the sequel it will be denoted by VERTEDGE. It requires two inputs, an image and a threshold value t. Applied to the preceding image f with threshold value $t = 3$, VERTEDGE outputs the image

$$\text{VERTEDGE}(f;\,3) = \begin{pmatrix} * & * & - & 1 & - & - \\ * & - & - & 1 & - & - \\ * & - & - & 1 & - & - \\ * & - & - & 1 & - & - \\ * & - & - & 1 & - & * \\ * & - & - & 1 & - & - \\ * & - & - & 1 & - & - \end{pmatrix}_{0,\,6}$$

The edge has been detected even though there is an obvious illumination gradient running top to bottom and light to dark.

The application of DY has produced no edge. This can be seen by the application of a detection sequence analogous to the one for DX. This sequence will be denoted HOREDGE and is given by the same block diagram as that for VERTEDGE except DY is used instead of DX. Nevertheless, DY does give some useful information regarding the image f of Example 3.1. All gray values of $\text{DY}(f)$ are less than or equal to zero

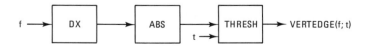

Figure 3.2 Block Diagram of VERTEDGE

except for one. This results from a process of increasing darkness as the pixels go from the top down. DY has revealed the illumination gradient!

A severe problem with any partial difference approach to edge detection is the extreme sensitivity of partial difference operators to noise. Indeed, consider the insertion of a single noise pixel into the image f that we have been discussing. For example, suppose $f(4, 4) = 9$, instead of $f(4, 4) = 1$, as originally given. Such a change would produce a third row of the output bound matrix for DX as follows:

$$* \quad -1 \quad 1 \quad -3 \quad 7 \quad -7$$

Therefore, the output of VERTEDGE would be

$$\begin{pmatrix} * & - & 1 & - & - \\ - & - & 1 & - & - \\ - & - & 1 & 1 & 1 \\ - & - & 1 & - & - \\ - & - & 1 & - & * \\ - & - & 1 & - & - \\ - & - & 1 & - & - \end{pmatrix}_{1,\,6}$$

Hence the vertical edge would be distorted and an improper stick figure would result. With any significant degree of high-frequency noise, the output image would be of no use. To remedy this sensitivity to high-frequency noise, it is often necessary to smooth an image prior to a partial difference transformation.

Both DX and DY are quite easy to represent in terms of the operators introduced earlier. DX is specified in Figure 3.3, and DY would be specified similarly. In Figure 3.3, the translate TRAN$(f; -1, 0)$ is simply subtracted from f to yield DX(f). The net effect is that all partial differences can be calculated in parallel.

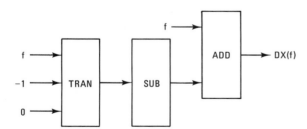

Figure 3.3 Block Diagram of DX

3.3 Gradient

Both partial difference operators DX and DY suffer from a dependence on directionality. DX can detect vertical edges and DY can detect horizontal edges. This can be a serious weakness when the desire is to detect *curved* edges, such as the boundary of a circular disk or of an ellipse.

Figure 3.4 gives an image and four edge images computed from it:

(a) Image f
(b) ABS[DX(f)]
(c) ABS[DY(f)]
(d) VERTEDGE(f; 3), which results from thresholding (b) at $t = 3$
(e) HOREDGE(f; 3), which results from thresholding (c) at $t = 3$

$$
\text{(a)} \quad f = \begin{pmatrix}
- & - & - & - & 1 & - & - & - & - & - & - \\
- & 1 & 1 & - & 4 & 4 & 4 & - & - & 1 & - \\
- & - & 4 & 4 & 4 & 3 & 4 & 4 & 3 & - & 1 \\
- & 4 & 3 & 4 & 4 & 4 & 4 & 4 & 4 & 4 & - \\
- & 3 & 4 & 4 & 3 & 4 & 4 & 3 & 4 & 3 & - \\
- & - & 4 & 4 & 4 & 4 & 4 & 4 & 4 & - & 1 \\
- & 1 & - & - & 4 & 4 & 3 & - & 1 & - & - \\
1 & - & - & - & - & - & - & - & - & - & 1
\end{pmatrix}_{2,4}
$$

$$
\text{(b)} \quad \text{ABS}[\text{DX}(f)] = \begin{pmatrix}
* & - & - & - & 1 & 1 & - & - & - & - & - \\
* & 1 & - & 1 & 4 & - & - & 4 & - & 1 & 1 \\
* & - & 4 & - & - & 1 & 1 & - & 1 & 3 & 1 \\
* & 4 & 1 & 1 & - & - & - & - & - & - & 4 \\
* & 3 & 1 & - & 1 & 1 & - & 1 & 1 & 1 & 3 \\
* & - & 4 & - & - & - & - & - & - & 4 & 1 \\
* & 1 & 1 & - & 4 & - & 1 & 3 & 1 & 1 & - \\
* & 1 & - & - & - & - & - & - & - & - & 1
\end{pmatrix}_{2,4}
$$

$$
\text{(c)} \quad \text{ABS}[\text{DY}(f)] = \begin{pmatrix}
- & 1 & 1 & - & 3 & 4 & 4 & - & - & 1 & - \\
- & 1 & 3 & 4 & - & 1 & - & 4 & 3 & 1 & 1 \\
- & 4 & 1 & - & - & 1 & - & - & 1 & 4 & 1 \\
- & 1 & 1 & - & 1 & - & - & 1 & - & 1 & - \\
- & 3 & - & - & 1 & - & - & 1 & - & 3 & 1 \\
- & 1 & 4 & 4 & - & - & 1 & 4 & 3 & - & 1 \\
- & 1 & - & - & 4 & 4 & 3 & - & 1 & - & 1 \\
* & * & * & * & * & * & * & * & * & * & *
\end{pmatrix}_{2,4}
$$

Figure 3.4 Image With Several Associated Edge Images

Figure 3.4 continued

(d) VERTEDGE(f; 3) =

$$
\begin{pmatrix}
* & - & - & - & - & - & - & - & - & - & - & - \\
* & - & - & - & 1 & - & - & 1 & - & - & - \\
* & - & 1 & - & - & - & - & - & - & 1 & - \\
* & 1 & - & - & - & - & - & - & - & - & 1 \\
* & 1 & - & - & - & - & - & - & - & - & 1 \\
* & - & 1 & - & - & - & - & - & - & 1 & - \\
* & - & - & - & 1 & - & - & 1 & - & - & - \\
* & - & - & - & - & - & - & - & - & - & -
\end{pmatrix}_{2,\,4}
$$

(e) HOREDGE(f; 3) =

$$
\begin{pmatrix}
- & - & - & - & 1 & 1 & 1 & - & - & - & - \\
- & - & 1 & 1 & - & - & - & 1 & 1 & - & - \\
- & 1 & - & - & - & - & - & - & - & 1 & - \\
- & - & - & - & - & - & - & - & - & - & - \\
- & 1 & - & - & - & - & - & - & - & 1 & - \\
- & - & 1 & 1 & - & - & - & 1 & 1 & - & - \\
- & - & - & - & 1 & 1 & 1 & - & - & - & - \\
* & * & * & * & * & * & * & * & * & * & *
\end{pmatrix}_{2,\,4}
$$

The image f represents the digitization of some elliptical shape consisting of similar gray values on a light background. Yet neither the application of DX or DY produces an edge that is elliptical. The application of DX reveals the edge pieces that tend to run vertically, while the application of DY reveals those that tend to run horizontally. Since the major axis of the ellipse lies horizontally, the edge tends to lie horizontally, and therefore DY reveals more than does DX.

To obtain a reasonable edge for the elliptical figure in image f by the use of DX and DY, it is necessary to utilize the difference operators in conjunction with one another so that the resulting operator is independent of directionality. To accomplish this end, we introduce a new operator, the *digital gradient*. The gradient is a different sort of image operator in that it has a single input image and two output images. Given an image f, GRAD(f) is defined by

$$\text{GRAD}(f) = [\text{DX}(f), \text{DY}(f)]$$

In other words, GRAD(f) is an *ordered pair* of images, where the notation [,] is used to denote an ordered pair. In a sense, GRAD(f) is a two-vector in which each component is an image. Several norms will be developed for this vector. Each gives a measure for the degree of overall change of gray level at the pixel at which GRAD(f) is being evaluated.

Given a vector $V = (x, y)$, there are three very common ways of defining the *norm*, or magnitude, of the vector. The first is called the l_∞-norm. It is given by

$$\|V\|_\infty = \max\{x, y\}$$

The second is the l_1-norm. It is given by

$$\|V\|_1 = |x| + |y|$$

Finally, there is the l_2-norm, or the usual vector magnitude utilized in elementary calculus. It is given by

$$\|V\|_2 = (x^2 + y^2)^{\frac{1}{2}}$$

Each of the three preceding norms can be applied to the gradient vector (DX, DY). The result is three different measures of the magnitude of the gradient (three different measures of the magnitude of the bidirectional gray-value change). In other words, each norm leads to an operator that has a single input image and a single output image, where each pixel of the output image has as its gray value the appropriate gradient magnitude at the corresponding input pixel.

The l_∞-norm leads to the operator GRADMAG0 defined by the block diagram

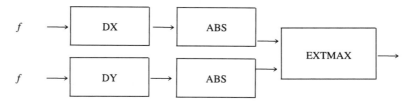

The diagram follows exactly the definition of the l_∞-norm, except that an extended maximum is taken at the end. This is done so that most of the stars resulting from the application of DX and DY are filled in. Applied to the image f of Figure 3.4, GRADMAG0 yields the output of Figure 3.5(a). In a manner analogous to the application of the partial difference operators, clarity is gained by thresholding the output of GRADMAG0. The result is the edge detector we shall call GRADEDGE0. The output of GRADEDGE0 for the image f and the threshold value $t = 3$ is given in Figure 3.5(b).

The l_1-norm leads to the operator GRADMAG1 defined by the block diagram

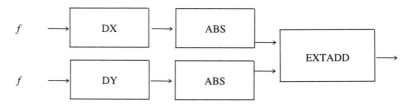

This diagram follows directly from the definition of the l_1-norm. Applied to the image f of Figure 3.4, GRADMAG1 outputs the image of Figure 3.5(c). Once again the gradient

(a) GRADMAG0(f) =

$$
\begin{pmatrix}
- & 1 & 1 & 1 & 3 & 4 & 4 & - & - & 1 & - \\
- & 1 & 3 & 4 & 4 & 1 & - & 4 & 3 & 1 & 1 \\
- & 4 & 4 & - & - & 1 & 1 & - & 1 & 4 & 1 \\
- & 4 & 1 & 1 & 1 & - & - & 1 & - & 1 & 4 \\
- & 3 & 1 & - & 1 & 1 & - & 1 & 1 & 3 & 3 \\
- & 1 & 4 & 4 & - & - & 1 & 4 & 3 & 4 & 1 \\
- & 1 & 1 & - & 4 & 4 & 3 & 3 & 1 & 1 & 1 \\
* & 1 & - & - & - & - & - & - & - & - & 1
\end{pmatrix}_{2,\,4}
$$

(b) GRADEDGE0(f; 3) =

$$
\begin{pmatrix}
- & - & - & - & 1 & 1 & 1 & - & - & - & - \\
- & - & 1 & 1 & 1 & - & - & 1 & 1 & - & - \\
- & 1 & 1 & - & - & - & - & - & - & 1 & - \\
- & 1 & - & - & - & - & - & - & - & - & 1 \\
- & 1 & - & - & - & - & - & - & - & 1 & 1 \\
- & - & 1 & 1 & - & - & - & 1 & 1 & 1 & - \\
- & - & - & - & 1 & 1 & 1 & 1 & - & - & - \\
- & - & - & - & - & - & - & - & - & - & -
\end{pmatrix}_{2,\,4}
$$

(c) GRADMAG1(f) =

$$
\begin{pmatrix}
- & 1 & 1 & - & 4 & 5 & 4 & - & - & 1 & - \\
- & 2 & 3 & 5 & 4 & 1 & - & 8 & 3 & 2 & 2 \\
- & 4 & 5 & - & - & 2 & 1 & - & 2 & 7 & 2 \\
- & 5 & 2 & 1 & 1 & - & - & 1 & - & 1 & 4 \\
- & 6 & 1 & - & 2 & 1 & - & 2 & 1 & 4 & 4 \\
- & 1 & 8 & 4 & - & - & 1 & 4 & 3 & 4 & 2 \\
- & 2 & 1 & - & 8 & 4 & 4 & 3 & 2 & 1 & 1 \\
- & 1 & - & - & - & - & - & - & - & - & 1
\end{pmatrix}_{2,\,4}
$$

(d) GRADMAG2(f) =

$$
\begin{pmatrix}
- & 1 & 1 & - & 3.2 & 4.1 & 4 & - & - & 1 & - \\
- & 1.4 & 9 & 4.1 & 4 & 1 & - & 5.7 & 3 & 1.4 & 1.4 \\
- & 4 & 4.1 & - & - & 1.4 & 1 & - & 1.4 & 5 & 1.4 \\
- & 4.1 & 1.4 & 1 & 1 & - & - & 1 & - & 1 & 4 \\
- & 4.2 & 1 & - & 1.4 & 1 & 1 & 1.4 & 1 & 3.2 & 3.2 \\
- & 1 & 5.7 & 4 & - & - & 1 & 4 & 3 & 4 & 1.4 \\
- & 1.4 & 1 & - & 5.7 & 4 & 3.2 & 3 & 1.4 & 1 & 1 \\
* & 1 & - & - & - & - & - & - & - & - & 1
\end{pmatrix}_{2,\,4}
$$

Figure 3.5 GRADMAG Images Associated with Image in Figure *3.4*

magnitude operator output must be thresholded. The result is the edge detector we shall refer to as GRADEDGE1. For the image f that we have been considering, GRAD-EDGE1$(f; 3)$ = GRADEDGE0$(f; 3)$. In general, this is not so. It happens to be so in this case for the threshold value $t = 3$. It should be obvious from looking at the output images GRADMAG0(f) and GRADMAG1(f) that another threshold value might give differing outputs.

Finally, the l_2-norm leads to the operator GRADMAG2 defined by the block diagram

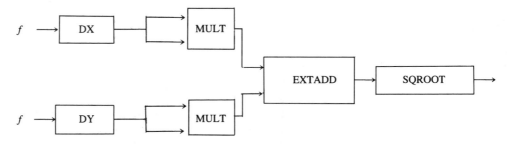

In this diagram SQROOT is an operator that outputs at each pixel the square root of the corresponding input pixel gray value. The edge detector GRADEDGE2 is obtained by thresholding the output of GRADMAG2. Figure 3.5(d) gives the output GRADMAG2(f) for the input f of Figure 3.4. Once again, thresholding at $t = 3$ gives the image of Figure 3.5(b).

Prior to leaving this section, it might be appropriate to consider an example where the edge is a zone of transition between two regions of homogeneity. Such situations were discussed at the end of Section 3.1.

Example 3.2

Consider the image

$$f = \begin{pmatrix} - & - & 3 & 5 & 9 & 9 & 9 & 9 \\ - & - & - & 3 & 6 & 9 & 9 & 9 \\ - & - & - & - & 2 & 6 & 9 & 9 \\ - & - & - & 3 & 7 & 9 & 9 & 9 \\ - & - & 3 & 6 & 9 & 9 & 9 & 9 \end{pmatrix}_{4, -2}$$

Then

$$\text{GRADMAG2}(f) = \begin{pmatrix} - & - & 4.2 & 2.8 & 5 & - & - & - \\ - & - & - & 4.2 & 5 & 4.2 & - & - \\ - & - & - & 3 & 5.3 & 5 & 3 & - \\ - & - & 3 & 4.2 & 4.4 & 2 & - & - \\ * & - & 3 & 3 & 3 & - & - & - \end{pmatrix}_{4, -2}$$

The gradient has revealed the zone of transition. Measuring horizontally, it is either three or four pixels wide.

3.4 Gradient-type Edge Detectors

It is possible to view the three gradient edge-detection schemes of Section 3.3 from a general perspective. We begin this by re-examining the partial difference operators DX and DY. Consider the masks

$$G1 = (-1 \quad \textcircled{1})$$

and

$$G2 = \begin{pmatrix} \textcircled{1} \\ -1 \end{pmatrix}$$

If we apply the moving-average filter operator FILTER to an image f with input mask $G1$, we obtain at each pixel in the domain of f the output gray value

$$[\text{FILTER}(f; G1)](i, j) = [(-1) \times f(i - 1, j)] + [1 \times f(i, j)]$$
$$= f(i, j) - f(i - 1, j)$$
$$= [\text{DX}(f)](i, j)$$

Likewise,

$$[\text{FILTER}(f; G2)](i, j) = [\text{DY}(f)](i, j)$$

Hence both partial difference operators can be viewed as filters. Moreover, the first filter measures change in the x direction and the second measures change in the y direction. We refer to the two filters as *gradient filters*.

Once the filtering has been accomplished, one of three norms is applied to the resulting gradient vector. But these norms can be applied to any input image vector, whether or not the components result from filtering. Hence we can consider three norm operators on input image pairs:

1) MAXNORM(f, g)
2) ONENORM(f, g)
3) TWONORM(f, g)

These image norms are defined pixelwise by the vector norms, $\|V\|_\infty$, $\|V\|_1$, and $\|V\|_2$, given in Section 3.3. TWONORM is known as the *root sum square* norm. Depending on heuristic considerations, one of the images, GRADMAG0, GRADMAG1, or GRADMAG2, is employed. The resulting image is thresholded to produce a binary edge image. The entire process is depicted in Figure 3.6, where the operation NORM refers to one of the three previously described magnitude operators.

Of note in Figure 3.6 is the role played by $G1$ and $G2$. These masks determine the gradient measuring to be implemented by the filtering operations. The two filters output a gradient pair, which is then normed and thresholded. We could obtain a different edge-detection scheme by varying the input masks $G1$ and $G2$. The masks chosen thus far are those defined by the partial difference operators DX and DY. Others are possible.

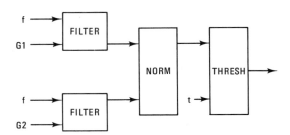

Figure 3.6 Gradient-type Edge Detector

Consider the *Prewitt masks* given by

$$P1 = \begin{pmatrix} -1 & 0 & 1 \\ -1 & \textcircled{0} & 1 \\ -1 & 0 & 1 \end{pmatrix}$$

and

$$P2 = \begin{pmatrix} 1 & 1 & 1 \\ 0 & \textcircled{0} & 0 \\ -1 & -1 & -1 \end{pmatrix}$$

The first Prewitt mask is a variant of the difference operator DX. It is different in that change is measured on both sides of the pixel at which the measure is being taken. It also differs in that the Prewitt gradient measure at pixel (i, j) is affected by the x direction changes one pixel above and one pixel below. This *spreading* of the measure makes the measure less sensitive to noise. The second Prewitt mask is a variant of the difference operator DY. Similar comments apply.

Whereas the usual gradient is defined by

$$\text{GRAD}(f) = [\text{FILTER}(f; G1), \text{FILTER}(f; G2)]$$

the *Prewitt gradient* is given by

$$\text{PREWITT}(f) = [\text{FILTER}(f; P1), \text{FILTER}(f; P2)]$$

In terms of pixel gray values, assuming that all relevant gray values are defined,

$$[\text{FILTER}(f; P1)](i, j) = f(i + 1, j + 1) + f(i + 1, j) + f(i + 1, j - 1)$$
$$- f(i - 1, j + 1) - f(i - 1, j) - f(i - 1, j - 1)$$

and

$$[\text{FILTER}(f; P2)](i, j) = f(i - 1, j + 1) + f(i, j + 1) + f(i + 1, j + 1)$$
$$- f(i - 1, j - 1) - f(i, j - 1) - f(i + 1, j - 1)$$

If, in the edge-detection scheme of Figure 3.6, the Prewitt masks $P1$ and $P2$ are utilized instead of the partial difference masks $G1$ and $G2$, then the three possible output images of NORM will be called PREWMAG0, PREWMAG1, and PREWMAG2, depending on whether the l_∞-norm, the l_1-norm, or the l_2-norm is applied. We shall refer to the corresponding outputs of THRESH as PREWEDGE0, PREWEDGE1, and PREWEDGE2.

It is helpful to note that we are using the numeric designations 0, 1, and 2 in a fashion consistent with the norming technique applied to the usual gradient GRAD. We shall continue to do so for succeeding gradient-type operators that fit the scheme of Figure 3.6.

Figure 3.7 gives an image f, the image f filtered with respect to both Prewitt masks, and the edge-detection images obtained by finding the three different norms of the Prewitt gradient. Recall that FILTER is obtained by placing the center of the mask over the appropriate pixel and then applying DOT. If all pixels of f under the fitted mask have defined gray values, the output of DOT is defined; otherwise, it is undefined. For instance,

$$[\text{FILTER}(f; P1)](4, -2) = \text{DOT}\left[\begin{pmatrix} -1 & 0 & 1 \\ -1 & 0 & 1 \\ -1 & 0 & 1 \end{pmatrix}_{3, -1} , \begin{pmatrix} 4 & 4 & 4 \\ 0 & 4 & 4 \\ 0 & 0 & 3 \end{pmatrix}_{3, -1} \right]$$

$$= -4 + 4 + 4 + 3 = 7$$

Figure 3.7 also gives the thresholded image PREWEDGE0(f; 7), which has been obtained by using $t = 7$ and applying THRESH to PREWMAG0(f). Similar thresholded results are obtainable for PREWEDGE1 and PREWEDGE2.

Closely akin to the Prewitt edge detectors are the Sobel edge detectors. These are also produced by the detection scheme of Figure 3.6, the difference being the use of the *Sobel masks S*1 and *S*2 in place of the Prewitt masks. The Sobel masks are given by

$$S1 = \begin{pmatrix} -1 & 0 & 1 \\ -2 & ⓪ & 2 \\ -1 & 0 & 1 \end{pmatrix}$$

and

$$S2 = \begin{pmatrix} 1 & 2 & 1 \\ 0 & ⓪ & 0 \\ -1 & -2 & -1 \end{pmatrix}$$

The *Sobel gradient* is given by

$$\text{SOBEL}(f) = [\text{FILTER}(f; S1), \text{FILTER}(f; S2)]$$

Due to the similarity between the Sobel masks and the Prewitt masks, we shall leave the associated gradient edge-detection operators to the exercises. As with the gradient and the Prewitt gradient, there will be three gradient magnitude images and three corresponding edge images.

Another commonly employed edge-detection gradient is the *Roberts gradient*. It is generated by the *Roberts masks*

$$R1 = \begin{pmatrix} -1 & 0 \\ 0 & ① \end{pmatrix}$$

and

$$R2 = \begin{pmatrix} 0 & 1 \\ -1 & ⓪ \end{pmatrix}$$

(a) f = $\begin{pmatrix} - & - & 3 & 4 & 4 & 4 & 4 & 4 & 4 \\ - & - & - & 4 & 4 & 4 & 4 & 4 & 4 \\ - & - & - & - & 4 & 4 & 4 & 4 & 4 \\ - & - & - & - & - & 3 & 4 & 4 & 4 \\ - & - & - & - & - & - & 4 & 4 & 4 \\ * & - & - & - & - & - & - & 4 & 4 \end{pmatrix}_{0,\,0}$

(b) FILTER(f; P1) = $\begin{pmatrix} * & * & * & * & * & * & * & * & * \\ * & 3 & 8 & 9 & 4 & - & - & - & * \\ * & - & 4 & 8 & 7 & 4 & 1 & - & * \\ * & - & - & 4 & 7 & 8 & 5 & - & * \\ * & - & - & - & 3 & 8 & 9 & 4 & * \\ * & * & * & * & * & * & * & * & * \end{pmatrix}_{0,\,0}$

(c) FILTER(f; P2) = $\begin{pmatrix} * & * & * & * & * & * & * & * & * \\ * & 3 & 7 & 7 & 4 & - & - & - & * \\ * & - & 4 & 8 & 9 & 5 & 1 & - & * \\ * & - & - & 4 & 8 & 8 & 4 & - & * \\ * & - & - & - & 3 & 7 & 7 & 4 & * \\ * & * & * & * & * & * & * & * & * \end{pmatrix}_{0,\,0}$

(d) PREWMAG0(f) = $\begin{pmatrix} 3 & 8 & 9 & 4 & - & - & - \\ - & 4 & 8 & 9 & 5 & 1 & - \\ - & - & 4 & 8 & 8 & 5 & - \\ - & - & - & 3 & 8 & 9 & 4 \end{pmatrix}_{1,\,-1}$

(e) PREWMAG1(f) = $\begin{pmatrix} 6 & 15 & 16 & 8 & - & - & - \\ - & 8 & 16 & 16 & 9 & 2 & - \\ - & - & 8 & 15 & 16 & 9 & - \\ - & - & - & 6 & 15 & 16 & 8 \end{pmatrix}_{1,\,-1}$

Figure 3.7 Image with Associated Prewitt Edge Images

Figure 3.7 continued

$$(f) \quad \text{PREWMAG2}(f) = \begin{pmatrix} 4.2 & 10.6 & 11.4 & 5.7 & - & - & - \\ - & 5.7 & 11.3 & 11.4 & 6.4 & 1.4 & - \\ - & - & 5.7 & 10.6 & 11.3 & 6.4 & - \\ - & - & - & 4.2 & 10.6 & 11.4 & 5.7 \end{pmatrix}_{1,-1}$$

$$(g) \quad \text{PREWEDGE0}(f; 7) = \begin{pmatrix} - & 1 & 1 & - & - & - & - \\ - & - & 1 & 1 & - & - & - \\ - & - & - & 1 & 1 & - & - \\ - & - & - & - & 1 & 1 & - \end{pmatrix}_{1,-1}$$

The *Roberts gradient* is given by

$$\text{ROBERTS}(f) = [\text{FILTER}(f; R1), \text{FILTER}(f; R2)]$$

At each pixel (i, j), assuming that all relevant gray values are defined, the outputs of the two Roberts difference operators are

$$[\text{FILTER}(f; R1)](i, j) = f(i, j) - f(i - 1, j + 1)$$

and

$$[\text{FILTER}(f; R2)](i, j) = f(i, j + 1) - f(i - 1, j)$$

Once again, by choosing the appropriate norming operation, we can obtain three possible Roberts gradient magnitude images and three corresponding edge images (after thresholding). Figure 3.8 gives the results of applying the Roberts masks to the image f of Figure 3.7. It also gives the gradient magnitude image for the norm ONENORM. In accordance with previous terminology, this is called ROBMAG1(f).

Many other such gradient-type edge detectors can be created by simply utilizing the scheme of Figure 3.6. We have introduced only the most common. The use of larger masks tends to reduce the effect of noise while spreading the region of detection. Although the first effect is beneficial, the latter might lead to an increased incidence of false detection.

3.5 Compass Gradients

Each of the gradient-type edge detectors of Section 3.5 involved the use of exactly two masks. With the gradient, Prewitt gradient, and Sobel gradient, there was one mask responding to change in the x direction and one responding to change in the y direction. With the Roberts gradient, one mask responded to change in the $-45°$ direction and the other responded to change in the $+45°$ direction.

$$\text{FILTER}(f; R1) = \begin{pmatrix} * & * & * & * & * & * & * & * & * \\ * & - & - & 1 & - & - & - & - & - \\ * & - & - & - & - & - & - & - & - \\ * & - & - & - & - & -1 & - & - & - \\ * & - & - & - & - & - & 1 & - & - \\ * & - & - & - & - & - & - & - & - \\ * & - & - & - & - & - & - & - & - \end{pmatrix}_{0,0}$$

$$\text{FILTER}(f; R2) = \begin{pmatrix} * & * & * & * & * & * & * & * & * \\ * & - & 3 & 4 & - & - & - & - & - \\ * & - & - & 4 & 4 & - & - & - & - \\ * & - & - & - & 4 & 4 & 1 & - & - \\ * & - & - & - & - & 3 & 4 & - & - \\ * & - & - & - & - & - & 4 & 4 & - \end{pmatrix}_{0,0}$$

$$\text{ROBMAG1}(f) = \begin{pmatrix} - & 3 & 5 & - & - & - & - & - \\ - & - & 4 & 4 & - & - & - & - \\ - & - & - & 4 & 5 & 1 & - & - \\ - & - & - & - & 3 & 5 & - & - \\ - & - & - & - & - & 4 & 4 & - \end{pmatrix}_{1,-1}$$

Figure 3.8 Roberts Edge Images of Image In Figure *3.7*

Another way to proceed is to look for masks that respond to changes in all directions that are integral multiples of 45°. In essence, the methodology is to filter by applying masks that respond well to change in a particular *compass direction*. Since there are eight 45° directions, each procedure involves filtering by eight different masks, each mask being a 45° *cycling* of the previous mask (see Figures 3.10 through 3.12). Once this has been accomplished, a maximum norm is applied to the eight outputs to obtain an image that indicates the gray level rate of change at each pixel. As in Figure 3.6, this image can then be thresholded to produce an edge image. Indeed, if Figure 3.6 were modified to include eight filtering operations with eight different masks, it would apply directly to the compass gradient method, except in this new technique only the norming operator MAXNORM is utilized. Figure 3.9 gives the appropriate block diagram for the input masks $M1, M2, \ldots, M8$.

The *Prewitt compass gradient* is defined by the masks of Figure 3.10. Notice that each can be obtained from the preceding mask by a 45° cycling of the gray values. The *Kirsh* operator uses the masks of Figure 3.11. Other well-known masks for compass gradient edge detection are the *three-level* masks and the *five-level* masks. The three-level masks are generated by cycling the Prewitt mask $P1$, and the five-level masks are generated by cycling the Sobel mask $S1$. The eight three-level masks are shown in Figure 3.12. Due to symmetry and the use of the absolute value, one need only apply the first four three-level masks and the first four five-level masks when using these mask sets. In each case, filtering by the second four masks and then applying the absolute value operator merely gives a repetition of the outputs obtained from the first four masks.

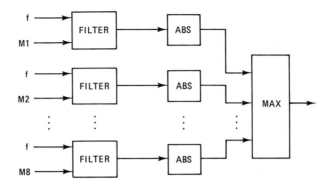

Figure 3.9 Detection Scheme Block Diagram

$$
\begin{pmatrix} -1 & 1 & 1 \\ -1 & -2 & 1 \\ -1 & 1 & 1 \end{pmatrix}
\qquad
\begin{pmatrix} 1 & 1 & 1 \\ -1 & -2 & 1 \\ -1 & -1 & 1 \end{pmatrix}
\qquad
\begin{pmatrix} 1 & 1 & 1 \\ 1 & -2 & 1 \\ -1 & -1 & -1 \end{pmatrix}
$$

$$
\begin{pmatrix} 1 & 1 & 1 \\ 1 & -2 & -1 \\ 1 & -1 & -1 \end{pmatrix}
\qquad
\begin{pmatrix} 1 & 1 & -1 \\ 1 & -2 & -1 \\ 1 & 1 & -1 \end{pmatrix}
\qquad
\begin{pmatrix} 1 & -1 & -1 \\ 1 & -2 & -1 \\ 1 & 1 & 1 \end{pmatrix}
$$

$$
\begin{pmatrix} -1 & -1 & -1 \\ 1 & -2 & 1 \\ 1 & 1 & 1 \end{pmatrix}
\qquad
\begin{pmatrix} -1 & -1 & 1 \\ -1 & -2 & 1 \\ 1 & 1 & 1 \end{pmatrix}
$$

Figure 3.10 Prewitt Compass Gradient Masks

$$
\begin{pmatrix} -5 & 3 & 3 \\ -5 & 0 & 3 \\ -5 & 3 & 3 \end{pmatrix}
\qquad
\begin{pmatrix} 3 & 3 & 3 \\ -5 & 0 & 3 \\ -5 & -5 & 3 \end{pmatrix}
\qquad
\begin{pmatrix} 3 & 3 & 3 \\ 3 & 0 & 3 \\ -5 & -5 & -5 \end{pmatrix}
$$

$$
\begin{pmatrix} 3 & 3 & 3 \\ 3 & 0 & -5 \\ 3 & -5 & -5 \end{pmatrix}
\qquad
\begin{pmatrix} 3 & 3 & -5 \\ 3 & 0 & -5 \\ 3 & 3 & -5 \end{pmatrix}
\qquad
\begin{pmatrix} 3 & -5 & -5 \\ 3 & 0 & -5 \\ 3 & 3 & 3 \end{pmatrix}
$$

$$
\begin{pmatrix} -5 & -5 & -5 \\ 3 & 0 & 3 \\ 3 & 3 & 3 \end{pmatrix}
\qquad
\begin{pmatrix} -5 & -5 & 3 \\ -5 & 0 & 3 \\ 3 & 3 & 3 \end{pmatrix}
$$

Figure 3.11 Kirsh Compass Gradient Masks

$$\begin{pmatrix} -1 & 0 & 1 \\ -1 & \textcircled{0} & 1 \\ -1 & 0 & 1 \end{pmatrix} \quad \begin{pmatrix} 0 & 1 & 1 \\ -1 & \textcircled{0} & 1 \\ -1 & -1 & 0 \end{pmatrix} \quad \begin{pmatrix} 1 & 1 & 1 \\ 0 & \textcircled{0} & 0 \\ -1 & -1 & -1 \end{pmatrix}$$

$$\begin{pmatrix} 1 & 1 & 0 \\ 1 & \textcircled{0} & -1 \\ 0 & -1 & -1 \end{pmatrix} \quad \begin{pmatrix} 1 & 0 & -1 \\ 1 & \textcircled{0} & -1 \\ 1 & 0 & -1 \end{pmatrix} \quad \begin{pmatrix} 0 & -1 & -1 \\ 1 & \textcircled{0} & -1 \\ 1 & 1 & 0 \end{pmatrix}$$

$$\begin{pmatrix} -1 & -1 & -1 \\ 0 & \textcircled{0} & 0 \\ 1 & 1 & 1 \end{pmatrix} \quad \begin{pmatrix} -1 & -1 & 0 \\ -1 & \textcircled{0} & 1 \\ 0 & 1 & 1 \end{pmatrix}$$

Figure 3.12 Eight Three Level Masks

We shall now apply the detection scheme of Figure 3.9 to the image f of Figure 3.13 using the three-level masks. The outputs of the filtering by the first four masks, $L1$, $L2$, $L3$, and $L4$, are also given in Figure 3.13, along with the final output of the operation, THREELEVEL(f). Only the first four masks are necessary for THREELEVEL. (All eight are required for the Prewitt compass gradient and the Kirsh edge-detection scheme.) Since the operation DOT is to be employed with a square mask (in FILTER), the outside pixels of the original image will become starred. Other values are calculated by direct use of the dot product. For example,

$$[\text{FILTER}(f; L2)](2, 2) = \text{DOT}\left[\begin{pmatrix} - & - & - \\ 2 & 2 & - \\ 2 & 2 & - \end{pmatrix}_{1,3}, \begin{pmatrix} 0 & 1 & 1 \\ -1 & 0 & 1 \\ -1 & -1 & 0 \end{pmatrix}_{1,3} \right]$$

$$= -2 + -2 + -2 = -6$$

To obtain the final output, simply take the absolute value of the gray values in the filtered images and then apply the maximum operator. For instance,

$$[\text{THREELEVEL}(f)](1, 2) = \max(0, 4, 6, 4) = 6$$

As with the gradient-type edge detectors of Section 3.4, the operators of this section can be followed by a thresholding operation to obtain an edge image.

3.6 Textural Edge Detection

Thus far we have considered edge detection by finding zones of transition between regions of homogeneous gray level. We can also consider edges between regions of differing texture. Consider the image f of Figure 3.14 together with its pictorial representation. It is clear to the eye that the image contains a square consisting of a horizontal gray-level pattern on a background consisting of a vertical gray-level pattern. It is also clear that the square is darker than its ground, although this darkness is not directly due to hom-

$$
f = \begin{pmatrix}
- & - & - & - & - & - \\
- & - & - & - & - & - \\
- & - & - & - & - & - \\
2 & 2 & 2 & - & - & - \\
2 & 2 & 2 & - & - & - \\
2 & 2 & 2 & - & - & -
\end{pmatrix}_{0,\,5}
$$

$$
\text{FILTER}(f; \text{L1}) = \begin{pmatrix}
- & - & - & - \\
- & -2 & -2 & - \\
- & -4 & -4 & - \\
- & -6 & -6 & -
\end{pmatrix}_{1,\,4}
$$

$$
\text{FILTER}(f; \text{L2}) = \begin{pmatrix}
- & - & - & - \\
-4 & -4 & -2 & - \\
-4 & -6 & -4 & - \\
- & -4 & -4 & -
\end{pmatrix}_{1,\,4}
$$

$$
\text{FILTER}(f; \text{L3}) = \begin{pmatrix}
- & - & - & - \\
-6 & -4 & -2 & - \\
-6 & -4 & -2 & - \\
- & - & - & -
\end{pmatrix}_{1,\,4}
$$

$$
\text{FILTER}(f; \text{L4}) = \begin{pmatrix}
- & - & - & - \\
-4 & -2 & - & - \\
-4 & - & 2 & - \\
- & 4 & 4 & -
\end{pmatrix}_{1,\,4}
$$

$$
\text{THREELEVEL}(f) = \begin{pmatrix}
* & * & * & * & * & * \\
* & - & - & - & - & * \\
* & 6 & 4 & 2 & - & * \\
* & 6 & 6 & 4 & - & * \\
* & - & 6 & 6 & - & * \\
* & * & * & * & * & *
\end{pmatrix}_{0,\,4}
$$

Figure 3.13 Use of THREELEVEL

ogeneity of gray level. Nevertheless, this textural darkness can be exploited to locate the edge between the figure and its background. If the image is smoothed (gray levels averaged), then a new image will result in which the square and its background will each be essentially homogeneous with respect to gray level. It is then possible to apply a gradient technique to this enhanced image to determine the textural edge. In fact, Figure 3.14 contains a walk-through of such a detection scheme. It applies (shown vertically) the detection sequence SMOOTH, THRESH, and GRADMAG0. The result is a reasonably good estimate of the textural boundary that the eye discerns in the pictorial of f.

The method can be summarized by the following diagram:

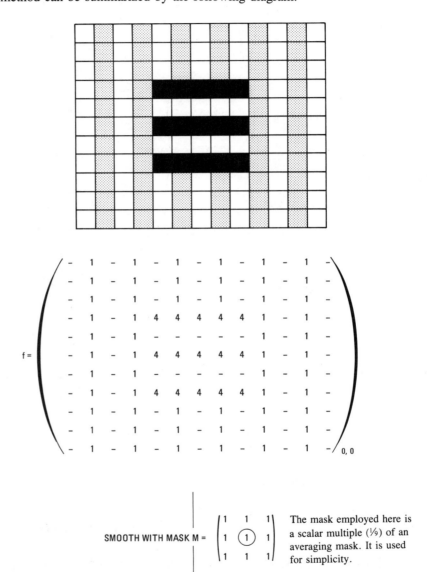

Figure 3.14 Picture with Pictorial Representation and Operation Trace

Figure 3.14 continued

$$
\begin{pmatrix}
3 & 6 & 3 & 6 & 3 & 6 & 3 & 6 & 3 & 6 & 3 \\
3 & 6 & 7 & 13 & 14 & 16 & 14 & 13 & 7 & 6 & 3 \\
3 & 6 & 7 & 12 & 13 & 14 & 13 & 12 & 7 & 6 & 3 \\
3 & 6 & 11 & 19 & 24 & 24 & 24 & 19 & 11 & 6 & 3 \\
3 & 6 & 7 & 11 & 12 & 12 & 12 & 11 & 7 & 6 & 3 \\
3 & 6 & 11 & 19 & 24 & 24 & 24 & 19 & 11 & 6 & 3 \\
3 & 6 & 7 & 12 & 13 & 14 & 13 & 12 & 7 & 6 & 3 \\
3 & 6 & 7 & 13 & 14 & 16 & 14 & 13 & 7 & 6 & 3 \\
3 & 6 & 3 & 6 & 3 & 6 & 3 & 6 & 3 & 6 & 3 \\
\end{pmatrix}_{1, -1}
$$

THRESH WITH t = 10

$$
\begin{pmatrix}
- & - & - & - & - & - & - & - & - & - & - \\
- & - & - & 1 & 1 & 1 & 1 & 1 & - & - & - \\
- & - & - & 1 & 1 & 1 & 1 & 1 & - & - & - \\
- & - & 1 & 1 & 1 & 1 & 1 & 1 & 1 & - & - \\
- & - & - & 1 & 1 & 1 & 1 & 1 & - & - & - \\
- & - & 1 & 1 & 1 & 1 & 1 & 1 & 1 & - & - \\
- & - & - & 1 & 1 & 1 & 1 & 1 & - & - & - \\
- & - & - & 1 & 1 & 1 & 1 & 1 & - & - & - \\
- & - & - & - & - & - & - & - & - & - & - \\
\end{pmatrix}_{1, -1}
$$

GRADMAG0 = MAXNORM[GRAD]

$$
\begin{pmatrix}
- & - & - & 1 & 1 & 1 & 1 & 1 & - & - & - \\
- & - & - & 1 & - & - & - & - & 1 & - & - \\
- & - & 1 & 1 & - & - & - & - & 1 & - & - \\
- & - & 1 & - & - & - & - & - & 1 & 1 & - \\
- & - & 1 & 1 & - & - & - & - & 1 & - & - \\
- & - & 1 & - & - & - & - & - & 1 & 1 & - \\
- & - & - & 1 & - & - & - & - & 1 & - & - \\
- & - & - & 1 & 1 & 1 & 1 & 1 & 1 & - & - \\
* & - & - & - & - & - & - & - & - & - & - \\
\end{pmatrix}_{1, -1}
$$

It depends heaily on the texturally defined regions having significantly different average gray levels. Yet this is not always the case.

Consider image g of Figure 3.15. It is clear that, in terms of vertical and horizontal pixel strings, g is texturally identical to image f of Figure 3.14. However, there is no significant average gray-level difference that will allow the use of a threshold operation after a smoothing operation. Indeed, smoothing will simply blur the entire image into an essentially constant mass. The preceding averaging technique is useless in this situation.

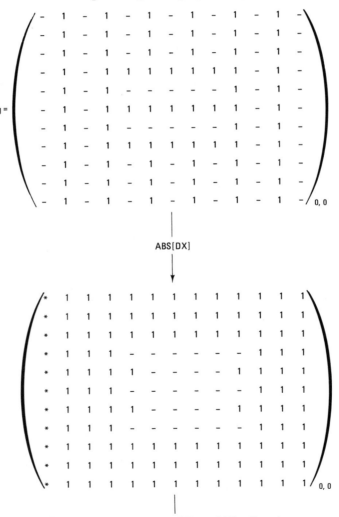

Figure 3.15 Walk-through of Textural Edge Detection

Figure 3.15 continued

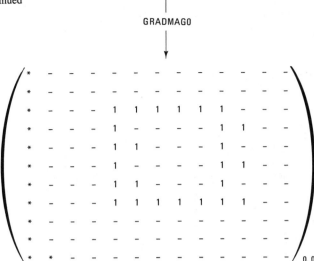

Suppose, however, that we have some knowledge regarding the type of textures that will appear within the image. For instance, suppose that we know the image will consist of vertical and horizontal strings of black and white pixels. In such a situation it is possible to preprocess the original image in a different manner than by simply smoothing and thresholding. In other words, we consider the following more general block diagram:

Here, the enhancement operation consists of some sequence of preprocessing transformations.

Given that we have prior knowledge concerning the vertical and horizontal textural differences within the image g of Figure 3.15, we might apply the difference operator DX before employing the edge detector. Figure 3.15 contains a walk-through of the resulting textural edge detection sequence

The resulting image is a fairly good representative of the textural edge discerned by the eye. It is essentially a rectangular perimeter.

The enhancement–detection method of determining textural edges is highly dependent upon good heuristics. A good knowledge-based determination must be made as to the enhancement operation sequence. Indeed, we might proceed with several parallel implementations of the methodology, where both the enhancement technique and the edge-detection scheme are varied. Our choice of GRADMAG0 (the use of the maximum norm) was merely for illustration. Another norm or another gradient-type detection method might lead to better results.

EXERCISES

3.1. Let

$$
f = \begin{pmatrix}
0 & 1 & 1 & 0 & 1 & 0 & 0 & 0 & 0 & 1 & 1 & 2 \\
1 & 0 & 1 & 0 & 1 & 0 & 0 & 0 & 0 & 7 & 0 & 1 \\
1 & 2 & 0 & 1 & 6 & 6 & 6 & 7 & 1 & 1 & 0 & 0 \\
* & 2 & 1 & 1 & 6 & 7 & 7 & 6 & 1 & 2 & 1 & 1 \\
1 & 1 & 7 & 5 & 6 & 7 & 5 & 7 & 6 & 6 & 0 & 0 \\
1 & 1 & 6 & 6 & 7 & 6 & 5 & 7 & 6 & 6 & 0 & 0 \\
1 & 2 & 0 & 0 & 7 & 7 & 8 & 6 & 1 & 1 & 1 & 1 \\
1 & 1 & 0 & 2 & 5 & 7 & 6 & 6 & 0 & 0 & 0 & 0 \\
0 & 0 & 1 & 0 & 1 & 0 & 0 & 0 & 1 & 0 & 0 & 0 \\
0 & 0 & 1 & 2 & 0 & 0 & 1 & 1 & 1 & 1 & 0 & 0
\end{pmatrix}_{0,6}
$$

Compute:

(a) VERTEDGE(f; 4)
(b) HOREDGE(f; 3)
(c) GRAD(f)
(d) GRADMAG1(f)
(e) GRADMAG2(f)
(f) GRADMAG0(f)

(g) PREWMAG1(f)
(h) PREWEDGE1(f; t),
    for t = 12, 16, 20, and 24
(i) SOBELMAG2(f)
(j) ROBMAG1(f)
(k) SOBELEDGE2(f; 20)

3.2. In a manner appropriate to Figure 3.6, define the operators GRADEDGE1, GRADEDGE2, and GRADEDGE0. Apply each of these operators to the image f of Exercise 3.1 with the threshold input t = 4.

3.3. Apply the edge-detection schema of Figure 3.9 to the image f of Exercise 3.1 for the following operators:

(a) Prewitt compass gradient (PREWCOMP)
(b) Sobel compass gradient (SOBELCOMP)
(c) Kirsh operator (KIRSH)
(d) Three-level operator (THREELEVEL)
(e) Five-level operator (FIVELEVEL)

3.4. Let

$$
g = \begin{pmatrix}
1 & 1 & 0 & 0 & 1 & 1 & 0 & 0 & 1 & 1 \\
0 & 0 & 1 & 1 & 0 & 0 & 1 & 1 & 0 & 0 \\
1 & 1 & 0 & 0 & 1 & 1 & 0 & 0 & 1 & 1 \\
0 & 0 & 1 & 1 & 0 & 0 & 1 & 1 & 0 & 0 \\
5 & 1 & 5 & 1 & 5 & 1 & 5 & 1 & 5 & 1 \\
5 & 1 & 5 & 1 & 5 & 1 & 5 & 1 & 5 & 1 \\
5 & 1 & 5 & 1 & 5 & 1 & 5 & 1 & 5 & 1 \\
5 & 1 & 5 & 1 & 5 & 1 & 5 & 1 & 5 & 1
\end{pmatrix}_{2,7}
$$

(a) Apply the textural edge-detection sequence SMOOTH, THRESH, and GRADMAG1 to g with input mask

$$M = \begin{pmatrix} 1 & 1 & 1 \\ 1 & \textcircled{1} & 1 \\ 1 & 1 & 1 \end{pmatrix}$$

Make your own choice of threshold value t.

(b) Repeat the procedure using SOBELMAG2 in place of GRADMAG1.

3.5. Apply an enhancement edge detector methodology with enhancement operator ABS(DY) to locate the textural edge in the image of Figure 3.15. Use the following edge detectors:

(a) GRADMAG1
(b) PREWMAG2
(c) KIRSH

3.6. Define the gradient operator NEWGRAD by

$$\text{NEWGRAD}(f) = [\text{FILTER}(f; Q1), \text{FILTER}(f; Q2)]$$

where the masks $Q1$ and $Q2$ are defined by

$$Q1 = \begin{pmatrix} -1 & 0 & 1 \\ -1 & 0 & 1 \\ -1 & \textcircled{0} & 1 \\ -1 & 0 & 1 \\ -1 & 0 & 1 \end{pmatrix}$$

$$Q2 = \begin{pmatrix} 1 & 1 & 1 & 1 & 1 \\ 0 & 0 & \textcircled{0} & 0 & 0 \\ -1 & -1 & -1 & -1 & -1 \end{pmatrix}$$

Using the norms MAXNORM, ONENORM, and TWONORM, define the operators NEWMAG0, NEWMAG1, and NEWMAG2 in a manner similar to PREWMAG0, PREWMAG1, and PREWMAG2. Then apply these three new gradient-type operators to the image f of Exercise 3.1.

3.7. Consider the mask

$$R = \begin{pmatrix} 3 & 3 & 3 \\ 0 & \textcircled{0} & 0 \\ -2 & -2 & -2 \end{pmatrix}$$

Find the eight 45° cyclings of R. Using the compass gradient detection scheme of Figure 3.9, define the operator NEWCOMP by letting $M1, M2, \ldots, M8$ be the 45° cyclings of R. Apply NEWCOMP to the image f of Exercise 3.1.

4

MORPHOLOGY

4.1 Definition

From a general scientific perspective, *morphology* is the study of form and structure. When we apply the latter terms specifically to image processing, we talk of pattern and texture. Consequently, at least insofar as the generic meaning of the word is involved, morphology has a natural place in the analysis of images.

Yet our viewpoint will be much more pointed. Whenever we talk of mathematical morphology, we shall be referring to a branch of image processing that was pioneered by G. Matheron in his studies of porous materials. The theory developed by Matheron is one of the most rigorous structures in the area of image processing.[1]

The germ of the morphological method is to analyze images in terms of shape and size by the use of elemental patterns chosen by the investigator. Due to the intricacy of texture, the manner in which these patterns are utilized is quite involved. Morphology calls on many areas of mathematics, including integral geometry, statistics, algebra, topology, analysis, and computer science. In this text, the algebraic and geometric operations that underlie morphology will be developed. Moreover, we shall give an introductory account of two particularly fruitful techniques utilized in morphology, granulometric distributions and the covariance.

4.2 Constant Images

An image that has only a single gray value is known as a *constant image*. For example, consider the image

[1]G. Matheron, *Random Sets and Integral Geometry*, John Wiley & Sons, Inc., New York, 1975.

$$S = \begin{pmatrix} 1 & 1 & * \\ 1 & * & ① \end{pmatrix}$$

In this image, a single gray value (1) appears; however, the symbol $*$ is also employed to indicate a lack of information for certain pixels. In practice, there will always be pixels with no known gray value, since real information is always finite in quantity. The image

$$S' = \begin{pmatrix} 1 & 1 & 1 \\ ① & 1 & 1 \end{pmatrix}$$

is a constant image. Recall that it has value $*$ outside the depicted frame; for example, $S'(0, -1) = *$.

When dealing with constant images, certain conventions will be adapted. We shall usually employ the letters S and T to denote the images, and the constant value of the image will almost always be 1 in this chapter.

Before we proceed with the basic properties of constant images, a point of potential confusion must be clarified: If a constant image has two "values," then why is it not called a binary image? The question is not superfluous; indeed, it goes to the heart of the definition of image. While it is true that the pixels of a constant image may be either 1 or $*$, it is also true that only one of these values is a gray value—only one represents positive information. On the other hand, a binary image has two gray values, usually 0 and 1, and consequently its pixels may have any one of three values: 0, 1, or $*$. The definition of image that we employ is faithful to the model that it represents, not to a convenient mathematical apparatus. Given that the value of S at (i, j) reflects the intensity registered by a sensor, it is clear that a binary sensor can yield three results, one of those results being no reading whatsoever. For such an occurrence, we use the symbol $*$. On the other hand, if a sensor can merely become activated or remain deactivated, this is a true two-valued case, and faithful modeling requires us to use the gray value 1 and the nongray value $*$. The lack of activation on the part of the sensor does not yield positive information; indeed, the sensor could simply be inoperative, or, more trivially, the pixel (i, j) might be outside the field of sensors altogether. In accordance with these considerations, we say that pixel (i, j) is *activated* if $S(i, j) \neq *$, and it is *deactivated* if $S(i, j) = *$.

Constant images have a natural set theoretic interpretation. We can view the grid of pixels as a universal class of locations and say that a set is defined by the collection of all pixels having nonstar value. Indeed, under this classification the image S is simply a set, and a pixel may either be in the set or outside the set. Moreover, the notion of subimage introduced earlier is, in this instance, equivalent to the notion of subset.

This leads us to the concept of a *complementary image*, where a technique analogous to the sign-magnitude representation of negative numbers will prove to be useful. If $T = (a_{pq})_{rt}$ is a bound matrix representation of T, then the complementary image T^c will have the *complementary bound matrix* representation $(b_{pq})^c_{rt}$, defined by

$b_{pq} = *$ if $a_{pq} = 1$ and (p, q) is within the bound matrix frame

$b_{pq} = 1$ if $a_{pq} = *$ and (p, q) is within the bound matrix frame

$T^c(p, q) = 1$ for all (p, q) outside the frame

Whereas the location of the 1's within the complementary bound matrix must be kept in computer memory, the value 1 for all pixels outside the frame can be represented by a single word. In reality, the situation with T^c, the complementary image, is no different than that with T itself. By convention, we assume the value $T(p, q) = *$ for any pixel (p, q) outside the frame. Yet such a value has no specific location in memory. We simply operate "as though it were," our operators being defined in such a manner as to give us both consistency and a virtually infinite image. For example, consider the image

$$T = \begin{pmatrix} 1 & 1 & 1 & * \\ 1 & \circledast & 1 & 1 \\ 1 & 1 & 1 & * \end{pmatrix}; \quad \text{then} \quad T^c = \begin{pmatrix} * & * & * & 1 \\ * & \textcircled{1} & * & * \\ * & * & * & 1 \end{pmatrix}^c$$

When working with constant images, two operations are of particular importance. They are the minimum operation MIN and the extended maximum operation EXTMAX. For constant images with constant gray value 1, these play the role of intersection and union, respectively. For such images, MIN outputs a constant image (with gray value 1) whose domain is the intersection of the two input domains, and EXTMAX outputs a constant image (with gray value 1) whose domain is the union of the two input domains. Because of these intersection and union properties, we introduce the special notation

$$S \wedge T = \text{MIN}(S, T)$$

and

$$S \vee T = \text{EXTMAX}(S, T)$$

It is important to note that the operation EXTMAX, when performed on constant images having different gray values, might produce an output image that is not constant. However, this cannot occur as long as the input images have constant gray value 1. Example 4.1 illustrates the intersection and union properties for two such images. Example 4.2, on the other hand, shows what can happen when the two input images have different constant gray values. Except for this latter example, all constant images throughout the remainder of this chapter will have gray values equal to 1.

Example 4.1

Consider the images S and T:

$$S = \begin{pmatrix} 1 & 1 & * \\ 1 & * & \circledast \end{pmatrix}, \quad T = \begin{pmatrix} * & 1 & 1 & 1 & * \\ * & 1 & \circledast & 1 & 1 \\ * & 1 & 1 & 1 & * \end{pmatrix}$$

Then

$$S \vee T = \begin{pmatrix} 1 & 1 & 1 & 1 & * \\ 1 & 1 & \circledast & 1 & 1 \\ * & 1 & 1 & 1 & * \end{pmatrix}$$

$$S \wedge T = \begin{pmatrix} * & 1 & * & * & * \\ * & * & \circledast & * & * \\ * & * & * & * & * \end{pmatrix}$$

Example 4.2

Let

$$S = \begin{pmatrix} 2 & 2 \\ \circledast & 2 \end{pmatrix}, \quad T = \begin{pmatrix} 3 & 3 & 3 \\ 3 & 3 & * \\ 3 & ③ & 3 \end{pmatrix}$$

Then

$$S \vee T = \begin{pmatrix} 3 & 3 & 3 \\ 3 & 3 & 2 \\ 3 & ③ & 3 \end{pmatrix}$$

$$S \wedge T = \begin{pmatrix} * & * & * \\ * & 2 & * \\ * & \circledast & 2 \end{pmatrix}$$

4.3 Minkowski Algebra

The algebraic foundation of all morphological analysis consists of two basic set theoretic operations on pairs of constant images having gray value 1. The first of these operations is known as *Minkowski addition* and is defined by

$$S \boxplus E = \bigvee_{(i, j) \in D_S} \text{TRAN}(E; i, j)$$

where D_S stands for the domain of S. In the language of set theory, the image E is translated by each pair in the image S (each pair with value 1), and the resulting images are unioned, the union of constant images being the extended maximum of those images. The new image will be a "larger" image than S and one where the "small" holes of S have been filled, the latter change being a textural alteration. If the origin is contained in E, then the original image S will be a subimage of the new image. This new image, $S \boxplus E$, is called the *dilation* of S by E.

Intuitively, the image E plays the role of a template; the *center* of the template is the pixel of the bound matrix representing E that is located at the origin. The Minkowski sum is found by placing the center of the template over each of the activated pixels (those having value 1) of S and then taking the union of all the resulting copies of E. We produce these copies of E by using the translation operation. In morphological terminology, the template E is referred to as a *structuring element*, and it is precisely this template representation that impels us to utilize bound matrices with origin specification when considering morphology. Example 4.3 illustrates the technique.

Example 4.3

Consider the two images S and E, where

$$S = \begin{pmatrix} * & 1 & * & 1 & * \\ * & 1 & 1 & * & 1 \\ \circledast & 1 & 1 & 1 & * \end{pmatrix} \quad \text{and} \quad E = \begin{pmatrix} 1 & * \\ 1 & \textcircled{1} \end{pmatrix} \leftarrow \text{origin or center}$$

The domain of S is

$$D_S = \{(1, 2), (1, 1), (1, 0), (2, 1), (2, 0), (3, 2),$$

$$(3, 0), (4, 1)\}$$

The translation operation should be used eight times (once for each element in D_S). We first use it to move the center of E to $(1, 0)$. Thus the translation of E by $(i, j) = (1, 0)$ yields the image

$$\text{TRAN}(E; 1, 0) = \begin{pmatrix} 1 & * \\ \textcircled{1} & 1 \end{pmatrix}$$

This shows that $S \boxplus E$ must have a 1 at $(0, 0)$, $(1, 0)$, and $(0, 1)$. Also,

$$\text{TRAN}(E; 1, 2) = \begin{pmatrix} 1 & * \\ 1 & 1 \\ * & * \\ \circledast & * \end{pmatrix}$$

Thus $S \boxplus E$ must have a 1 at $(0, 2)$, $(0, 3)$, and $(1, 2)$. When the additional six translations have been formed and the union has been taken, the resulting image is the Minkowski addition:

$$S \boxplus E = \begin{pmatrix} 1 & * & 1 & * & * \\ 1 & 1 & 1 & 1 & * \\ 1 & 1 & 1 & 1 & 1 \\ \textcircled{1} & 1 & 1 & 1 & * \end{pmatrix}$$

Note that E has value 1 at the origin and hence S is a subimage of the dilation. (It is recommended that the reader also form the image E on cellophane or some other transparent material and overlay translates of this image on S to visually obtain $S \boxplus E$. See Figure 4.1.)

The block diagram for Minkowski addition, or dilation, is

$$S \to \boxed{\qquad \text{DILATE} \qquad} \longrightarrow S \boxplus E$$
$$E \to$$

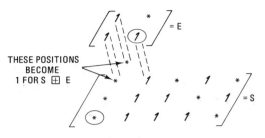

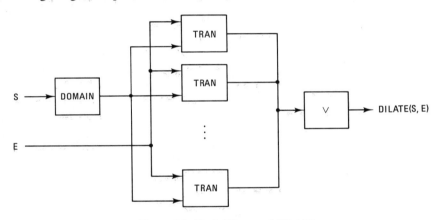

Figure 4.1 Illustration of Dilation Operation

The operation is binary since it requires the input of two images and yields a single image. In line with the block diagram and our usual notation style, we will often write DILATE(S, E) to represent the dilation of S by E. Figure 4.2 gives an implementation of Minkowski addition in terms of the more primitive operators from which it is formed. For purposes of concurrent processing and associated vision understanding architecture, note the high degree of parallelism in that figure.

Figure 4.2 Block Diagram of DILATE

Before proceeding with the basic properties of Minkowski addition, we define its dual operation, *Minkowski subtraction*. This, too, is an operation on constant images. It is defined in the following manner. Let $-E = \{(-i, -j) : (i, j) \in E\}$. It should be recognized that $-E$ is nothing more than a 180° counterclockwise rotation of E; thus $-E = \text{NINETY}^2(E)$. We define the Minkowski subtraction $S \boxminus E$ by

$$[S \boxminus E](i, j) = \begin{cases} 1, & \text{if } \text{TRAN}(-E; i, j) \lor S = S \\ *, & \text{otherwise} \end{cases}$$

The appearance of the minus sign (i.e. the occurrence of $-E$, the 180° rotation of E) is a consequence of theoretical considerations and should not cause any undue concern. In fact, the operation of *erosion* by a structuring element E, the operation with which we are mainly concerned, is precisely the Minkowski subtraction of $-E$. Consequently, for erosion, the minus sign does not appear on the right side. (Two successive 180° rotations produce the original image.) To be precise, the erosion of S by E is defined by

$$[\text{ERODE}(S, E)](i, j) = [S \boxminus (-E)](i, j) = \begin{cases} 1, & \text{if TRAN}(E; i, j) \vee S = S \\ *, & \text{otherwise} \end{cases}$$

Erosion, as opposed to dilation, will yield a "smaller" image than the original. Moreover, the erosion will be a subimage of the original if the origin is an activated pixel of the structuring element. Finally, $T \vee S = S$ if and only if T is a subimage of S.

Like dilation, the erosion of S by E, ERODE(S, E), can be described intuitively by template translation, and it is again advised that a physical model be employed to help see this (see Figure 4.3). The center of the template is placed successively over each activated pixel of S. If, for a given pixel, say (i, j), the translated copy of E, TRAN$(E; i, j)$, is a subimage of S, then (i, j) is activated in the erosion; otherwise, (i, j) is given the value $*$ in the eroded image. From this description it should be clear that, whereas dilation "fills in small holes" and "makes the image grow," erosion eliminates those

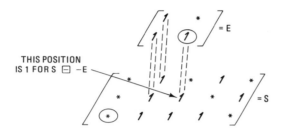

Figure 4.3 Illustration of Erosion Operation

parts of the image that are small in comparison to the structuring element. The elimination is highly dependent on the shape of that element.

The block diagram for erosion is given by

$$\begin{array}{ccc} S & \longrightarrow & \\ E & \longrightarrow & \boxed{\text{ERODE}} \longrightarrow \text{ERODE}(S, E) \end{array}$$

An expanded block diagram will be given after an explanation of the duality between Minkowski addition and Minkowski subtraction is provided in Section 4.5.

Example 4.4

Referring to Example 4.3, the translation TRAN$(E; 1, 2)$ is certainly not a subimage of S. Therefore, $(1, 2)$ will not be activated in the eroded image. On the other hand,

$$\text{TRAN}(E; 2, 1) = \begin{pmatrix} * & 1 & * \\ * & 1 & 1 \\ \circledast & * & * \end{pmatrix}$$

is a subimage of S. Hence $(2, 1)$ will be activated in ERODE$(S, E) = S \boxminus (-E)$. When all translations to activated pixels of S have been completed and the inclusions checked, we obtain

$$\text{ERODE}(S, E) = \begin{pmatrix} * & * & 1 & * \\ \circledast & * & 1 & 1 \end{pmatrix}$$

4.4 Opening and Closing

The operations of *opening* and *closing* are introduced in this section. For both practical and theoretical reasons, the two not necessarily being distinct, the morphological operation of opening is the most significant. It is essentially a filtering (not to be confused with moving-average filter) operation that removes from the activated portion of a constant image those regions in which we cannot fit the given structuring element; it leaves those in which we can make the fit. Opening differs from erosion in that we are not concerned with the fit of the template relative to the center, but of the template taken as a whole. The operation of opening is sometimes referred to as a *sizing* operation. This terminology is quite appropriate.

Given two images S and E, the former to be opened and the latter to do the opening, the opening operation is defined by

$$\text{OPEN}(S, E) = \bigvee \{\text{TRAN}(E; i, j) : \text{TRAN}(E; i, j) \vee S = S\}$$

From the definition it should be clear that a pixel is activated in the opened image if and only if it is a part of a *fitted* copy of E, the *structuring element*. Moreover, it is obvious that the larger the structuring element E, the smaller the opening. In other words, E is a subimage of E' implies $\text{OPEN}(S, E')$ is a subimage of $\text{OPEN}(S, E)$.

Example 4.5

Consider the image S and the structuring element E of Example 4.3. There are three translations of E that fit into S. They are $\text{TRAN}(E; 2, 0)$, $\text{TRAN}(E; 3, 0)$, and $\text{TRAN}(E; 2, 1)$. They are precisely the translations that yielded the erosion given in Example 4.4. The union, or extended maximum, of these translations gives the opening:

$$\text{OPEN}(S, E) = \begin{pmatrix} * & 1 & * & * \\ * & 1 & 1 & * \\ \circledast & 1 & 1 & 1 \end{pmatrix}$$

The block diagram representing the opening is given by

$$\begin{array}{c} S \\ E \end{array} \begin{array}{c} \longrightarrow \\ \longrightarrow \end{array} \boxed{\text{OPEN}} \longrightarrow \text{OPEN}(S, E)$$

Once again, we shall forego the block diagram that gives the implementation until a more appropriate setting.

To motivate the manner in which the opening yields textural information by way of its geometric formulation, another example will be given, this one utilizing linear structuring elements. A *linear structuring element* is either a column of 1's, in which case it is called *vertical*, or a row of 1's, in which case it is called *horizontal*. Since the center of the template is irrelevant insofar as the opening is concerned, we shall usually assume that it lies at the foot of a vertical linear structuring element and to the extreme left of a horizontal linear structuring element.

Example 4.6

Let

$$
S = \begin{pmatrix} * & 1 & * & * & 1 & 1 \\ 1 & \textcircled{1} & 1 & * & 1 & 1 \\ 1 & 1 & * & * & 1 & 1 \\ 1 & * & * & * & 1 & 1 \\ 1 & * & * & * & 1 & * \end{pmatrix},
$$

$$
E = \begin{pmatrix} 1 \\ 1 \\ \textcircled{1} \end{pmatrix}, \quad \text{and} \quad E' = (\textcircled{1} \quad 1 \quad 1)
$$

Opening S by E yields

$$
\text{OPEN}(S, E) = \begin{pmatrix} * & 1 & * & * & 1 & 1 \\ 1 & \textcircled{1} & * & * & 1 & 1 \\ 1 & 1 & * & * & 1 & 1 \\ 1 & * & * & * & 1 & 1 \\ 1 & * & * & * & 1 & * \end{pmatrix}
$$

This follows since OPEN(S, E) is given by the union, or extended maximum, of the following translates of E: TRAN(E; -1, -2), TRAN(E; -1, -3), TRAN(E; 0, -1), TRAN(E; 3, -1), TRAN(E; 3, -2), TRAN(E; 3, -3), TRAN(E; 4, -1), and TRAN(E; 4, -2). On the other hand, opening by E' yields

$$
\text{OPEN}(S, E') = (1 \quad \textcircled{1} \quad 1 \quad * \quad * \quad *)
$$

The only translate of E' that fits is TRAN(E'; -1, 0).

In Example 4.6, the activated pixels of S tend to form vertical strings. There appears to be vertical elongation. On the contrary, there is little or no horizontal elongation. The result is a greatly diminished image when S is opened by a horizontal linear element and little change when it is opened by a vertical element. Obviously, the result depends not only on the shape of the structuring element but also on the size. Had the vertical element been of greater length, it, too, could have resulted in an extensive diminution of the original image. It is precisely this ability of opening to distinguish textural differences that makes it so useful.

The dual operation to opening is closing. (The reason for the term *dual* will become evident in Section 4.5.) Whereas opening yields a filtered image, the nature of the filtering depending on the size and shape of the structuring element, closing yields an enlarged image. The closing is also a result of filtering, but in this case the filtering is accomplished on the complementary image.

Given the constant image S, we define the closing of S by the structuring element E in the following manner:

$$[\text{CLOSE}(S,\ E)](p,\ q) = \begin{cases} 1, & \text{if for all } (i,\ j) \text{ such that} \\ & [\text{TRAN}(E;\ i,\ j)](p,\ q) = 1, \\ & \text{TRAN}(E,\ i,\ j) \wedge S \neq \emptyset \\ *, & \text{otherwise} \end{cases}$$

(The null image $\emptyset$ has only stars.) According to the definition of closing, a pixel $(p,\ q)$ lies in the closing if and only if every translate of E containing $(p,\ q)$ intersects the original image S. Therefore to employ this definition directly, the structuring element must be translated to all pixels in the grid structure, an impossible task. However, this problem, like the problem of the complement, is only illusionary. Since the structuring element E is representable by its *minimal bound matrix containing the origin*, with dimensions, say, of u by v, we need only *augment* the minimal bound matrix of S by $(u - 1)$ rows on top and bottom and by $(v - 1)$ columns on each side. Certainly, any pixels outside this new frame can have no bearing on the computation of the closing. In the event that the center of E occurs in its minimal bound matrix, the most usual case, then u and v are the dimensions of that matrix.

Example 4.7

Consider images S and E of Example 4.3. Since the minimal bound matrix for E contains the center of E and since its dimensions are 2 by 2, S is written as the bound matrix

$$S = \begin{pmatrix} * & * & * & * & * & * \\ * & 1 & * & 1 & * & * \\ * & 1 & 1 & * & 1 & * \\ \circledast & 1 & 1 & 1 & * & * \\ * & * & * & * & * & * \end{pmatrix}$$

Treating

$$E = \begin{pmatrix} 1 & * \\ 1 & \textcircled{1} \end{pmatrix}$$

as a template and successively placing the center of E over the pixels of the augmented version of S, we obtain the closing

$$\text{CLOSE}(S,\ E) = \begin{pmatrix} * & * & * & * & * & * \\ * & 1 & 1 & 1 & * & * \\ * & 1 & 1 & 1 & 1 & * \\ \circledast & 1 & 1 & 1 & * & * \\ * & * & * & * & * & * \end{pmatrix}$$

Note that, in finding the closing, since E possesses only three activated pixels, each pixel in the augmented bound matrix representing S can occupy only three positions in the template. For example, there are three translates of E that have value 1 at $(1,\ 2)$. They are $\text{TRAN}(E;\ 1,\ 2),\text{TRAN}(E;\ 2,\ 2)$, and $\text{TRAN}(E;\ 2,\ 1)$. Since each of these translates has nonempty intersection with S, the pixel $(1, 2)$ is activated in the closing.

On the other hand, consider the pixel $(4, 2)$. It is not true that each of the three translates of E that has value 1 at $(4, 2)$ also has nonempty intersection with S. In particular, notice that

$$\text{TRAN}(E; 5, 2) \wedge S = \emptyset$$

even though $[\text{TRAN}(E; 5, 2)](4, 2) = 1$. Consequently,

$$[\text{CLOSE}(S, E)](4, 2) = *$$

Notice that the closing partly fills in small intrusions of the complement into the image itself; however, it does this in a far more sensitive manner than does the dilation.

The block diagram for the closing is given by

$$S \longrightarrow \boxed{\quad \text{CLOSE} \quad} \longrightarrow \text{CLOSE}(S, E)$$
$$E \longrightarrow$$

In Section 4.5, the basic properties of both the opening and closing will be presented. There, too, implementation will be achieved in terms of more fundamental operators.

Before terminating the present section, we would like to make a reference to Euclidean morphology, a subject not treated in detail in this text. If S were a two-dimensional Euclidean image, that is, a subset of the plane, and if E were a small disk, then the effect of opening S by E would be to roll the disk about the inside of the image S and to take as the opening all those points covered by the rolling disk. The closing would be accomplished in a dual manner by rolling the disk about the complementary image S^c. In either case, the net effect would be to filter out small irregularities in the boundary, one filtering taking place on the inside and the other taking place on the outside. Figure 4.4 gives an illustration of the procedure.

4.5 Properties

In this section we shall briefly outline the most fundamental properties of the four previously defined morphological operators. Since the duality properties involve the application of these operators to complementary images, it is necessary to explain the manner in which this is to be accomplished.

Consider an image S and a structuring element E, and suppose we wish to find the erosion by E of the complementary image S^c, denoted by either $S^c \boxminus (-E)$ or by $\text{ERODE}(S^c, E)$. In the eroded image, all pixels (i, j) for which the translated image $\text{TRAN}(E; i, j)$ is a subimage must be retained. Since all pixels outside the minimal bound matrix for S^c are assumed to be 1, we recognize that all pixels for which the translated image $\text{TRAN}(E; i, j)$ lies entirely outside the minimal bound matrix S^c will have the value 1 in the erosion. Therefore, in a manner similar to the implementation of the closing, we augment the minimal bound matrix of S^c by $(u - 1)$ rows on top and bottom and by

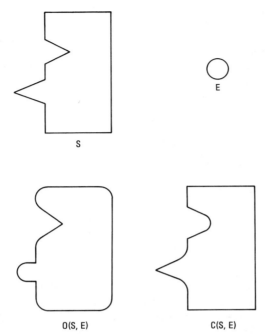

Figure 4.4 Euclidean Images and Associated Opening/Closing

$(v - 1)$ columns on each side, where u and v are the dimensions of the minimal origin containing bound matrix representing E; however, in this case the augmented pixels are given the gray value 1. We then proceed to erode this augmented form of S^c by E, realizing that, when we are done, the complement symbol must be retained, since all pixels outside the augmented frame continue to have gray value 1.

Example 4.8

Let S and E be as in Example 4.3. Then S^c is given by

$$S^c = \begin{pmatrix} 1 & * & 1 & * & 1 \\ 1 & * & * & 1 & * \\ ① & * & * & * & 1 \end{pmatrix}^c$$

Since the minimal bound matrix for E is 2 by 2 and since it already contains the origin, the necessary augmented version of S^c is given by

$$S^c = \begin{pmatrix} 1 & 1 & 1 & 1 & 1 & 1 \\ 1 & * & 1 & * & 1 & 1 \\ 1 & * & * & 1 & * & 1 \\ ① & * & * & * & 1 & 1 \\ 1 & 1 & 1 & 1 & 1 & 1 \end{pmatrix}^c$$

Recalling that all pixels external to the frame have gray value 1 (since we are referring to S^c), we successively translate E about the augmented bound matrix and retain the value $S^c(i, j) = 1$ for any (i, j) for which

$$\text{TRAN}(E; i, j) \vee S^c = S^c$$

In other words, pixels (i, j) for which $\text{TRAN}(E; i, j)$ is a subimage of S^c constitute the erosion. For example, pixel $(1, -1)$ is activated in the eroded image since $\text{TRAN}(E; 1, -1)$ is a subimage of S^c. After performing all necessary translations throughout the augmented bound matrix for S^c, we obtain

$$\text{ERODE}(S^c, E) = \begin{pmatrix} 1 & 1 & 1 & 1 & 1 & 1 \\ 1 & * & * & * & * & 1 \\ 1 & * & * & * & * & * \\ \textcircled{1} & * & * & * & * & * \\ 1 & 1 & * & * & * & 1 \end{pmatrix}^c$$

In minimal form containing the origin, we have

$$\text{ERODE}(S^c, E) = \begin{pmatrix} 1 & * & * & * & * & 1 \\ 1 & * & * & * & * & * \\ \textcircled{1} & * & * & * & * & * \\ 1 & 1 & * & * & * & 1 \end{pmatrix}^c$$

Other operations are performed on S^c in a similar fashion. For instance, to compute the opening of S^c by a structuring element E, we again utilize the augmented form of the minimal bound matrix for S^c, once again augmenting by $(u - 1)$ rows on top and bottom and $(v - 1)$ rows on each side.

Example 4.9

Consider S and E as in Example 4.8. Once again the template E is translated about the augmented minimal bound matrix for S^c. Once this is done, the extended maximum, or union, of all those translates that are subimages of S^c is taken. The result is given by

$$\text{OPEN}(S^c, E) = \begin{pmatrix} 1 & 1 & 1 & 1 & 1 & 1 \\ 1 & * & * & * & 1 & 1 \\ 1 & * & * & * & * & 1 \\ \textcircled{1} & * & * & * & 1 & 1 \\ 1 & 1 & 1 & 1 & 1 & 1 \end{pmatrix}^c$$

The most fundamental properties of erosion and dilation are the following:

a) $S \boxplus T = T \boxplus S$ (commutativity of dilation)
b) $S \boxplus E = (S^c \boxminus E)^c$ (duality)
c) $S \boxminus E = (S^c \boxplus E)^c$ (duality)
d) $S \boxplus \text{TRAN}(E; p, q) = \text{TRAN}(S \boxplus E; p, q)$ (translation invariance)
e) $S \boxminus \text{TRAN}(E; p, q) = \text{TRAN}(S \boxminus E; p, q)$ (translation invariance)

Note that the properties involve Minkowski addition and subtraction directly. To rewrite them for dilation and erosion, simply recall that the erosion of S by E equals the Minkowski subtraction of S by $-E$. Then properties a through e appear as follows:

a) $DILATE(S, T) = DILATE(T, S)$

b) $DILATE(S, E) = ERODE(S^c, -E)^c$ or $DILATE(S, -E) = ERODE(S^c, E)^c$

c) $ERODE(S, E) = DILATE(S^c, -E)^c$ or $ERODE(S, -E), = DILATE(S^c, E)^c$

d) $DILATE[S, TRAN(E; p, q)] = TRAN[DILATE(S, E); p, q]$

e) $ERODE[S, -TRAN(E; p, q)] = TRAN[ERODE(S, -E); p, q]$

The duality properties allow us to interchange the role of the image and its complementary image. The translation properties allow us to either translate the structuring element and operate or to equivalently operate and then translate. This last property is of prime importance in image architecture and language development.

Example 4.10

Using the data of Example 4.8, where we found $ERODE(S^c, E)$, together with property b, we obtain

$$DILATE(S, -E) = ERODE(S^c, E)^c = \begin{pmatrix} * & 1 & 1 & 1 & * \\ * & 1 & 1 & 1 & 1 \\ \circledast & 1 & 1 & 1 & 1 \\ * & * & 1 & 1 & * \end{pmatrix}$$

The duality properties for the opening and closing are analogous to those same properties for erosion and dilation. We have

f) $OPEN(S, E)^c = CLOSE(S^c, E)$

g) $CLOSE(S, E)^c = OPEN(S^c, E)$

Property f says that opening the image and then complementing is equivalent to complementing the image and then closing; property e says that closing the image and then complementing is equivalent to complementing the image and then opening.

Example 4.11

Using the image S and the structuring element E of Example 4.3, we found in Example 4.9 the opening $OPEN(S^c, E)$. But in Example 4.7 we found the closing $CLOSE(S, E)$. Applying property g,

$$CLOSE(S, E)^c = COMPLEMENT \begin{pmatrix} * & 1 & 1 & 1 & * \\ * & 1 & 1 & 1 & 1 \\ \circledast & 1 & 1 & 1 & * \end{pmatrix}$$

$$= \begin{pmatrix} 1 & * & * & * & 1 \\ 1 & * & * & * & * \\ \textcircled{1} & * & * & * & 1 \end{pmatrix}^c$$

This agrees with the result obtained in Example 4.9 for $OPEN(S^c, E)$. The duality property holds.

Additional properties of the opening that play essential roles in both theory and application are the following:

    h) OPEN(S, E) is a subimage of S (anti-extensivity)

    i) S is a subimage of S' implies OPEN(S, E) is a subimage of OPEN(S', E)
          (increasing monotonicity)

    j) OPEN[OPEN(S, E), E] = OPEN(S, E)   (idempotence)

Note that property h says the opening yields a smaller image than the original. Using property j, it is seen that successive openings by the same structuring element have no effect after the first application.

The dual properties for the closing corresponding to properties h, i, and j are as follows:

    k) S is a subimage of CLOSE(S, E)   (extensivity)

    l) S is a subimage of S' implies CLOSE(S, E) is a subimage of CLOSE(S', E)
          (increasing monotonicity)

    m) CLOSE[CLOSE(S, E), E] = CLOSE(S, E)   (idempotence)

The last properties to be described relate the opening and closing to the dilation and the erosion; indeed, it will be these properties that allow us to implement the two higher-level operations in terms of the more primary operations. Specifically,

    n) OPEN(S, E) = $[S \boxminus (-E)] \boxplus E$
                = DILATE[ERODE(S, E), E]

    o) CLOSE(S, E) = $[S \boxplus (-E)] \boxminus E$
                 = ERODE[DILATE(S, $-E$), $-E$]

In words, the opening of S by E is the erosion of S by E followed by a dilation by E, and the closing of S by E is the dilation of S by the 180° rotation of E, followed by an erosion by the 180° rotation of E.

To conclude this section, we present block diagrams in Figure 4.5 for the erosion, the opening, and the closing, each dependent on previously implemented operators.

4.6 Granulometries

The key to the morphological analysis of images is the method of successively filtering and then measuring the residues. The particular method of filtering may vary (although it is customarily erosion or opening, or some related variant); but the methodology is essentially fixed, with the measure, at least in the digital case, being the number of activated pixels in the residue (see Figure 4.6). In this section, we shall consider the method of filtering by opening with successively increasing linear structuring elements.

EROSION IS GIVEN BY:

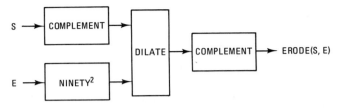

CLOSING IS GIVEN BY:

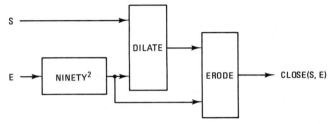

OPENING IS GIVEN BY:

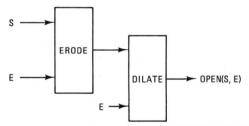

Figure 4.5 Block Diagrams of: ERODE, OPEN and CLOSE

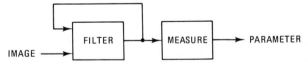

Figure 4.6 Block Diagram Illustration of Parameter Extraction

Consider the structuring elements $H(k)$ and $V(k)$, where $H(k)$ is a horizontal string of k activated pixels with the origin at the extreme left of the string, and $V(k)$ is a vertical string of k activated pixels with the origin at the base of the string (see Figure 4.7). Given a constant image S, consider the mappings

$$k \rightarrow \text{OPEN}(S, V(k))$$

and

$$k \rightarrow \text{OPEN}(S, H(k))$$

$$V(k) = \begin{pmatrix} 1 \\ \cdot \\ \cdot \\ \cdot \\ \cdot \\ 1 \\ \textcircled{1} \end{pmatrix} \qquad H(k) = (\ \textcircled{1}\ \ 1\ \dots\ 1)$$

Figure 4.7 Two Structuring Elements

for $k = 1, 2, 3, \dots$. These mappings are known as *linear digital granulometries*. Since opening by larger sets causes ever greater filtering, the granulometries are decreasing functions of k in that

$$\text{OPEN}(S, V(1)) \supset \text{OPEN}(S, V(2)) \supset \text{OPEN}(S, V(3)) \supset \dots$$

and

$$\text{OPEN}(S, H(1)) \supset \text{OPEN}(S, H(2)) \supset \text{OPEN}(S, H(3)) \supset \dots$$

Moreover, since we are starting with finite images, after some value of k the null image will result in each case.

What is of interest is the two mappings that are derived by composing the cardinality function CARD, which counts the number of elements in a set, together with the preceding granulometries. To be precise, we shall successively open with linear structuring elements and record the number of activated pixels in each case. Due to the decreasing nature of the granulometries, the resulting functions will also be decreasing and will reach 0 for some finite value of k. Formally, we define the functions

$$\psi_V(k) = \text{CARD}[\text{OPEN}(S, V(k))]$$

and

$$\psi_H(k) = \text{CARD}[\text{OPEN}(S, H(k))]$$

where CARD simply counts the number of activated pixels. Note that we have taken a slight liberty with the preceding definitions. To be strictly accurate, CARD counts the elements in the domain of an image and, therefore, $\psi_V(k)$ is actually the output of the following block diagram:

$$S \longrightarrow \boxed{\text{OPEN}} \longrightarrow \boxed{\text{DOMAIN}} \longrightarrow \boxed{\text{CARD}} \longrightarrow \psi_v(k)$$
$$V(k) \longrightarrow$$

A similar remark holds for $\psi_H(k)$. In the sequel, we shall continue to take the liberty of writing CARD of an image to mean the cardinality of the domain. In any event, the functions $\psi_V(k)$ and $\psi_H(k)$ satisfy the schema of Figure 4.6.

Example 4.12

Let S be given by

$$S = \begin{pmatrix} \circledast & 1 & 1 & 1 & * & * & 1 & * & 1 & 1 \\ 1 & 1 & 1 & * & * & * & 1 & 1 & 1 & 1 \\ 1 & 1 & 1 & * & * & * & 1 & 1 & 1 & 1 \\ 1 & * & 1 & * & * & * & 1 & * & 1 & * \\ 1 & 1 & 1 & 1 & * & * & 1 & * & 1 & * \\ 1 & 1 & 1 & 1 & * & * & 1 & * & 1 & * \\ * & 1 & 1 & 1 & * & * & * & * & 1 & * \end{pmatrix}$$

By taking successive openings, first horizontally and then vertically, we find

$$k = \quad 1 \quad 2 \quad 3 \quad 4 \quad 5 \quad 6 \quad 7 \quad 8$$

$$\psi_H(k) = 40 \quad 30 \quad 28 \quad 16 \quad 0 \quad 0 \quad 0 \quad 0$$

$$\psi_V(k) = 40 \quad 39 \quad 37 \quad 25 \quad 25 \quad 20 \quad 14 \quad 0$$

For instance, $\psi_V(6) = 20$ since there are 20 activated pixels in the image

$$\text{OPEN}(S, V(6)) = \begin{pmatrix} \circledast & * & 1 & * & * & * & 1 & * & 1 & * \\ * & * & 1 & * & * & * & 1 & * & 1 & * \\ * & * & 1 & * & * & * & 1 & * & 1 & * \\ * & * & 1 & * & * & * & 1 & * & 1 & * \\ * & * & 1 & * & * & * & 1 & * & 1 & * \\ * & * & 1 & * & * & * & 1 & * & 1 & * \\ * & * & 1 & * & * & * & * & * & 1 & * \end{pmatrix}$$

In Example 4.12, it is clear that $\psi_V(k)$ is less affected by small values of k than is $\psi_H(k)$. This means that opening by $H(k)$ has a greater filtering effect than opening by $V(k)$ for this example. Intuitively, there is a greater distribution of linear size in the vertical direction than in the horizontal direction. Indeed, measurement of a granulometry yields a measurement of the extent to which activated pixels are clustered relative to the shape of the structuring element.

Example 4.13

Consider the rectangular image

$$R = \begin{pmatrix} ① & 1 & 1 & 1 & 1 & 1 & 1 & 1 \\ 1 & 1 & 1 & 1 & 1 & 1 & 1 & 1 \\ 1 & 1 & 1 & 1 & 1 & 1 & 1 & 1 \end{pmatrix}$$

The functions $\psi_H(k)$ and $\psi_V(k)$ are given by

$$k = \quad 1 \quad 2 \quad 3 \quad 4 \quad 5 \quad 6 \quad 7 \quad 8 \quad 9$$

$$\psi_H(k) = 24 \quad 24 \quad 24 \quad 24 \quad 24 \quad 24 \quad 24 \quad 24 \quad 0$$

$$\psi_V(k) = 24 \quad 24 \quad 24 \quad 0 \quad 0 \quad 0 \quad 0 \quad 0 \quad 0$$

The fact that R is a rectangle with width 8 and height 3 is directly reflected by the result that $\psi_H(k)$ and $\psi_V(k)$ are constant and then jump down to 0 at 9 and 4, respectively.

It is common practice to normalize the functions $\psi_H(k)$ and $\psi_V(k)$ so that the resulting functions are distributions in the probabilistic sense. We define

$$\Phi_H(k) = 1 - \frac{\psi_H(k)}{\psi_H(1)} = 1 - \frac{CARD[OPEN(S, H(k))]}{CARD(S)}$$

and

$$\Phi_V(k) = 1 - \frac{\psi_V(k)}{\psi_V(1)} = 1 - \frac{CARD[OPEN(S, V(k))]}{CARD(S)}$$

The functions $\Phi_H(k)$ and $\Phi_V(k)$ are monotonically increasing, have leftmost value 0, and become 1 for some finite value of k. Moreover, by defining $\Phi(x)$ to be $\Phi(k)$ for any value x greater than $k - 1$ and less than or equal to k, a step function is obtained that is continuous from the left. As a result, the functions $\Phi_H(k)$ and $\Phi_V(k)$, called *size distributions*, are distributions in the usual sense. Figure 4.8 provides the graphs for the size distributions resulting from the image in Example 4.12.

Once again referring to Example 4.12, it should be noted that the granulometry $k \to OPEN(S, V(k))$ can be looked on as a *sieving process*. For each value of k, only those horizontal strings remain whose length is at least equal to k. The action is like a sequence of sieves; at each stage too small particles slide through the mesh of the sieve

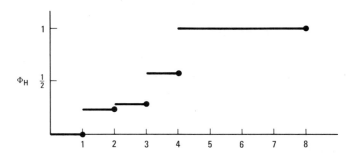

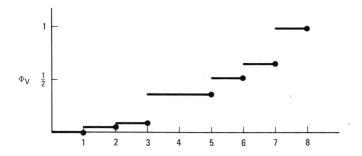

Figure 4.8 Size Distributions

and are lost. In considering the distribution $\Phi_H(k)$, we are computing the percentage of the original mass that is contained in the particles of linear horizontal size greater than $k - 1$; the mass contained in smaller horizontal lengths is filtered and discarded.

With regard to sieving, the idempotence property is of particular interest. OPEN[OPEN(S, E), E] = OPEN(S, E) shows that the repeated use of the same-sized sieve accomplishes nothing.

Although we have restricted ourselves to linear granulometries, others can be constructed using different-shaped structuring elements. Because we are utilizing a square grid structure, most relevant granulometric properties can be extracted by using either $H(k)$, $V(k)$, or a combination of the two. However, other parameterized families are certainly possible.

4.7 Size Distribution by Linear Erosion

Related to the granulometric size distributions are those size distributions generated by linear erosions. Let $V(k)$ and $H(k)$ be the linear structuring elements of Figure 4.7. Instead of considering the granulometries $k \rightarrow$ OPEN(S, $V(k)$) and $k \rightarrow$ OPEN(S, $H(k)$), we consider the mappings

$$k \rightarrow \text{ERODE}(S, V(K))$$

and

$$k \rightarrow \text{ERODE}(S, H(k))$$

The exact same procedure that was used to compute $\psi_H(k)$ and $\psi_V(k)$ is employed, only this time we define

$$\Lambda_H(k) = \text{CARD}[\text{ERODE}(S, H(k))]$$

and

$$\Lambda_V(k) = \text{CARD}[\text{ERODE}(S, V(k))]$$

Due to the similarity of the procedure, we shall content ourselves with one example.

Example 4.14

Let S be the image given in Example 4.12. By taking successive erosions and counting, we find

$$k = 1 \quad 2 \quad 3 \quad 4 \quad 5 \quad 6 \quad 7 \quad 8$$
$$\Lambda_H(k) = 40 \quad 21 \quad 12 \quad 4 \quad 0 \quad 0 \quad 0 \quad 0$$
$$\Lambda_V(k) = 40 \quad 30 \quad 21 \quad 13 \quad 9 \quad 5 \quad 2 \quad 0$$

For instance, $\Lambda_V(3) = 21$ since there are 21 activated pixels in the image

$$
\text{ERODE}(S,\ V(3))\ =\
\begin{pmatrix}
\circledast & * & * & * & * & * & * & * & * & * \\
* & * & * & * & * & * & * & * & * & * \\
* & 1 & 1 & * & * & * & 1 & * & 1 & 1 \\
1 & * & 1 & * & * & * & 1 & * & 1 & * \\
1 & * & 1 & * & * & * & 1 & * & 1 & * \\
1 & * & 1 & * & * & * & 1 & * & 1 & * \\
* & 1 & 1 & 1 & * & * & * & * & 1 & *
\end{pmatrix}
$$

As was done in the case of the granulometric size distributions, the functions $\Lambda_H(k)$ and $\Lambda_V(k)$ can be normalized. Since the methodology is identical to that of Section 4.6, the details are left as exercises.

4.8 Morphological Covariance

The granulometries and linear erosions of the previous two sections were generated by employing the horizontal and vertical linear structuring elements $H(k)$ and $V(k)$, together with the operations of opening and erosion, respectively. In this section, attention is focused on two structuring elements, each of which consists of only two activated pixels separated by a number of deactivated pixels. The structuring element $h(k)$ consists of two pixels in the horizontal direction with gray value 1 separated by $k - 2$ pixels valued $*$, where the leftmost activated pixel is situated at the origin. Correspondingly, the element $v(k)$ consists of two activated pixels in the vertical direction separated by $k - 2$ deactivated pixels, the lower of the two activated pixels being located at the origin. (See Figure 4.9, and note that in the case $k = 1$ the elements reduce to a single activated pixel.)

$$
v(k) =
\begin{pmatrix}
1 \\
* \\
\cdot \\
\cdot \\
\cdot \\
* \\
* \\
1
\end{pmatrix}
\qquad
h(k) = (\,\textcircled{1}\ *\ *\ \ldots\ *\ 1\,)
$$

Figure 4.9 Covariance Structuring Elements

The *horizontal digital covariance* function and the *vertical digital covariance* function are respectively obtained by successively eroding an image S by $h(k)$ and $v(k)$ and then counting the number of remaining activated pixels at each stage. We have

$$
C_h(k)\ =\ \text{CARD}[\text{ERODE}(S,\ h(k))]
$$

and

$$
C_v(k)\ =\ \text{CARD}[\text{ERODE}(S,\ v(k))]
$$

In block form, and precisely specifying the use of the domain function, we have, for the horizontal covariance function,

$$
S \longrightarrow \boxed{\text{ERODE}} \longrightarrow \boxed{\text{DOMAIN}} \longrightarrow \boxed{\text{CARD}} \longrightarrow C_h(k)
$$
$$
h(k) \longrightarrow
$$

The block form for the vertical covariance function is exactly the same except for the input $v(k)$ instead of $h(k)$.

Before examining some of the more interesting properties of the covariance, we give an example involving the horizontal covariance; indeed, since the vertical and horizontal covariance functions behave in like fashion, we shall limit ourselves to the study of the horizontal case and simply write $C(k)$ instead of $C_h(k)$.

Example 4.15

Let

$$S = \begin{pmatrix} ① & 1 & 1 & * & * & * & 1 & 1 & * & * & 1 & 1 & 1 \\ 1 & 1 & 1 & 1 & * & * & 1 & 1 & 1 & * & * & 1 & 1 \\ 1 & 1 & 1 & * & * & 1 & 1 & 1 & 1 & * & 1 & 1 & 1 \end{pmatrix}$$

To obtain the covariance function (horizontal case), we erode successively by $h(1)$, $h(2)$, $h(3)$, . . ., where

$$h(1) = (①), \qquad\qquad h(2) = (① \quad 1)$$
$$h(3) = (① \quad * \quad 1), \qquad h(4) = (① \quad * \quad * \quad 1)$$

and so on. We obtain the covariance function

$k =$	1	2	3	4	5	6	7	8	9	10	11	12	13	14
$C(k) =$	27	18	10	8	12	15	12	6	5	6	8	6	3	0

For instance, $C(3) = 10$ since

$$\text{ERODE}(S,\, h(3)) = \begin{pmatrix} ① & * & * & * & * & * & * & * & * & * & 1 \\ 1 & 1 & * & * & * & * & 1 & * & * & * & * \\ 1 & * & * & * & * & 1 & 1 & * & 1 & * & 1 \end{pmatrix}$$

In the computation of ERODE(S, $h(3)$), note that the value 1 was obtained for the pixel $(8, -2)$ since TRAN[$h(3)$; 8, -2] is a subimage of S. This pixel would not have been activated when working with the linear erosion since TRAN[$H(3)$; 8, -2] is not a subimage of S. The graph of $C(k)$ is given in Figure 4.10.

Examination of $C(k)$ in Example 4.15 shows a degree of periodicity in that there are local maximums at the k values 1, 6, and 11. These three local maximums correspond

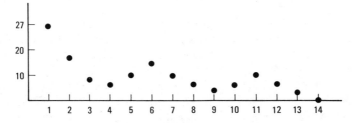

Figure 4.10 Graph of Covariance Function

to the three distinct component subimages of which S is composed. In other words, $C(k)$ has detected subimages distributed within the image. This is one way in which textural information is obtained from the covariance.

Some of the interesting properties of the covariance are as follows:

a) $C(1) = \text{CARD}(S)$

b) $C(k) = \text{CARD}[\text{ERODE}(S, -h(k))]$

c) $C(k) = \text{CARD}[S \wedge \text{TRAN}(S; -k + 1, 0)]$

Property a follows at once from the fact that erosion by a single pixel has no effect on the image, whereas property b results from the symmetric nature of the structuring element $h(k)$. Property c is the most interesting. It says that the covariance can be obtained by translating S exactly $k - 1$ units to the left, intersecting the resulting image, TRAN(S; $-k + 1, 0$), with S, and then taking the cardinality. This follows from the fact that the intersection is exactly equal to the image S eroded by the structuring element $h(k)$.

Example 4.16

Let

$$
S = \begin{pmatrix}
* & * & 1 & 1 & * & * & * & 1 & 1 & 1 \\
* & * & 1 & ① & 1 & * & * & 1 & 1 & * \\
* & * & * & 1 & 1 & * & * & * & 1 & 1
\end{pmatrix}
$$

Then

$$
\text{TRAN}(S; -2, 0) = \begin{pmatrix}
1 & 1 & * & * & * & 1 & 1 & 1 & * & * \\
1 & 1 & 1 & ⊛ & * & 1 & 1 & * & * & * \\
* & 1 & 1 & * & * & * & 1 & 1 & * & *
\end{pmatrix}
$$

and

$$
\text{ERODE}(S, h(3)) = \begin{pmatrix}
* & * & * & * & * & * & * & 1 & * & * \\
* & * & 1 & ⊛ & * & * & * & * & * & * \\
* & * & * & * & * & * & * & * & * & *
\end{pmatrix}
$$

It can be seen that

$$
\text{ERODE}(S, h(3)) = S \wedge \text{TRAN}(S; -2, 0)
$$

In Example 4.15, there was an observed quasi-periodicity of the covariance. The reason for this behavior is easily discerned from examining the intersections of S with its horizontal translates. Moreover, it should be observed that the local maxima are decreasing in Example 4.15.

Before this discussion is concluded, some comments concerning the use of morphological techniques for textural analysis are in order. First, it should be obvious that any interpretation of the granulometric distributions, the linear erosions, or the covariance must depend on extensive experience on the part of the investigator. The behavior of these functions, in that it is dependent on texture, is not describable in elementary geometric terms. Interpretation depends on not only the quantitative techniques described previously, but also on a deep understanding of the particular branch of science to which the techniques are to be applied.

In a second direction, we should take note of the difficulties inherent in the use of the size distributions and the covariance as image features from which to recognize an image as belonging to a certain class. For example, suppose we wish to classify an image taken from a slide of human liver tissue as displaying evidence of pathology. It may be that the covariance function computed from a slide of healthy tissue is quite different from that computed from a slide of pathological tissue; however, there must be some listing of tissue covariance functions in the data base, and we must have a quantitative measurement technique to apply to the experimental covariance function as it relates to the a priori functions stored in memory. Although this problem is beyond the scope of this text, it is characteristic of image classification based on the derivation of feature parameters through the quantitative analysis of empirical data, and it is a problem that is certainly not confined to mathematical morphology.

4.9 Skeleton

One way in which images are characterized is by the employment of various *thinning* methodologies. In these, a figure is replaced by a *thin* representative of itself. The purpose of such a procedure is twofold. First, it yields a less complex figure that might be used as an archetype for classification purposes. Second, if in later processing the new image containing only the thin figure can be used in place of the original image, then memory load requirements are reduced.

There are many thinning algorithms; however, we shall concentrate on the well-known *skeleton* or *medial axis* algorithm. To help to explain the intent, we shall consider the skeleton of a set in the Euclidean plane. The Euclidean skeleton of a set S is defined in the following manner. For each x in S, let $D(x)$ denote the largest disk centered at x such that $D(x)$ is a subset of S. Then x is in the skeleton of S if there does not exist a disk D_1, not necessarily centered at x, such that D_1 properly contains $D(x)$ and such that D_1 is contained in S. For example, consider the isosceles triangle in Figure 4.11(a). The skeleton is drawn in dark lines. Note that, whereas the point x lies in the skeleton, since $D(x)$ cannot be included in a larger disk still within the triangle [Figure 4.11(b)], the point w does not lie in the skeleton, since $D(w)$ is a subset of the disk D', which is itself a subset of the triangle [Figure 4.11(c)].

Figure 4.12 gives a good indication of some of the intuitive notions concerning the Euclidean skeleton. While the skeleton gives a decent replication of the shape of a figure that is already somewhat thin [Figure 4.12(a)], it is far less appropriate when applied to a *thick* figure [Figure 4.12(b)]. Moreover, different geometric figures may possess the same skeleton [Figure 4.12(c) and (d)]. Perhaps most importantly, the skeleton is extremely sensitive to noise. An infinitesimal distortion of the original shape can result in a vastly altered skeleton. For instance, in Figure 4.12(e) and (f), notice how the removal of a tiny section of the figure results in a drastically changed skeleton.

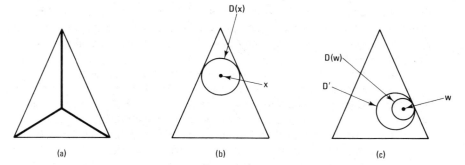

Figure 4.11 Determining Skeleton for Isosceles Triangle

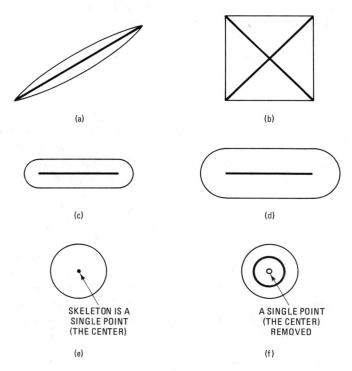

Figure 4.12 Skeleton For Various Pictures

In proceeding to a digital definition of the skeleton, we are immediately confronted with the impossibility of finding an exact analogue to a Euclidean disk. While there are several ways to give a digital version of Euclidean disks, we shall content ourselves with the collection of ''square disks'' given in Figure 4.13. Each of these is a constant image, or template, in which the origin is near the center of the domain. One might legitimately argue that a proper extension of the disk notion would require that we omit the even-

$$D_1 = \left(\textcircled{1} \right)$$

$$D_2 = \begin{pmatrix} 1 & 1 \\ \textcircled{1} & 1 \end{pmatrix}$$

$$D_3 = \begin{pmatrix} 1 & 1 & 1 \\ 1 & \textcircled{1} & 1 \\ 1 & 1 & 1 \end{pmatrix}$$

$$D_4 = \begin{pmatrix} 1 & 1 & 1 & 1 \\ 1 & 1 & 1 & 1 \\ 1 & \textcircled{1} & 1 & 1 \\ 1 & 1 & 1 & 1 \end{pmatrix}$$

$$D_5 = \begin{pmatrix} 1 & 1 & 1 & 1 & 1 \\ 1 & 1 & 1 & 1 & 1 \\ 1 & 1 & \textcircled{1} & 1 & 1 \\ 1 & 1 & 1 & 1 & 1 \\ 1 & 1 & 1 & 1 & 1 \end{pmatrix}$$

etc.

Figure 4.13 Square Disks of Increasing Size

numbered digital disks D_2, D_4, D_6, . . . , since for these the center of the template is not a true center in the sense of symmetry. If we were to do this, the resulting thinning procedure would often result in skeletons that were not sufficiently thin. In any event, note that for the even-numbered disks the center has been defined in a consistent fashion.

The definition of the digital skeleton can now be stated in a manner analogous to the corresponding Euclidean definition. Let T be a constant image (pixel values 1 or $*$). For any pixel (i, j) in the domain of T, the maximal disk for (i, j), MAXDISK(i, j), is the highest-numbered disk D_k, translated so that its new center is at (i, j), such that TRAN$(D_k; i, j)$ is a subimage of T. The skeleton of T, SKEL(T), is a constant image (1's and $*$'s) such that a pixel lies within the domain of SKEL(T) if and only if its maximal disk is not a proper subimage of any other translated disk that is itself a subimage of T. Intuitively, (i, j) is in the digital skeleton if and only if its maximal disk is not a proper subset of some other disk lying within T.

Example 4.17

Referring to image T of Figure 4.14(a), the maximal disk for the pixel $(1, 8)$ is given by

$$\text{MAXDISK}(1, 8) = \begin{pmatrix} 1 & 1 \\ 1 & 1 \end{pmatrix}_{1, 9}$$

This is schematically indicated in Figure 4.14(b). Also shown is the illustration of the maximal disks

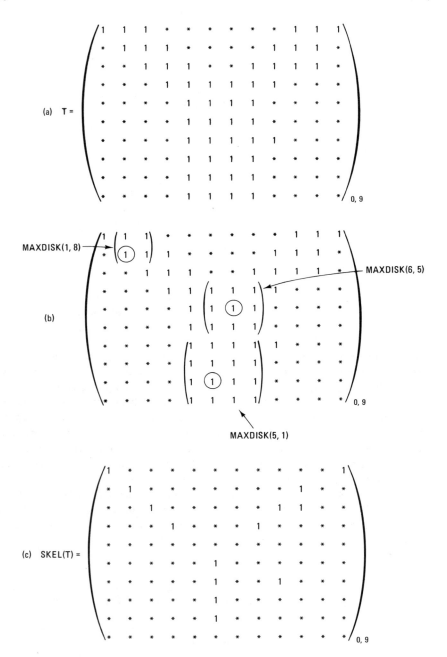

Figure 4.14 Image and Associated Skeleton Image

$$\text{MAXDISK(5, 1)} = \begin{pmatrix} 1 & 1 & 1 & 1 \\ 1 & 1 & 1 & 1 \\ 1 & 1 & 1 & 1 \\ 1 & 1 & 1 & 1 \end{pmatrix}_{4, \, 3}$$

and

$$\text{MAXDISK(6, 5)} = \begin{pmatrix} 1 & 1 & 1 \\ 1 & 1 & 1 \\ 1 & 1 & 1 \end{pmatrix}_{5, \, 6}$$

Pixels $(1, 8)$ and $(5, 1)$ lie in the domain of the skeleton of T, but pixel $(6, 5)$ does not. This latter claim follows from the fact that the domain of MAXDISK(6, 5) lies properly within the domain of TRAN(D_4; 5, 4), which is itself a subimage of T.

Finally, Figure 4.14(c) gives the skeleton SKEL(T). Assuming the underlying image to be the letter Y, the skeleton gives a farily good replication. Unfortunately, the pixel $(8, 3)$, which appears to be affected by noise, results in an extraneous activated pixel in the skeleton. Moreover, the skeleton is not *connected*. The fifth row of the bound matrix contains no activated pixels. As a result, the top section of the letter Y is separated from the bottom section. Such connectivity problems are common for the skeleton. They make its utilization highly problematic.

At this point, we wish to provide the implementation of the operator SKEL, whose block diagram is given by

$$f \longrightarrow \boxed{\text{SKEL}} \longrightarrow \text{SKEL}(f)$$

This implementation is given in Figure 4.15. In that figure, the number m is given by the minimum between the number of rows and columns of the minimal bound matrix for T. Although no proof will be presented for the specification of SKEL, it should be clear why the skeleton has been presented within the chapter on morphology. It is constructable from erosions and openings. In essence, the block diagram of Figure 4.15 works by finding the skeleton pixels that have maximal disk of edge length 1, then those with maximal disk of edge length 2, and so on. It then takes the set theoretic union of those pixel classes.

Figure 4.16 provides a walk-through of the first three branches of Figure 4.15 with input image R. For the remaining branches, $k = 4, 5,$ and 6, the first erosion yields the empty image. This will usually be the case for values of k near to the value m unless the minimal bound matrix consists of mostly activated pixels, with all deactivated pixels near the outer edge of the matrix. Notice also that the image $S \wedge T^c$ is the image whose activated pixels are those contained in the domain of S minus (set theoretic subtraction) the domain of T.

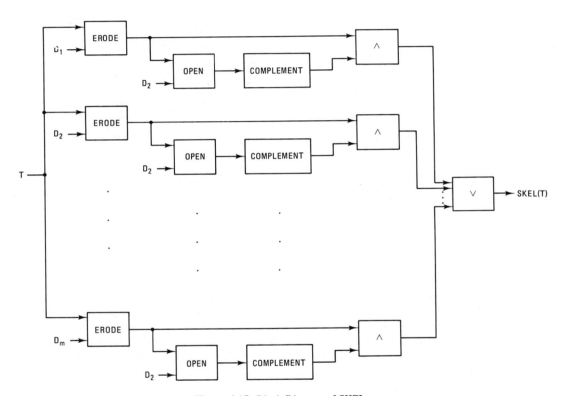

Figure 4.15 Block Diagram of SKEL

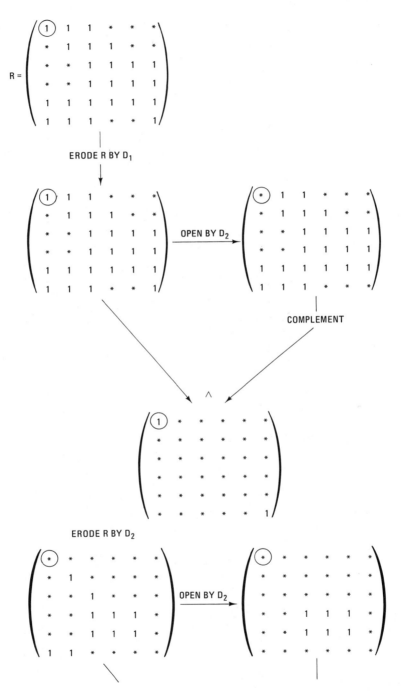

Figure 4.16 Walk-through for SKEL Operation

Figure 4.16 Continued

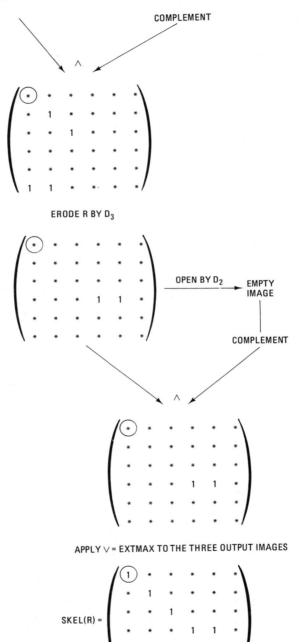

COMPLEMENT

ERODE R BY D_3

OPEN BY D_2 → EMPTY IMAGE

COMPLEMENT

APPLY $\vee$ = EXTMAX TO THE THREE OUTPUT IMAGES

SKEL(R) =

EXERCISES

4.1. The following images are used in Exercises 4.1 through 4.4:

$$S = \begin{pmatrix} 1 & 1 & 1 & 1 & 1 & * \\ 1 & 1 & 1 & * & * & * \\ 1 & 1 & 1 & 1 & * & * \\ * & * & 1 & 1 & 1 & 1 \\ * & \circledast & 1 & 1 & 1 & 1 \\ * & * & 1 & 1 & 1 & * \end{pmatrix}$$

$$T = \begin{pmatrix} \textcircled{1} & 1 & 1 & 1 & 1 & 1 & 1 \\ 1 & 1 & * & * & 1 & * & 1 \\ * & * & * & * & 1 & 1 & 1 \end{pmatrix}$$

and

$$E = \begin{pmatrix} 1 & 1 \\ \textcircled{1} & 1 \end{pmatrix}$$

Find

(a) S^c	**(g)** ERODE(S, E)
(b) $S \wedge T$	**(h)** ERODE(T, E)
(c) $S \vee T$	**(i)** OPEN(S, E)
(d) TRAN(E; 1, 2)	**(j)** OPEN(T, E)
(e) DILATE(S, E)	**(k)** CLOSE(S, E)
(f) DILATE(T, E)	**(l)** CLOSE(T, E)

4.2. Find the following morphological outputs without using properties b, c, f, and g in the chapter:

(a) DILATE(S^c, E)	**(c)** OPEN(S^c, E)
(b) ERODE(S^c, E)	**(d)** CLOSE(S^c, E)

4.3. Find the following morphological outputs by using properties b, c, f, and g in the chapter:

(a) DILATE(T^c, E)	**(c)** OPEN(T^c, E)
(b) ERODE(T^c, E)	**(d)** CLOSE(T^c, E)

4.4. Using properties n and o in the chapter, find

(a) CLOSE(S, E)	**(b)** OPEN(S, E)

4.5. Using the image S of Exercise 4.1, find

(a) $\psi_V(k)$	**(e)** Graph of $\Phi_V(k)$
(b) $\psi_H(k)$	**(f)** Graph of $\Phi_H(k)$
(c) $\Phi_V(k)$	**(g)** $\Lambda_H(k)$
(d) $\Phi_H(k)$	**(h)** $\Lambda_V(k)$

4.6. Using a technique similar to that employed in obtaining $\Phi_V(k)$ from $\psi_V(k)$ and $\Phi_H(k)$ from $\psi_H(k)$, define the two distributions

$$\Omega_V(k) = 1 - \frac{\Lambda_V(k)}{\Lambda_V(1)} = 1 - \frac{\text{CARD}[\text{ERODE}(S, V(k))]}{\text{CARD}(S)}$$

and $\Omega_H(k)$. Find $\Omega_V(k)$ and $\Omega_H(k)$ for the image S of Exercise 4.1.

4.7. Find

    (a) The morphological covariance functions $C_h(k)$ and $C_v(k)$ for the image S of Exercise 4.1.

    (b) Repeat part (a) for the image T of Exercise 4.1.

4.8. Define the morphological edge detector (for constant images) MOREDGE(S) by

$$\text{MOREDGE}(S) = \text{CLOSE}(S, E) \wedge \text{OPEN}(S, E)^c$$

where E is the structuring element

$$E = \begin{pmatrix} 1 & 1 & 1 \\ 1 & \textcircled{1} & 1 \\ 1 & 1 & 1 \end{pmatrix}$$

(In terms of domains, MOREDGE is given by the set theoretic subtraction of the closing minus the opening.) Apply MOREDGE to the following image:

$$R = \begin{pmatrix}
* & * & * & * & * & 1 & * & * & * & * & * \\
* & * & * & * & 1 & 1 & 1 & * & * & * & * \\
* & * & * & 1 & 1 & 1 & 1 & 1 & * & * & * \\
* & * & 1 & 1 & 1 & 1 & 1 & 1 & 1 & * & * \\
* & 1 & 1 & 1 & 1 & 1 & 1 & 1 & 1 & 1 & * \\
1 & \textcircled{1} & 1 & 1 & 1 & 1 & 1 & 1 & 1 & 1 & 1 \\
* & 1 & 1 & 1 & 1 & 1 & 1 & 1 & 1 & 1 & * \\
* & * & 1 & 1 & 1 & 1 & 1 & 1 & 1 & * & * \\
* & * & * & 1 & 1 & 1 & 1 & 1 & * & * & *
\end{pmatrix}$$

4.9. For the following figure U, find SKEL(U) by performing a walk-through of Figure 4.15.

$$U = \begin{pmatrix}
1 & 1 & 1 & 1 & * & * & * & * \\
1 & 1 & 1 & * & * & * & * & * \\
1 & 1 & 1 & * & * & * & * & * \\
1 & 1 & 1 & * & * & * & * & * \\
1 & 1 & 1 & * & * & * & * & * \\
1 & 1 & 1 & * & * & * & * & * \\
1 & 1 & 1 & 1 & 1 & 1 & * & * \\
1 & 1 & 1 & 1 & 1 & 1 & 1 & 1 \\
1 & 1 & 1 & 1 & 1 & 1 & 1 & \textcircled{1}
\end{pmatrix}$$

5

TOPOLOGICAL OPERATIONS

This chapter presents some of the basic concepts of digital image topology. Although some familiarity with Euclidean topology would be helpful in appreciating the anomalies of the digital scheme, no prerequisite knowledge is required. Therefore, there will be no investigation of the relationship between the two models. Regarding the subject matter of the chapter, there might be some question as to whether or not the study of curves should be restricted to the chapter on edge detection. There are two reasons for not taking such an approach: (1) The study of curves in the present chapter is more topological in nature. (2) The methodology used in this study is of a tracking nature, whereas in strictly edge techniques there tends to be a reliance on gray-level gradation and filtering.

5.1 Vertical Tracking

In this section, a particular tracking methodology will be introduced which tracks a sequence of dark pixels on a lighter background. The technique employs a vertical tracking scheme but could just as well be utilized for horizontal tracking.

Intuitively, the purpose and methodology of vertical tracking can be described rather simply. We pick as a starting point for a *curve* any pixel whose gray level exceeds some predetermined *signal* value. Once a pixel has been chosen, the pixels in the immediate neighborhood N below it are searched for dark pixels. The exact configuration of N is a methodological choice depending on the purposes of the image engineer. Moreover, there is usually a higher gray-value requirement for a signal pixel than for those following a pixel already chosen for a curve. The purpose is to find curves which have some sort of continuity, not merely a collection of dark pixels; otherwise, we could simply threshold the entire image and stop there.

Referring to the image in Figure 5.1 and using signal value $s = 10$, the signal pixels can be found by applying THRESH with the threshold value being s. In THRESH(f; 10), there are exactly five black pixels.

The next stage of the tracking algorithm depends on the size of the neighborhoods to be searched. Here there are many possibilities, including *multi-tiered* neighborhoods having various *cut-off* gray values. If we wish to ensure "connectivity" of the curve, only the three pixels immediately below an already chosen pixel should be searched. Often, however, this strict requirement is loosened somewhat to avoid curves ending too abruptly. Second, the neighborhood might be tiered in the sense that different pixels within the neighborhood possess different cut-off points. This condition usually results from a decision to have lower cut-off points for pixels nearer to, or directly below, an already chosen *curve pixel*. Third, there must be some condition for choosing among two or more pixels in the row immediately below a curve pixel when both have gray values exceeding their respective cut-off values. This can most easily be accomplished by choosing the pixel with the maximum gray level. However, suppose there are two, or even three, pixels in the same row having the maximum gray value. Should we include them all, at the cost of a "thick" curve, or should a mechanism be devised for choosing among them, at the cost of perhaps losing a horizontal shift in the curve? The variations on the scheme are practically endless. Probably the best way to grasp the overall technique is to exhaustively study a vertical tracking algorithm as applied to a particular image.

Let f be the image of Figure 5.1 and let the signal value be $s = 10$. Given a curve pixel (i, j), one already chosen, the neighborhood $N(i, j)$ below (i, j) will be the three pixels immediately below (i, j) in each of the two succeeding rows. $N(i, j)$ will be tiered in the following manner:

$$N_1(i, j) = \{(i, j - 1)\}$$

$$N_2(i, j) = \{(i - 1, j - 1), (i + 1, j - 1)\}$$

$$N_3(i, j) = \{(i - 1, j - 2), (i, j - 2), (i + 1, j - 2)\}$$

$$f = \begin{pmatrix} 0 & 2 & 1 & 4 & 10 & 4 & 6 & 11 & 2 \\ 2 & 3 & 4 & 2 & 7 & 3 & 9 & 9 & 2 \\ 3 & 1 & 4 & 9 & 8 & 8 & 4 & 2 & 1 \\ * & 10 & 2 & 8 & 9 & 5 & 8 & 1 & 2 \\ 8 & 8 & 4 & 3 & 7 & 2 & 2 & 8 & 1 \\ 6 & 9 & 3 & 4 & 6 & 6 & 1 & 0 & 8 \\ 1 & 7 & 4 & 3 & 7 & 9 & 2 & 1 & 1 \\ 2 & 9 & 2 & 1 & 2 & 10 & 2 & 1 & 1 \\ 2 & 2 & 8 & 2 & 2 & 9 & 2 & 1 & 3 \\ 1 & 1 & 10 & 2 & 2 & 1 & 3 & 1 & 0 \end{pmatrix}_{0, 9}$$

Figure 5.1 Image to be Tracked

where the respective cut-off gray values are $c_1 = 7$, $c_2 = 8$, and $c_3 = 9$ (see Figure 5.2). The cut-off gray values of subsequent tiers, as is common, get progressively larger.

A method of tracking will now be described:

1) Check N_1 and N_2. Take the set of pixels in these two tiers which have gray values exceeding or equal to the respective cut-off values c_1 and c_2.

2) If the set obtained from step 1 is nonempty, choose all pixels as curve pixels which possess the maximum gray value over the neighborhood $N_1 \cup N_2$, the row immediately below pixel (i, j).

3) If the set obtained from step 1 is empty, form the set of all pixels in N_3 whose gray values are greater than or equal to c_3.

4) Choose as curve pixels all pixels in N_3 which possess the maximum gray value among pixels in N_3.

5) If the set resulting from step 3 is empty, then (i, j) is *terminal*. The tracked curve containing it terminates at (i, j).

When all tracking has terminated, the algorithm is complete. Second, if a signal pixel, one whose gray value exceeds or is equal to 10, should be chosen during the neighborhood processing, it should not be used during further processing stemming from the branch upon which it was found; otherwise, there will be redundant processing, since two branches of the parallel processing scheme, the new branch for the signal pixel and the original branch containing the signal pixel, will be overlayed. It should be noted that the *tracked curves* can have "holes" and therefore are not curves at all. This abuse of terminology should create no dilemma.

Continuing the example, the tracking procedure will be applied to the signal pixel $(4, 9)$, which is in the top row of the bound matrix and has gray value 10. Applying step 1, only the pixel directly below, pixel $(4, 8)$, has gray value satisfying the appropriate cut-off value. Note that $(4, 8)$ is in N_1 and $c_1 = 7$.

Pixel $(4, 8)$ is now the curve pixel of concern. In the row directly beneath it, all three pixels under consideration have sufficiently high gray values in their respective tiers. Therefore, step 2 is applied and pixel $(3, 7)$, whose gray value is 9, is chosen since it has the darker value of gray.

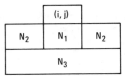

Figure 5.2 Neighborhood Structure for VERTRACK

Under pixel $(3, 7)$, there are two candidate pixels. Once again step 2 is applied. This time pixel $(4, 6)$ is chosen. [Note in Figure 5.3, which gives the final result of the overall tracking algorithm, that it is at pixel $(4, 6)$ where two curves join.] Steps 1 and 2 give pixel $(4, 5)$, with gray value 7, as the next one down.

Now apply the procedure to pixel $(4, 5)$. Since no pixel in N_1 or in N_2 [in the row immediately below $(4, 5)$] satisfies the respective cut-off criteria, step 3 is applied. Since

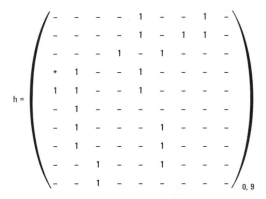

$$h = \begin{pmatrix} - & - & - & - & 1 & - & - & 1 & - \\ - & - & - & - & 1 & - & 1 & 1 & - \\ - & - & - & 1 & - & 1 & - & - & - \\ * & 1 & - & - & 1 & - & - & - & - \\ 1 & 1 & - & - & 1 & - & - & - & - \\ - & 1 & - & - & - & - & - & - & - \\ - & 1 & - & - & - & 1 & - & - & - \\ - & 1 & - & - & - & 1 & - & - & - \\ - & - & 1 & - & - & 1 & - & - & - \\ - & - & 1 & - & - & - & - & - & - \end{pmatrix}_{0, \, 9}$$

Figure 5.3 Output of Tracking Algorithm

only pixel (5, 3) has gray value exceeding or equal to $c_3 = 9$, that pixel is selected for the curve.

Proceeding, the procedure encounters a pixel with gray value 10. Moreover, it alone is chosen in its row. Hence, processing along the branch can cease since one curve has merged with another.

To display the final result of the tracking, a black and white image is produced with gray value 1 representing the chosen pixels and 0 (denoted by $-$) representing the pixels which have not been chosen. The output h of the preceding tracking process is given in Figure 5.3.

Many vertical tracking schemes are possible; however, the given scheme appears to employ many of the various conditions which can be imposed. For future reference, it will be given the name VERTRACK. As an operator, it requires five inputs:

1) An image f
2) A signal value, which is a real number
3) Three cut-off values, which are real numbers

Therefore, using the appropriate operator notation, $h = \text{VERTRACK}(f; s, c_1, c_2, c_3)$. Notice that the three neighborhoods (tiers) are not inputs since their description is part of the definition of VERTRACK.

Although many vertical and horizontal tracking schema can be devised, they all suffer from certain inherent drawbacks besides the usual one concerning the choice of appropriate threshold values. VERTRACK is directional in nature, and therefore the orientation of the image affects the output. In general, the operation of any tracking algorithm is highly dependent on the tiering structure employed. That structure must represent a balance between the desire for continuity, the desire not to have a number of very short curves strewn about the output image, and the desire for thinness. For instance, in the image of Figure 5.1, two pixels are chosen in the row beneath pixel (7, 9), the pixel in the top row of the image having gray level 11. Suppose the tracking algorithm VERTRACK had been defined so as to choose between pixels (6, 8) and (7, 8), each having gray value 9, and it chose the one directly below (7, 9). Then the resulting branch would have terminated, and the merging with the branch starting at pixel (4, 9) would not have been revealed. The price for not making such decisions regarding pixels which share the maximum gray level can be seen in the extreme left column, where pixel (0, 5) appears extraneous.

Another problem with VERTRACK is that it can "lose track" of one curve when two curves cross and continue on, or it can miss an entire branch of a curve which splits into two. For instance, in the curve of Figure 5.1, pixel (5, 7), having gray value 8, is chosen. Immediately below it, both pixels of N_2 exceed or equal the cut-off value $c_2 = 8$. Nevertheless, as a consequence of the maximum criterion, only pixel (4, 6), having gray value 9, is chosen. The result is that pixels (6, 6), (7, 5), and (8, 4), each having gray value 8, and apparently forming a straight line running downward and left to right, are omitted from the output image h. Although this omission could have been avoided by a slight alteration of the algorithm, such a change could easily lead to the problem of "thick" curves. The trade-offs are ever present.

A final problem with VERTRACK, and perhaps the most profound, concerns an output which does not appear to reveal curves at all, but rather a *region*. Take the situation where several Euclidean curves run vertically and are close together in the underlying predigital continuous model. The digital representation problem, or *digitization* problem, as it is known, emerges fully: Going from the continuous world to the digital world tends to "thicken" thin sets (see Figure 5.4). This interesting and deep problem goes beyond the level of the present text. And by this statement we do not mean to imply that there is a universally acceptable solution to the digitization dilemma. Indeed, there are structural limitations intrinsic to digitization.

A digital representation of four underlying continuous curves:

$$
f = \begin{pmatrix}
1 & 10 & 3 & 10 & 11 & 2 & 12 \\
1 & 2 & 10 & 9 & 9 & 9 & 1 \\
2 & 1 & 9 & 9 & 9 & 9 & 2 \\
1 & 1 & 9 & 9 & 8 & 7 & 1 \\
1 & 1 & 9 & 8 & 9 & 9 & 0
\end{pmatrix}_{3,\,2}
$$

(a)

The output of VERTRACK using signal input and cut-off inputs as above:

$$
h = \begin{pmatrix}
- & 1 & - & 1 & 1 & - & 1 \\
- & - & 1 & 1 & 1 & 1 & - \\
- & - & 1 & 1 & 1 & 1 & - \\
- & - & 1 & 1 & 1 & - & - \\
- & - & 1 & - & 1 & 1 & -
\end{pmatrix}_{3,\,2}
$$

(b)

Figure 5.4 Thick Region

One alteration of VERTRACK which might be of benefit would be the filling of the holes left by the algorithm whenever it jumps to the subneighborhood N_3 (the second row below a curve pixel) and there is a pixel in N_3 with gray value exceeding or equal to c_3. This can be done most simply by including the pixel directly beneath the curve pixel under consideration. Such a variation in the VERTRACK algorithm would make the tracked curve continuous, a property normally desired in a curve. If this were done to the image of Figure 5.1, then the pixel (4, 4) would be given the value 1 in Figure 5.3. Had a more elaborate tracking procedure been employed, a more sophisticated hole filling technique would have been appropriate.

The specification of VERTRACK in terms of more primitive operators is somewhat complex and can be presented with greater clarity if a new operator is first introduced. Analogous to PIXSUM, which takes a single image as an input and outputs the arithmetic sum of the image's gray values, the operator PIXMAX takes in an image and yields the maximum value of its gray values.

Example 5.1

Let f be given by

$$f = \begin{pmatrix} 4 & * & 5 \\ 3 & -2 & 7 \end{pmatrix}_{2,\, 4}$$

Then PIXMAX(f) = 7.

The block diagram for PIXMAX, with input f and output h, is given in Figure 5.5. The object of the implementation is to execute a group of parallel translations in such a way as to yield a collection of images, each of which has a unique gray value of the original at the origin. These images are input into MAX, whose output has the correct value of PIXMAX at the origin. SELECT followed by RANGE then yields the output for PIXMAX.

Figure 5.6 gives the desired specification of VERTRACK, where the operation PRO, whose block diagram is provided in Figure 5.7, is a procedure designed to select the next pixel, given a particular curve pixel. Because of the complexity of the algorithm, several assumptions will be made so that the essentials are not obscured. It is assumed that all gray values are nonnegative. The halting criterion resulting from the encounter with a signal pixel is not included. In addition, boundary conditions will be ignored: we assume that no stars occur in the neighborhood structure, $N_1 \cup N_2 \cup N_3$. Although the inclusion of boundary conditions in the algorithm would not present serious difficulties, excluding them results in expositional clarity. Perhaps the best way to grasp the algorithm executed by Figure 5.6 is to follow a walk-through.

The first THRESH of Figure 5.6 simply picks out the signal pixels. One copy is sent on to the end to be included in the final output of VERTRACK and the other moves on through the algorithm. TRAN and DOMAIN yield the set consisting of pixel locations beneath already chosen curve pixels. For each such location, a SELECT gives the 2 by 3 restriction of f immediately below the appropriate curve pixel. Each restriction enters a copy of PRO.

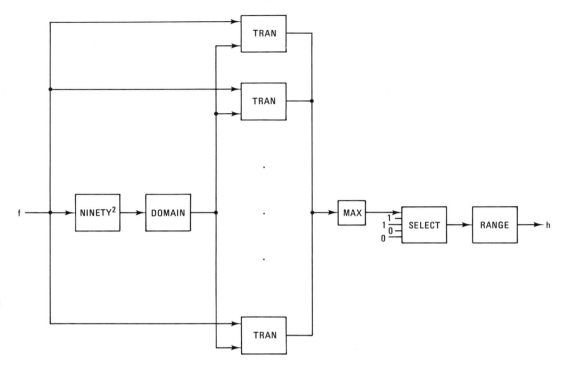

Figure 5.5 Block Diagram for PIXMAX

Once a restriction is in PRO, DOMAIN outputs pixel locations for the upper-left corner of each neighborhood. Notice that only the first, second, third, and fifth elements of the array output by DOMAIN are utilized. It is in such an instance that the output of DOMAIN being an array instead of simply a set is advantageous. SELECT creates a single image for each such neighborhood. If we consider signal pixel (4, 9), having gray value 10, SELECT produces the image

$$\begin{pmatrix} 2 & 7 & 3 \\ 9 & 8 & 8 \end{pmatrix}_{3, 8}$$

This image now enters the procedure PRO of Figure 5.7. There it is split into four images, one for N_1, two for N_2 (a split neighborhood), and one for N_3. These are given respectively by

$$(7)_{4, 8}, \quad (2)_{3, 8} \quad \text{and} \quad (3)_{5, 8}, \quad (9 \quad 8 \quad 8)_{3, 7}$$

TRUNC truncates each image at the appropriate cut-off value. The results are given by

$$(7)_{4, 8}, \quad (0)_{3, 8} \quad \text{and} \quad (0)_{5, 8}, \quad (9 \quad 0 \quad 0)_{3, 7}$$

EXTADD has the effect of bringing the singleton images of the row beneath (4, 9) back into a single image. PIXMAX then finds the maximum gray value of each of the two

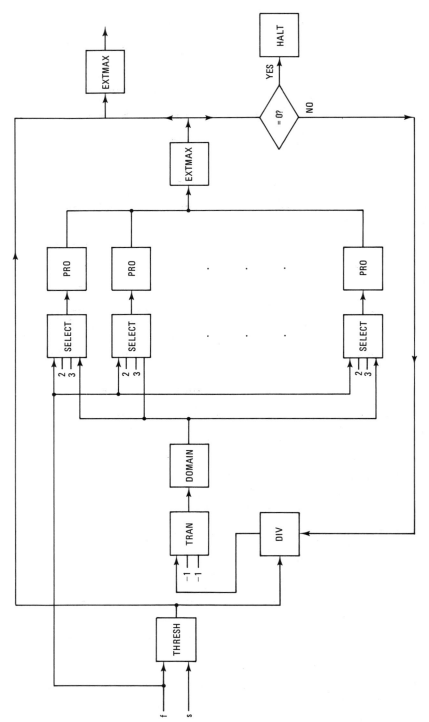

Figure 5.6 Block Diagram for VERTRACK

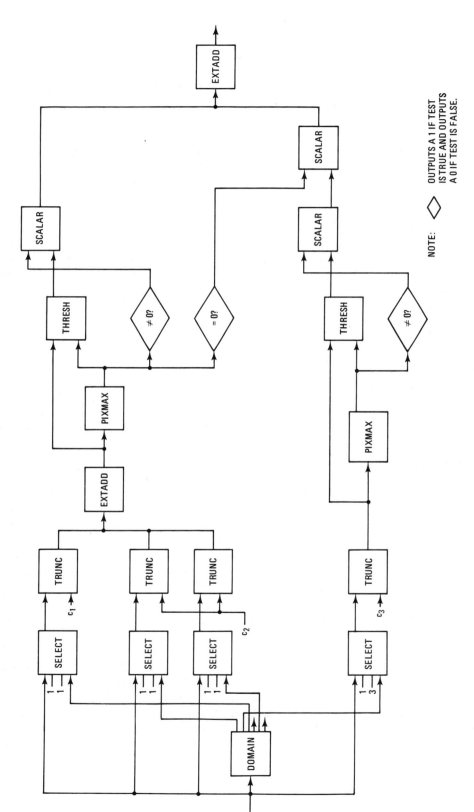

Figure 5.7 Block Diagram for PRO

images. THRESH, with the appropriate output of PIXMAX being the threshold value, yields the following two images:

$$(0 \quad 1 \quad 0)_{3,\,8} \quad \text{and} \quad (1 \quad 0 \quad 0)_{3,\,7}$$

Each image is tested to see whether or not it is an image with the only gray value being 0, CONST$(g; 0)$, where g is the appropriate image. Since neither is a zero image, the test $\langle \neq 0 \ ? \ \rangle$ puts out a 1 in each case. (The output is 0 if the test is false.) Each is scalar multiplied by this output to yield:

$$(0 \quad 1 \quad 0)_{3,\,8} \quad \text{and} \quad (1 \quad 0 \quad 0)_{3,\,7}$$

However, the lower image must go through another step. It can only contribute a nonzero term if the upper image is the zero image. This is the role of the test $\langle = 0 \ ? \ \rangle$. In this instance, it outputs 0. Thus, the second scalar on the bottom yields a zero image. EXTADD then has inputs

$$(0 \quad 1 \quad 0)_{3,\,8} \quad \text{and} \quad (0 \quad 0 \quad 0)_{3,\,7}$$

The image

$$\begin{pmatrix} 0 & 1 & 0 \\ 0 & 0 & 0 \end{pmatrix}_{3,\,8}$$

is then fed into the EXTMAX of the main diagram, together with the outputs of the other PRO operations. This output enters EXTMAX with the previous images which have arrived at this point. If all outputs of PRO are zero images, the entire algorithm halts.

5.2 Region Growing

A common image-processing task is to separate out a particular region of the overall image on the basis of gray value or texture. The image is segmented into a feature region and a background region. Simple truncation will not do. For one thing, the term *region* usually applies to a *connected domain*, a term to be rigorously defined momentarily. And for another, truncation only applies to segmentation by minimum gray level. The general method to be described is far ranging; however, like the section on tracking, only a single algorithm will be precisely specified.

Two pixels are called *direct (strong) neighbors* if they share a common side. The direct neighbors of pixel (i, j) are pixels $(i, j - 1)$, $(i, j + 1)$, $(i + 1, j)$, and $(i - 1, j)$. Two pixels are called *indirect (weak) neighbors* if they share exactly one common corner. The indirect neighbors of pixel (i, j) are pixels $(i - 1, j - 1)$, $(i - 1, j + 1)$, $(i + 1, j - 1)$, and $(i + 1, j + 1)$ (see Figure 5.8). Two pixels are simply called *neighbors* if they are either direct or indirect neighbors.

A *path* is a sequence of pixels $p_1, p_2, \ldots, p_n$ such that p_k is a neighbor of p_{k+1} for $k = 1, 2, \ldots, n - 1$. Pixel p_1 is called the *initial* pixel and p_n is the *terminal* pixel. A path is called *simple* if no pixel is repeated, except perhaps the first and last, and if no pixel has more than two direct neighbors. It is called *closed* if the first and last pixels coincide.

X DIRECT NEIGHBOR
O INDIRECT NEIGHBOR   **Figure 5.8** Neighbors of A Pixel

Example 5.2

The labeled pixels in the following grid can be sequenced to form several paths.

$$
\begin{array}{cccccc}
- & - & b & - & - & - \\
- & a & - & c & e & - \\
- & h & - & f & d & - \\
- & - & g & - & - & - \\
\end{array}
$$

Some examples are

$$P_1: \quad a,\ b,\ c,\ d,\ e,\ c,\ f,\ g$$

$$P_2: \quad a,\ b,\ c,\ d,\ e,\ f,\ g$$

$$P_3: \quad a,\ b,\ c,\ d,\ e,\ c,\ f,\ g,\ h,\ a$$

$$P_4: \quad a,\ b,\ c,\ d,\ e,\ f,\ g,\ h,\ a$$

P_2 is simple, P_3 is closed, and P_4 is simple and closed. For those familiar with the definition of a simple Euclidean path, notice that, if the lattice points of P_2 were joined in order by straight lines, the resulting path would not be simple in the Euclidean sense. Once again, digitization has created an apparent anomaly.

A collection of pixels is said to be *connected* if for any two pixels in the collection there exists a path of pixels in the collection such that one is the initial pixel and the other is the terminal pixel of the path. A connected set of pixels is usually called a *region*.

Example 5.3

In the following binary image f, the black pixels form a connected set.

$$
f = \begin{pmatrix}
- & - & 1 & - & - & - & 1 \\
- & - & 1 & - & 1 & 1 & - \\
- & - & 1 & - & 1 & 1 & 1 \\
- & - & - & 1 & 1 & - & - \\
\end{pmatrix}_{3,\ -1}
$$

In the image g, the collection of black pixels is not connected.

$$
g = \begin{pmatrix}
- & - & 1 & - & - & - & - \\
1 & 1 & 1 & - & - & - & - \\
1 & 1 & - & - & 1 & - & - \\
- & - & - & 1 & 1 & 1 & - \\
- & - & - & - & 1 & 1 & 1 \\
\end{pmatrix}_{-4,\ 2}
$$

A region-growing algorithm starts with a region and yields a larger region after some number of steps. A more precise characterization will be given after the discussion of GROW, a particular region-growing technique. The purpose of GROW is to start with a given pixel (i, j) and to generate a region containing (i, j) whose average gray value is close to that of (i, j). The degree of closeness is determined by some input parameter t. The output of GROW is a constant image where the desired region is precisely the set of activated pixels.

Consider an image f and a pixel (i, j) in the domain of f. Let $R_0 = \{(i, j)\}$. Define R_0' to be the set of all pixels not in R_0 but with a neighbor in R_0. Let AVERAG(R_0) be the unweighted average of the gray values of the pixels of R_0. The region R_1 is defined to be the region R_0 together with all those pixels (u, v) in R_0' for which the gray value $f(u, v)$ differs from the average AVERAG(R_0) by less than or equal to the input parameter t. In other words,

$$|f(u, v) - \text{AVERAG}(R_0)| \leq t$$

The real number t will be referred to as a *uniformity* parameter since it is employed to define what is meant by the uniformity of gray level.

Once R_1 has been determined, the process is repeated. R_1' is the collection of all pixels outside R_1 with a neighbor in R_1. R_2 is defined to be the region R_1 together with all those pixels (u, v) in R_1' for which the gray value $f(u, v)$ differs from AVERAG(R_1), the unweighted average of f over R_1, by less than or equal to t. In other words,

$$|f(u, v) - \text{AVERAG}(R_1)| \leq t$$

The process is continued inductively until a point is reached where the new set generated is the same as the set from which it is grown: $R_{k+1} = R_k$. The algorithm is then halted.

The image f of Figure 5.9, with input pixel $(i, j) = (4, 3)$ and uniformity parameter $t = 2$, will be used to demonstrate the methodology of the algorithm GROW. The initial region is $R_0 = \{(4, 3)\}$. The *test* region R_0' is the outside of the square neighborhood SQUARE(4, 3). The image f restricted to that test region is the image

$$f_0' = \begin{pmatrix} 1 & 2 & 7 \\ 6 & * & 5 \\ 7 & 13 & 7 \end{pmatrix}_{3, 4}$$

Since R_0 only consists of one pixel, AVERAG(R_0) $= 6 = f(4, 3)$. Applying the uniformity condition to the pixels of R_0' yields the following image, which equals 1 at

$$f = \begin{pmatrix} 1 & 1 & 2 & 0 & 14 & 6 & 1 & 1 \\ 14 & 0 & 2 & 1 & 0 & 5 & 13 & 0 \\ 6 & 6 & 1 & 1 & 2 & 7 & 0 & 1 \\ 1 & 7 & 2 & 6 & 6 & 5 & 1 & 14 \\ 2 & 2 & 1 & 7 & 13 & 7 & 1 & 2 \\ 1 & 14 & 11 & 6 & 5 & 6 & 14 & 3 \\ 2 & 3 & 3 & 6 & 5 & 5 & 3 & 3 \end{pmatrix}_{(0, 6)}$$

Figure 5.9 Image to be Region Grown

the pixels of the test region which satisfy the uniformity condition and is star valued at those which do not:

$$\begin{pmatrix} * & * & 1 \\ 1 & * & 1 \\ 1 & * & 1 \end{pmatrix}_{3,\ 4}$$

Therefore, the new region R_1 is precisely the set of activated pixels in the image

$$f_1 = \begin{pmatrix} * & * & 1 \\ 1 & 1 & 1 \\ 1 & * & 1 \end{pmatrix}_{3,\ 4}$$

In other words, R_1 is precisely equal to DOMAIN(f_1). It should be recognized for specification purposes that the constant image depicting the region R_1 is obtained from the corresponding image representing R_0 and the acceptable pixels in the test region R_0' by the application of EXTMAX. Also, just as R_1 is given by the domain of f_1, R_0 is given by the domain of f_0, where

$$f_0 = (1)_{4,\ 3}$$

Now that R_1 has been determined, the test region R_1' must be examined. The image f restricted to R_1', the set of pixels outside R_1 having at least one neighbor inside R_1, is given by

$$f_1' = \begin{pmatrix} * & * & 0 & 5 & 13 \\ 1 & 1 & 2 & * & 0 \\ 2 & * & * & * & 1 \\ 1 & * & 13 & * & 1 \\ 11 & 6 & 5 & 6 & 14 \end{pmatrix}_{2,\ 5}$$

Moreover, AVERAG(R_1) = 6.33. Application of the uniformity condition to the pixels in the domain of the preceding image yields

$$\begin{pmatrix} * & * & * & 1 & * \\ * & * & * & * & * \\ * & * & * & * & * \\ * & * & * & * & * \\ * & 1 & 1 & 1 & * \end{pmatrix}_{2,\ 5}$$

Therefore, R_2 is determined by the activated pixels in

$$f_2 = \begin{pmatrix} * & * & * & 1 & * \\ * & * & * & 1 & * \\ * & 1 & 1 & 1 & * \\ * & 1 & * & 1 & * \\ * & 1 & 1 & 1 & * \end{pmatrix}_{2,\ 5}$$

Continuing, f restricted to R_2' is

$$f_2' = \begin{pmatrix} * & * & 14 & 6 & 1 \\ * & * & 0 & * & 13 \\ 1 & 1 & 2 & * & 0 \\ 2 & * & * & * & 1 \\ 1 & * & 13 & * & 1 \\ 11 & * & * & * & 14 \\ 3 & 6 & 5 & 5 & 3 \end{pmatrix}_{2, 6}$$

Using the fact that $\text{AVERAG}(R_2) = 6$, $R_3 = \text{DOMAIN}(f_3)$, where

$$f_3 = \begin{pmatrix} * & * & * & 1 & * \\ * & * & * & 1 & * \\ * & * & * & 1 & * \\ * & 1 & 1 & 1 & * \\ * & 1 & * & 1 & * \\ * & 1 & 1 & 1 & * \\ * & 1 & 1 & 1 & * \end{pmatrix}_{2, 6}$$

Since the next run through the loop gives $R_4 = R_3$, R_3 is the desired region. Therefore, the output of the algorithm GROW is given by

$$h = \begin{pmatrix} * & * & 1 \\ * & * & 1 \\ * & * & 1 \\ 1 & 1 & 1 \\ 1 & * & 1 \\ 1 & 1 & 1 \\ 1 & 1 & 1 \end{pmatrix}_{3, 6}$$

And $R_G = \text{DOMAIN}(h)$ is the fully grown region.

In the precise specification of GROW, the primary input will be a nonempty image f. The secondary input will be an image $f_0 = (1)_{i, j}$, where (i, j) is the single pixel in the domain of f. The tertiary input will be the uniformity parameter t. Hence, GROW will have the block diagram

$$f \longrightarrow \boxed{}$$
$$f_0 \longrightarrow \boxed{\quad \text{GROW} \quad} \longrightarrow \text{GROW}(f, f_0; t)$$
$$t \longrightarrow \boxed{}$$

In the preceding verbal description of GROW, the average of f over the region R_k has been denoted by $\text{AVERAG}(R_k)$. Since the average under consideration is unweighted, it is equal to the sum of the pixel gray levels divided by the area of the image (the number of pixels in the domain). Hence it is obtained by a simple arithmetic division:

$$\text{AVERAG}(R_k) = \frac{\text{PIXSUM}[\text{REST}(f, f_k)]}{\text{AREA}[\text{REST}(f, f_k)]}$$

The implementation of GROW, which is somewhat involved, is presented in Figure 5.10. At the highest level, it is a loop structure which is initiated with the secondary input f_0 and is re-initiated at each stage, with the secondary input being the output of the previous stage.

When a secondary input f_k enters the loop, it is translated in the eight neighboring directions by TRAN. When these translations, together with f_k itself, are sent to EXTMAX, the net effect is to union all nine domains. Put precisely, EXTMAX yields a constant image whose domain is the union of the domains of the nine inputs. Its output is a constant image whose domain consists of those pixels which have a neighbor in the domain of f_k or are in f_k. (Note that only in the case of $k = 0$ is there a need to include f_0 as an input to EXTMAX; for k greater than 0, it is automatically included under the eight translations.) The sequence SUB, EXTADD (with co-input coming from EXTMAX), and DIV yields a constant image with domain equal to those pixels which have neighbors in f_k but are not in f_k themselves. In other words, this sequence of operations removes the domain of f_k from the output of EXTMAX. This leaves an image whose domain, after DIV, is the required test region R'_k. This image is input into MULT together with f to provide the image f'_k, which is f restricted to the test region R'_k. The chain in Figure 5.10 which runs along the bottom, REST, SUB, AVERAG, and SCALAR, outputs a constant image which has gray value $-$ AVERAG(R_k) and domain equal to the test region. The sequence ADD, ABS, SUB, and THRESH produces an image which has domain equal to the test region, is equal to 1 wherever the inequality

$$|f(i, j) - \text{AVERAG}(R_k)| \leq t$$

is satisfied, and equals 0 wherever the inequality is not satisfied. (Note the use of SUB to negate the gray values and the corresponding use of THRESH with input $-t$ to give a thresholding at less than or equal to t.) DIV turns the 0's to stars. The image under consideration now has the property that each activated pixel is to be included in the final output image. EXTMAX takes this image together with the original secondary input of the loop to yield the loop output f_{k+1}, which has domain R_{k+1}. It does this because it acts like a union operator with respect to the domains of constant input images. Finally, the output f_{k+1} is tested to see if it is strictly greater in area than the previous output. If so, it is sent back to initiate another run through the loop; if not, the process is halted, since the final output of GROW has been determined to be f_{k+1}.

Figure 5.11 gives a walk-through of the second stage of GROW with the primary input

$$f = \begin{pmatrix} * & 1 & 5 & 1 \\ 9 & 5 & 1 & 9 \\ 9 & 1 & 6 & 1 \end{pmatrix}_{0,\,2}$$

and the secondary input

$$f_0 = (1)_{2,\,0}$$

The uniformity parameter is $t = 2$. The flow of the data is downward. The walk-through must be followed with close attention to the block diagram in Figure 5.10. The flow diagram begins with f_1.

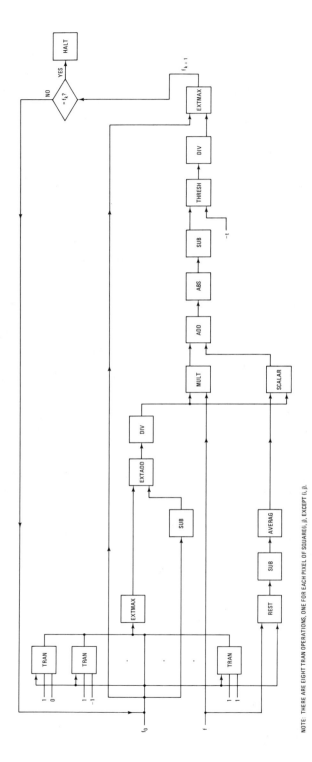

Figure 5.10 Block Diagram of GROW Algorithm

NOTE: THERE ARE EIGHT TRAN OPERATIONS, ONE FOR EACH PIXEL OF SQUARE(i, j), EXCEPT (i, j).

GROW is an example of a region-growing methodology that is quite general in its structure. Numerous changes could be made in GROW to give somewhat different algorithms that still maintain certain fundamental features. For instance, the input region could be a set of pixels rather than simply a single pixel. The test region could be either

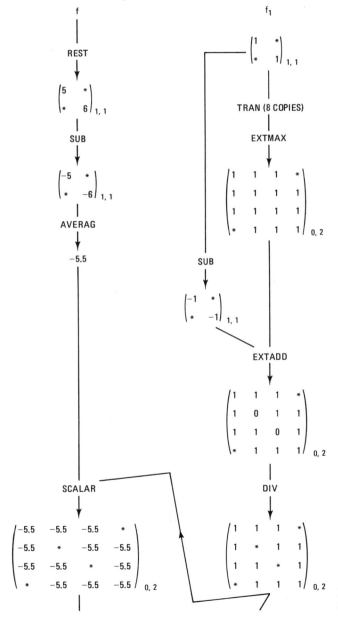

Figure 5.11 Walk-through of Second Stage of GROW Algorithm

Figure 5.11 Continued

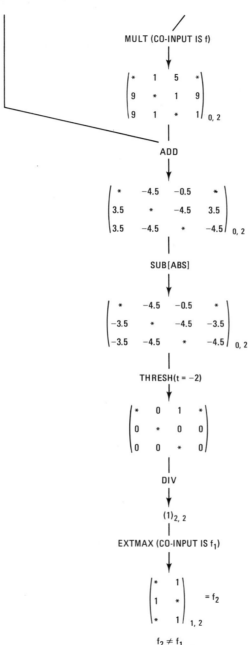

MULT (CO-INPUT IS f)

$$\begin{pmatrix} * & 1 & 5 & * \\ 9 & * & 1 & 9 \\ 9 & 1 & * & 1 \end{pmatrix}_{0,\,2}$$

ADD

$$\begin{pmatrix} * & -4.5 & -0.5 & * \\ 3.5 & * & -4.5 & 3.5 \\ 3.5 & -4.5 & * & -4.5 \end{pmatrix}_{0,\,2}$$

SUB[ABS]

$$\begin{pmatrix} * & -4.5 & -0.5 & * \\ -3.5 & * & -4.5 & -3.5 \\ -3.5 & -4.5 & * & -4.5 \end{pmatrix}_{0,\,2}$$

THRESH(t = −2)

$$\begin{pmatrix} * & 0 & 1 & * \\ 0 & * & 0 & 0 \\ 0 & 0 & * & 0 \end{pmatrix}$$

DIV

$$(1)_{2,\,2}$$

EXTMAX (CO-INPUT IS f_1)

$$\begin{pmatrix} * & 1 \\ 1 & * \\ * & 1 \end{pmatrix}_{1,\,2} = f_2$$

$$f_2 \neq f_1$$

RETURN f_2 TO START NEW LOOP

more than just the neighboring pixels, or perhaps less. The uniformity condition might be some other measure than simply the difference between a single gray value and the unweighted average gray value of the region currently being enlarged. If we were interested in finding a region with a common texture, it would be prudent to begin with a fairly large region. Whatever uniformity condition is being applied, the value assigned to the region (that being the average in GROW) must be representative of the desired textural properties.

We might characterize the previous methodology by the following four steps:

1) An initial region R_0 is chosen as input.
2) After the region R_k is determined, a test region R'_k is determined by a predefined procedure.
3) A uniformity condition is applied to R'_k to determine whether all, or part, of it will be adjoined to R_k to form the newly enlarged region R_{k+1}.
4) If $R_{k+1} = R_k$, the algorithm terminates. Otherwise, a new loop is begun.

Aside from the obvious difficulties in choosing an appropriate uniformity condition other than the one presented in GROW, the general region-growing technique outlined herein suffers from its dependence on the choice of initial region. Given the same data, two different image engineers can arrive at different regions even if they apply the same uniformity condition, as long as they do not use the same input region. Nevertheless, the technique is quite useful for picking out connected domains of uniform gray value and, in certain instances, uniform texture.

5.3 Curve Filling

In each run through of the loop in algorithm GROW, it was necessary to find all the pixels in the domain of f which had a neighbor in R_k but were not in R_k themselves. This particular operation is a variant of a standard topological procedure, that of finding the *boundary* of a constant image.

Let S be a constant image. The boundary of S, BOUND(S), is the constant image whose domain is such that each pixel within it has a neighbor in the domain of S but is not in the domain of S itself. Two points should be noted. First, for those who are familiar with the boundary of a Euclidean set, BOUND is a digital version of that notion; however, it is only one of several possible digital alternatives, each suffering from its own digitization shortcomings. Second, the concept of boundary, as defined herein, is often called the *external* boundary, since BOUND(S) has a domain of pixels which are external to the domain of S.

Example 5.4

Let

$$
S = \begin{pmatrix}
* & * & * & * & * & * & * & * & * \\
* & * & * & 1 & * & 1 & * & * & * \\
* & * & * & 1 & * & 1 & * & * & * \\
* & * & 1 & 1 & 1 & 1 & 1 & * & * \\
* & 1 & 1 & 1 & 1 & 1 & 1 & 1 & * \\
* & * & * & * & * & 1 & 1 & * & * \\
* & 1 & 1 & * & * & * & * & 1 & * \\
* & 1 & 1 & 1 & * & * & * & * & * \\
* & * & * & * & * & * & * & * & *
\end{pmatrix}_{0,\,8}
$$

Then

$$
\mathrm{BOUND}(S) = \begin{pmatrix}
* & * & 1 & 1 & 1 & 1 & 1 & * & * \\
* & * & 1 & * & 1 & * & 1 & * & * \\
* & 1 & 1 & * & 1 & * & 1 & 1 & * \\
1 & 1 & * & * & * & * & * & 1 & 1 \\
1 & * & * & * & * & * & * & * & 1 \\
1 & 1 & 1 & 1 & 1 & * & * & 1 & 1 \\
1 & * & * & 1 & 1 & 1 & 1 & * & 1 \\
1 & * & * & * & 1 & * & 1 & 1 & 1 \\
1 & 1 & 1 & 1 & 1 & * & * & * & *
\end{pmatrix}_{0,\,8}
$$

The boundary (external boundary) of a constant image *encloses* that image. Due to the discreteness of the grid, this enclosing at times appears paradoxical. For instance, in Example 5.4 the image S can intuitively be viewed as the union of two disjoint, connected subimages S_1 and S_2, where S_1 is the image consisting of five black pixels in the lower-left corner of the bound matrix for S, and S_2 consists of the remaining activated pixels of S. Rigorously,

$$
S = S_1 \bigvee S_2 = \mathrm{EXTMAX}(S_1,\, S_2)
$$

In accordance with Euclidean intuition, the boundaries of S_1 and S_2 should be disjoint. This is not the case. As is often the problem, digitization yields thick sets where one would desire a thin set. More precisely, Euclidean points have no diameter, whereas pixels are squares with edges having a fixed positive length. Redefining the boundary in some other manner might solve this particular anomaly; however, the new definition would have its own problems.

The implementation of BOUND appears as a subroutine in the specification of GROW. It is presented in Figure 5.12, where EXTMAX yields the union of all pixels which are either in S or have a neighbor in S.

A significant issue addressed in image processing is the *filling* of a region determined by a given simple closed curve. The problem, in its most general form, is extremely delicate due to the customary intricacies of digitization.

In Figure 5.13, the image S has a domain which is a simple closed curve. Like a star, the symbol # denotes the value at a pixel where the gray value is undefined. It appears

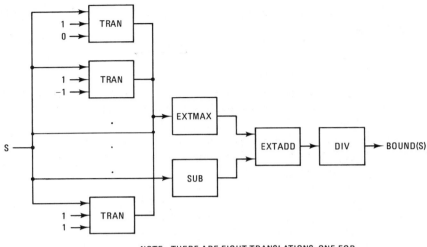

NOTE: THERE ARE EIGHT TRANSLATIONS, ONE FOR
EACH NEIGHBOR OF PIXEL (i, j)

Figure 5.12 Block Diagram of BOUND Algorithm

that the #-value pixels are *interior* to the curve S. Yet if I denotes the constant image with those pixels activated, it is certainly not true that $S = \text{BOUND}(I)$. Suppose we were to argue that the notion of *internal* boundary should be applied, where the internal boundary of $S \lor I$ is the collection of pixels in the domain of $S \lor I$ that have neighbors outside the domain of $S \lor I$. Would S then be the boundary of $S \lor I$? Certainly not! Pixel $(1, 1)$ is in the domain of $S \lor I$ and it has a neighbor outside that domain. Yet it is not in S. Another argument might be to use the internal boundary notion but include a pixel if and only if it has a direct neighbor outside the domain. This would also fail since pixel $(4, 1)$ is in the domain of $S \lor I$ and does not have a direct neighbor outside that domain, but is nevertheless in the domain of S! It is possible to point out many such seeming pathologies. Yet the problem is inherent in the digitization scheme. To obtain rigorous results, precise definitions must be generated, and theorems must be carefully checked against those definitions. There is certainly no definitive, universally accepted approach to the matter. In this text, we shall demonstrate one algorithm for filling a particular type of curve and shall leave the multitude of other approaches to the literature.

An image is said to be *directly connected* if, for any two pixels in its domain, there is a path $p_1, p_2, \ldots, p_n$ between the two given pixels such that p_k is a direct neighbor of p_{k+1} for $k = 1, 2, \ldots, n - 1$. Intuitively, for a directly connected image, it is

$$S = \begin{pmatrix} 1 & * & * & * & 1 & * & * & * \\ 1 & 1 & * & 1 & 1 & * & * & * \\ 1 & \# & 1 & \# & \# & 1 & 1 & * \\ 1 & \# & \# & \# & 1 & 1 & \# & 1 \\ * & 1 & 1 & 1 & 1 & * & 1 & * \end{pmatrix}_{0,\,4}$$

Figure 5.13 Simple Closed Curve-Type Image

possible to go from any one pixel in the domain to any other by a sequence of horizontal and vertical steps.

A constant image C is said to be *grid convex* if three conditions are satisfied:

1) C is directly connected.
2) If two pixels in the same column of the minimal bound matrix representing C are activated, then so are all pixels in the column that lies between them (vertical convexity).
3) If two pixels in the same row of the minimal bound matrix representing C are activated, then so are all pixels in the row that lies between them (horizontal convexity).

Figure 5.14 gives a grid convex image. From this example, it should be clear that grid convexity and Euclidean convexity are quite different notions. Yet there is one sense in which they are the same. If P and Q are any two activated pixels of a grid convex image that lie in the same column or the same row, then all pixels between them are activated. Since there are only two principal directions on the grid, vertical and horizontal, the definition of grid convexity remains essentially true to the underlying notion of convexity. Figure 5.15 presents an image that fails to be grid convex because it violates condition 1 of the definition, even though it is connected.

An algorithm will now be introduced that fills a curve—the external boundary of a grid convex image. The procedure is quite straightforward. It begins with the top row of the minimal bound matrix and searches from left to right. It then proceeds row by row through the bound matrix. In a given row, one of two situations can occur:

1) A single string of activated pixels is encountered.
2) Two strings of activated pixels are encountered with a single string of nonactivated pixels between them.

If condition 1 occurs, there are no pixels to be filled. If condition 2 occurs, all pixels between the two that were encountered must be filled (be activated). When the algorithm is complete, all pixels of the image S whose boundary was the original curve will be activated. And only those will be activated. This algorithm will be called FILL.

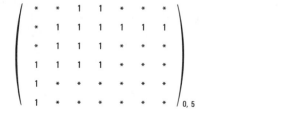

Figure 5.14 Grid Convex Image

Figure 5.15 Not Grid Convex

Example 5.5

Let

$$T = \begin{pmatrix} * & 1 & 1 & 1 & * & * & * \\ 1 & 1 & * & 1 & 1 & * & * \\ 1 & * & * & * & 1 & 1 & 1 \\ 1 & * & * & * & * & * & 1 \\ 1 & 1 & 1 & 1 & * & * & 1 \\ * & * & * & 1 & * & 1 & 1 \\ * & * & * & 1 & 1 & 1 & 1 \end{pmatrix}_{0,6}$$

The search of the first row locates only a single string of 1's. Hence no pixels are filled. In the second row, two strings of activated pixels are found. There is a single pixel, (2, 5), between them. Hence that single pixel is activated. In the third row there is a string of one activated pixel, followed by three successive nonactivated pixels, followed by a string of three activated pixels. Hence the three nonactivated pixels are activated in the output image. When the process is complete, the output can be represented by

$$T \longrightarrow \boxed{\text{FILL}} \rightarrow \begin{pmatrix} * & * & * & * & * & * & * \\ * & * & 1 & * & * & * & * \\ * & 1 & 1 & 1 & * & * & * \\ * & 1 & 1 & 1 & 1 & 1 & * \\ * & * & * & * & 1 & 1 & * \\ * & * & * & * & 1 & * & * \\ * & * & * & * & * & * & * \end{pmatrix}_{0,6}$$

Before proceeding to the implementation of FILL, some comments are in order. The conditions required for the application of FILL-like algorithms can be weakened. For instance, the procedure clearly works if the image is just horizontally convex since the search is horizontal. By using a vertical search instead, we can apply the underlying algorithm to a vertically convex region. In general, extensions of the technique require attention to the relevant factors concerning digital topology.

The block diagram expansion of FILL makes use of a template-matching procedure based on the template images

$$h(k) = (1 \quad * \quad \ldots \quad * \quad * \quad 1)_{0,0}$$

the same constant images that were used to generate the morphological covariance. It also utilizes the images

$$h'(k) = (1 \quad 0 \quad \ldots \quad 0 \quad 0 \quad 1)_{0,0}$$

which are related to the $h(k)$ by

$$\text{DIV}[h'(k)] = h(k)$$

Since the curve T is the boundary of a grid convex region, at most one such template can be *fit* in each row of the minimal bound matrix of T. The germ of the process is to successively fit

$$h(3) = (1 \quad * \quad 1)_{0, 0}$$

$$h(4) = (1 \quad * \quad * \quad 1)_{0, 0}$$

and so on. Figure 5.16 presents the procedural loop TEMPPRO, which takes a given template $h'(k)$ and outputs certain pixels in FILL(T). These are filled because they occur in a string of $(k - 2)$ stars between two strings of 1's in the boundary image T.

TEMPPRO translates the template $h'(k)$ to all pixels in the domain of T and restricts T in each case to the domain of the translated template. The sequence SUB, DIV, and EXTADD subtracts, in the extended sense, the template $h(k)$, not $h'(k)$, from the restricted image. If the resulting image is the zero image, $\langle = 0 \, ? \rangle$, on the domain of the translated template, there must have been a perfect fit and the procedure continues. If the zero image does not result, the template did not fit and the particular branch of the procedure is halted. If there was a fit, the sequence EXTMULT and DIV yields a constant image which has activated pixels precisely on the desired region. Finally, EXTADD produces an image of region pixels discovered by fitting the template $h(k)$. Notice that the stipulation is made that, if no inputs arrive at EXTADD, then TEMPPRO outputs the empty image.

Utilizing TEMPPRO, it is rather easy to specify FILL (see Figure 5.17). The template $h'(3)$ is entered into TEMPPRO together with T. The output is sent to EXTADD to be added to succeeding outputs of the loop. Meanwhile, the lower loop of Figure 5.17 is changing $h'(k)$ to $h'(k + 1)$ and feeding the new template back to TEMPPRO. This lower loop is equipped with a counter to halt the operation FILL after the template $h'(n)$ is utilized by TEMPPRO, where n is the number of columns of the minimal bound matrix representing T.

5.4 Template Matching

The operator FILL accomplishes the task of filling the region interior to a curve by successively, and in parallel, checking to see whether or not the template $h(k)$ fits into the given constant image. Not only can the template-matching technique be used to find copies of specific shapes in a constant image, but it can also be applied to more general gray-valued subimages within a given image.

In this section, rather than work with constant images, we shall utilize binary, or black and white, images. Binary images have two possible gray values, 0 and 1. However, they also have the value $*$ both outside the minimal bound matrix and at nonactivated pixels within the minimal bound matrix. While it is easier to work with constant images, in template matching the intuition often has to do with black shapes on white backgrounds, or common gradations of shading. In any event, if a binary image is input into DIV, the output is a constant image with its activated pixels in exactly the same location as the black values of the input image.

A simple example of template matching can be exhibited by considering the binary image S of Figure 5.18, together with the templates T_1 and T_2 of Figure 5.19. The algorithm proceeds by translating T_1 and T_2 so that their origin pixels lie on black pixels of the image. Those for which there is a match are recorded, and the output of the

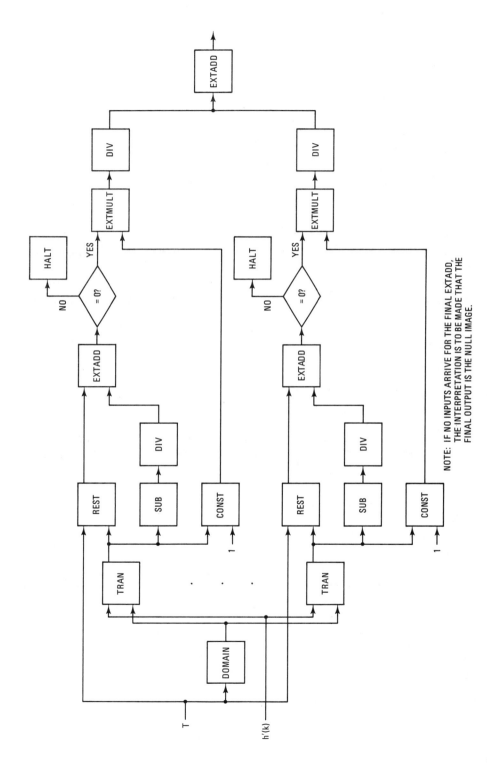

Figure 5.16 Block Diagram for TEMPPRO Algorithm

NOTE: IF NO INPUTS ARRIVE FOR THE FINAL EXTADD,
THE INTERPRETATION IS TO BE MADE THAT THE
FINAL OUTPUT IS THE NULL IMAGE.

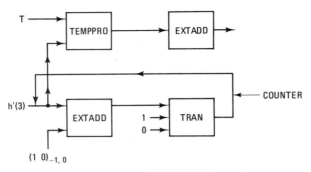

$(1\ 0)_{-1,\ 0}$

THIS LOOP IS EQUIPPED WITH A COUNTER.
AFTER n − 3 RUNS, WHERE n IS THE NUMBER
OF COLUMNS OF THE MINIMAL BOUND MATRIX
FOR T, IT ISSUES A HALT.

Figure 5.17 Block Diagram of FILL Algorithm

algorithm is a listing of pixels, one for each match, together with the number of the
template which matched at that pixel. For the example being considered, the list is

$$(1,\ 1)\quad 2$$
$$(7,\ 1)\quad 1$$
$$(10,\ 1)\quad 1$$

But such a list is itself an image. To be precise,

$$\text{CREATE}\,([\,(1,\ 1),\ (7,\ 1),\ (10,\ 1)\,];\ [2,\ 1,\ 1])$$

is an image containing exactly the same information as the list. Therefore, it is appropriate
to consider the algorithm as an image-to-image operator, called COPY, with three inputs:

1) An image S
2) Two secondary input images, T_1 and T_2

In the preceding example,

$$\text{COPY}(S,\ T_1,\ T_2) = (2\ \ *\ \ *\ \ *\ \ *\ \ *\ \ 1\ \ *\ \ *\ \ 1)_{1,\ 1}$$

Several points concerning the preceding algorithm should be noted. First, the output
of COPY is an encoding of the number 211, which appears in the image S. This encoding

$$S = \begin{pmatrix} - & - & - & - & - & - & - & - & - & - & - & - \\ - & 1 & 1 & 1 & 1 & - & - & 1 & - & - & 1 & - \\ - & - & - & - & 1 & - & - & 1 & - & - & 1 & - \\ - & 1 & 1 & 1 & 1 & - & - & 1 & - & - & 1 & - \\ - & 1 & - & - & - & - & - & 1 & - & - & 1 & - \\ - & 1 & 1 & 1 & 1 & - & - & 1 & - & - & 1 & - \\ - & - & - & - & - & - & - & - & - & - & - & - \end{pmatrix}_{0,\ 6}$$

Figure 5.18 Binary Image

$$
T_2 = \begin{pmatrix}
- & - & - & - & - & - \\
- & 1 & 1 & 1 & 1 & - \\
- & - & - & - & 1 & - \\
- & 1 & 1 & 1 & 1 & - \\
- & 1 & - & - & - & - \\
- & \textcircled{1} & 1 & 1 & 1 & - \\
- & - & - & - & - & -
\end{pmatrix}
\qquad
T_1 = \begin{pmatrix}
- & - & - \\
- & 1 & - \\
- & 1 & - \\
- & 1 & - \\
- & 1 & - \\
- & \textcircled{1} & - \\
- & - & -
\end{pmatrix}
$$

Figure 5.19 Template Images

can be transmitted so that the 211 can be graphically displayed at the destination point. Second, if we were interested in *reading* the numerals from 0 to 9, then COPY could be altered to require ten secondary input images, or templates. Third, the technique can be used to read letters or, more generally, any collection of disjoint shapes. For instance, the preceding output might indicate the word BEE if template T_1 contained the shape of an E and template T_2 contained the shape of a B. Moreover, if the output of the algorithm were altered so as to allow more than one template number per pixel, it could locate overlapping, or nondisjoint, shapes. Then, however, the output would not be an image. Finally, and most troublesomely, the algorithm is extremely sensitive to noise. The occurrence of a black pixel where there should be a white one, or a white one or undefined one where there should be a black, can cause the loss of an entire letter. This difficulty must be addressed.

Suppose that, instead of requiring a perfect template match, some *error* were allowed in the determination of a fit. For example, the template must match except for one pixel, or perhaps two, or even more. While it is unlikely that this would result in the recording of extraneous matches, especially in real situations where a shape might consist of hundreds of black pixels, it would restrain the loss of matches due to noise. In a sense, COPY is simply a special case of this form of algorithm. In COPY the error must be 0, while in this new operator it is given by some input parameter q. The new operator will be called MATCH. Once again the shapes will be assumed to be disjoint so that the output can be an image. As before, we shall only consider the case where there are two input templates. Hence, the block diagram for MATCH is given by

Applying MATCH to the image R in Figure 5.20 with the templates of Figure 5.19 and input parameter $q = 2$, we obtain the same output that was obtained for the image S of Figure 5.18. However, that was obtained with input parameter $q = 0$. If COPY had been used on R, there would have been no output (or, more correctly, the empty image).

The implementation of the operator MATCH will be given in two stages. Figure 5.21 gives the specification for a procedure called SUMSQ, which is an acronym for

$$
R = \begin{pmatrix}
- & - & - & 1 & - & - & - & * & - & - & - & - \\
- & 1 & 1 & 1 & 1 & - & - & 1 & - & - & 1 & - \\
- & - & - & - & 1 & - & - & 1 & - & - & - & - \\
- & 1 & 1 & 1 & 1 & - & - & 1 & 1 & - & 1 & - \\
- & 1 & - & - & 1 & - & - & 1 & - & - & 1 & - \\
- & 1 & 1 & 1 & 1 & - & - & 1 & - & - & 1 & - \\
- & - & - & - & - & - & - & - & - & - & * & \\
\end{pmatrix}_{0,\,6}
$$

Figure 5.20 Image for which MATCH is to be Applied

sum square. This procedure takes a template T and successively places it over the domain of an image R. At each pixel (i, j), it computes, in an extended sense, the sum

$$
[\mathrm{SUMSQ}(R, T)](i, j) = \sum_{(u,\,v)\ \text{in}\ D_{i,j}} [R(u, v) - T_{i,j}(u, v)]^2
$$

where $T_{i,j}$ is the template translated to pixel (i, j), and $D_{i,j}$ is the domain of the translated template. In the case of MATCH, SUMSQ will output the number of pixels (u, v) in the domain of the translated template at which either $R(u, v) = 1$ and $T_{i,j}(u, v) = 0$, or $R(u, v) = 0$ or $*$ and $T_{i,j}(u, v) = 1$. It is precisely this sum that we desire to be less than or equal to the input parameter q.

The block diagram of Figure 5.21 is quite straightforward. Since the match need not be perfect, all positions in the domain of R must be checked. TRAN takes the template T to the correct location. REST restricts R to the domain of the translated template. SUB followed by EXTADD gives a pixelwise subtraction. Two copies of that output are sent to MULT to get a square of the difference. PIXSUM gives the summation in the sum square, and CREATE puts the value of the sum square for a given location of the template into precisely that location. Finally, EXTADD outputs an image consisting of the sum square values at each pixel.

To obtain MATCH, we simply input R and the appropriate templates into the block diagram of Figure 5.22. Thresholding minus the sum square bound matrix at $-q$ gives a bound matrix that has a 1 wherever the sum square, or in this case the number of nonmatching pixels, is less than or equal to q and has a 0 wherever the sum square is greater than q. DIV takes this bound matrix and makes it constant. Scalar multiplying by the appropriate template subscript and then extend adding gives a bound matrix that has value 1 where T_1 fits, value 2 where T_2 fits, and a $*$ everywhere else. This is precisely what was desired.

As constructed for binary images, MATCH chooses a pixel (i, j) as a *match pixel* if and only if

$$
[\mathrm{SUMSQ}(R, T)](i, j) \leq q
$$

where q is a given input parameter. For the case of binary images, SUMSQ simply counts the number of pixels where the translated template has value 1 and the image does not, together with the number of pixels where the image has value 1 and the translated template does not. But SUMSQ need not be restricted to applications involving only binary images.

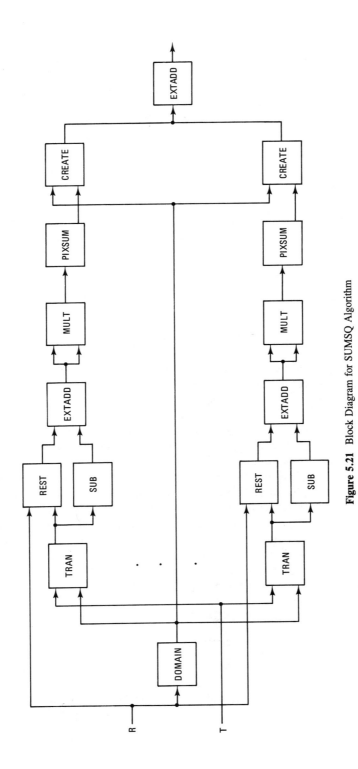

Figure 5.21 Block Diagram for SUMSQ Algorithm

159

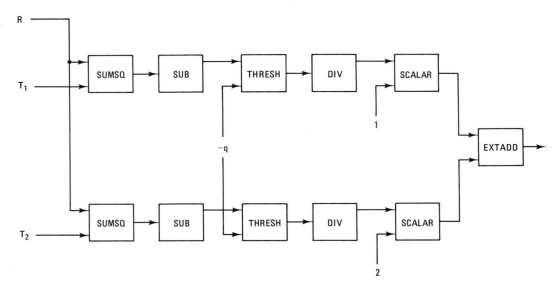

Figure 5.22 Block Diagram For MATCH Algorithm

Suppose R is a general gray-scale image and T is a template utilizing the same gray scale as R. Notice that in the definition of SUMSQ there is a summation of the terms

$$[R(u,\, v) \, - \, T_{i,\,j}(u,\, v)]^2$$

Since each such term involves a square, and hence cannot be negative, each gives a measure of the absolute difference between the template gray value and that of the original image. Therefore, the summation over the domain of the translated template as a whole provides a measure of the degree to which the template fits the image: the closer the fit, the smaller the value of SUMSQ at the pixel $(i,\, j)$; the worse the fit, the larger the value. As a result, SUMSQ can be utilized as a procedure to judge the quality of fit at a given pixel for general gray-valued images. But this means that MATCH, with SUMSQ as a subroutine, can be employed as a template-matching operation for general images.

For instance, consider the image f of Figure 5.23 and the template g_1 of Figure 5.24. Intuitively, g_1 is a vertical rectangle that gets progressively darker from top to bottom. Some straightforward calculations yield

$$[\text{SUMSQ}(f,\, g_1)](0,\, 0) \, = \, 59$$

$$[\text{SUMSQ}(f,\, g_1)](1,\, 0) \, = \, 5$$

$$[\text{SUMSQ}(f,\, g_1)](5,\, 0) \, = \, 13$$

If we were to proceed through the entire MATCH operation, altered so as to have only one input template, with f, g_1, and $q = 15$, the output would be

$$f = \begin{pmatrix} 0 & 0 & 0 & 1 & 0 & 9 & 0 & 0 \\ 0 & 1 & 1 & 1 & 1 & 1 & 1 & 9 \\ 2 & 1 & 2 & 2 & 0 & 2 & 2 & 0 \\ 7 & 3 & 3 & 1 & 0 & * & 3 & 1 \\ 0 & 4 & 4 & 0 & * & 4 & 4 & 1 \\ 0 & 5 & 7 & 9 & 0 & 5 & 7 & 0 \end{pmatrix}_{0,5}$$

$$g_1 = \begin{pmatrix} 1 & 1 \\ 2 & 2 \\ 3 & 3 \\ 4 & 4 \\ 5 & 5 \end{pmatrix}_{0,4} = \begin{pmatrix} 1 & 1 \\ 2 & 2 \\ 3 & 3 \\ 4 & 4 \\ \boxed{5} & 5 \end{pmatrix}$$

Figure 5.23 Image to be Used in Matching Algorithm   **Figure 5.24** Templates for Use in MATCH

$$\text{MATCH}(f, g_1; 15) = (1 \quad * \quad * \quad * \quad 1)_{1, 0}$$

For a walk-through demonstrating the appearance of a gray value of 1 for pixel (1, 0) in the preceding outcome, see Figure 5.25. The walk-through is vertical, and it employs the block diagram of Figure 5.22 for MATCH, together with the procedure SUMSQ of Figure 5.21. (Note that MATCH is only applied to the single pixel under consideration, not the entire output of SUMSQ.)

The major deficiency with MATCH, as with other similar variants of it, is that the choice of the input parameter q is heuristic. An obvious difficulty is the dependence of the output of SUMSQ on the gray-scale quantization. If that scale involves large values, SUMSQ may be large even if the template fits well. The reverse situation holds for the use of small scales. The answer in this direction appears to be a uniform use of gray scale. Perhaps a universal agreement on quantization scales running from 0 (white) to 1 (black) would be helpful. This would agree with the black and white scale and would effectuate good methodology in other areas such as morphology. As yet, the discipline of image processing is new and no such agreement is at hand.

Another problem with SUMSQ, and hence with MATCH, is the relativity of its output insofar as the area (domain size) of the template is concerned. Obviously, the greater the domain of the template, the more terms there will be in the sum square summation. One way of handling this problem is to simply divide the output of SUMSQ by the cardinality of the template domain prior to entering it into MATCH. This would mean that the average value of the squares of the gray-value differences would be compared to q. Intuitively, the match would be determined by the *average fit*. In this way, the input parameter q would have a more uniform interpretation, especially if combined with some standard quantization scale.

A more mathematically fruitful manner of handling both of the previous problems at one time is to introduce the concept of image *norm*. Given an image f, the norm of f is defined by

$$\text{NORM}(f) = \left(\sum_{(i, j) \text{ in } D_f} [f(i, j)]^2 \right)^{1/2}$$

where D_f is the domain of f. NORM(f) gives a quantitative measure of the absolute gray levels. If it happens, as is most customary, that the gray values run from 0 upward, then

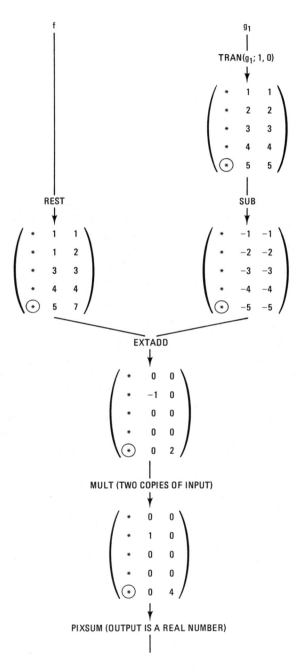

Figure 5.25 This figure gives a walk-through of MATCH for the image of f of Figure 5.23, the template g_1 of Figure 5.24, parameter $q = 15$ and pixel $(1, 0)$.

Figure 5.25 Continued

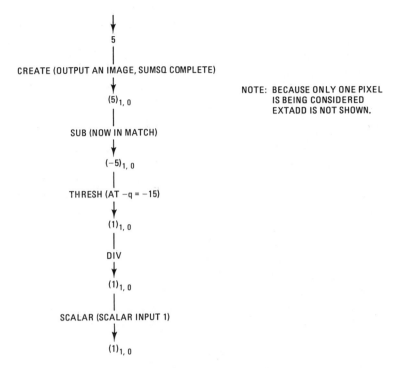

NOTE: BECAUSE ONLY ONE PIXEL
IS BEING CONSIDERED
EXTADD IS NOT SHOWN.

NORM(f) gives an overall quantification of the darkness of the image. Several properties of NORM should be noted:

a) NORM(f) $\geq$ 0.

b) NORM(f)^2 = DOT(f, f)

c) NORM[SCALAR($r; f$)] = $|r| \times$ NORM(f)

d) NORM $\left[\text{SCALAR} \left(\dfrac{1}{\text{NORM}(f)}; f \right) \right]$ = 1, if NORM(f) $\neq$ 0.

e) NORM[EXTADD(f, g)] $\leq$ NORM(f) + NORM(g).

Property a states that the norm is never negative, and property b states that the square of the norm is equal to the dot product (Section 2.2) of the image with itself. Property c says simply that the norm of a real-number scalar multiplied times an image is simply the absolute value of the real number times the norm of the image itself. Property d is merely property c applied to $1/\text{NORM}(f)$ and f. Those familiar with the vector norm (or vector magnitude) in vector algebra should recognize properties a through d as analogues of similar vector norm properties. Property e should also be familiar. It is the image version of the triangle inequality, which states the norm of a sum is less than or equal to the sum of the norms. However, in the image case, we use extended addition instead of straight image addition. Note that this creates no loss, since

$$\text{NORM}[\text{ADD}(f, g)] \leq \text{NORM}[\text{EXTADD}(f, g)]$$

In applying the procedure SUMSQ in MATCH, it would be helpful to have some *normalized* measure of difference between the image and the template so as to diminish the effect of the template domain size and the quantization scale. Both ends can be accomplished at once by considering a normalized version of the sum square. The technique is to divide the output of SUMSQ by the square of the sum of the norms at each pixel. More precisely, the multiplication is a scalar multiplication:

$$\text{SCALAR}\left[\left(\frac{1}{\text{NORM}[\text{REST}(f, g_1)] + \text{NORM}[g_1]}\right)^2 ; \text{SUMSQ}(f, g_1)\right]$$

This new output, a normalized version of SUMSQ, tends to be more of an absolute measure. A large value of SUMSQ due to a high-valued quantization scale or a large template is offset by the division, since either situation increases the divisor to a similar degree. This last comment can be demonstrated in a quantitative manner. In fact, the normalized version of SUMSQ has all pixel values between 0 and 1. A pixel value of the output of the normalized version near 0 indicates a good match at that pixel, while a value not near 0 indicates a bad match. Although the situation is still relative, it is no longer dependent on domain size and quantization scale.

Example 5.6

Let f be the image of Figure 5.23 and g_1 be the template image of Figure 5.24. Figure 5.25 presents a walk-through for MATCH for the pixel $(1, 0)$. As part of the walk-through, the procedure SUMSQ is executed at $(1, 0)$. The output for this procedure is the singleton image

$$(5)_{1, 0}$$

Referring to Figure 5.25, let h denote the image beneath REST and l the image beneath SUB. If the normalized version of SUMSQ were to be applied, there would be a scalar multiplication by the quantity

$$\frac{1}{[\text{NORM}(h) + \text{NORM}(l)]^2} = \frac{1}{[131^{1/2} + 110^{1/2}]^2} = 0.0021$$

Scalar multiplying this quantity times the singleton image output of SUMSQ yields

$$(0.0105)_{1, 0}$$

The extreme closeness of 0.0105 to 0 is a reflection of the excellent match at $(1, 0)$.

The normalized sum square approach remains relative, which tells us that the method is still problematic. Although it has solved some of the problems inherent in template matching, others remain. To see this, consider what happens in Example 5.7. There can be no better indication that MATCH must always be employed with caution, even when we rely on the normalized version of the subroutine SUMSQ.

Example 5.7

Let

$$f = (1 \quad 0 \quad 0 \quad 0 \quad 0 \quad 0 \quad 0)_{0,\,0}$$

and

$$g = (0 \quad 0 \quad 0 \quad 0 \quad 0 \quad 0 \quad 0)_{0,\,0}$$

It certainly appears that g is a pretty good match for f, especially if the gray scale were to run from 0 to 255. Yet in this instance

$$[\text{SUMSQ}(f, g)](0, 0) = 1$$

$$\text{NORM}(f) = 1$$

$$\text{NORM}(g) = 0$$

Therefore, the normalized sum square at pixel $(0, 0)$ would have value 1, which would apparently indicate a very poor match if we could rely totally on the normalized sum square technique. Notice, however, that in this example, dividing the sum square by the number of pixels in the domain of g yields the output $\frac{1}{6}$, a much better indication of the excellent match, especially with a gray scale running to 255.

EXERCISES

5.1. Let

$$f = \begin{pmatrix} 0 & 1 & 2 & 4 & 9 & 0 & 4 & 9 & 4 \\ * & 1 & 2 & 4 & 6 & 4 & 7 & 6 & 4 \\ * & 2 & 1 & 4 & 7 & 7 & 0 & 5 & 5 \\ 7 & 8 & 1 & 1 & 2 & 2 & 7 & 4 & 2 \\ 2 & 9 & 1 & 8 & 2 & 2 & 6 & 5 & 4 \\ 7 & 2 & 2 & 8 & 7 & 7 & 5 & 4 & 1 \\ 2 & 7 & 2 & 6 & 1 & 1 & 7 & 1 & 1 \end{pmatrix}_{4,\,-3}$$

Compute VERTRACK(f; 9, 6, 7, 8).

5.2. Let

$$g = \begin{pmatrix} 2 & 4 & 9 & 5 & 5 & 4 \\ 2 & 8 & 7 & 3 & 3 & 3 \\ 1 & 1 & 7 & 2 & * & 1 \\ 1 & 7 & 2 & 2 & 2 & 0 \end{pmatrix}_{1,\,0}$$

Find VERTRACK(g; 9, 6, 7, 8) by doing a walk-through of Figure 5.6. In doing the walk-through, also do a walk-through of the procedure PRO in Figure 5.7 wherever that procedure is called.

5.3. Define a new vertical tracking algorithm VERTRACK2 by using the tiering scheme

(i, j)
N_1
N_2

Compute VERTRACK2(f; 9, 7, 8) for the image f of Exercise 5.1.

5.4. Apply the algorithm GROW to the image

$$h = \begin{pmatrix} 4 & 5 & 7 & 3 & 5 & 13 \\ 5 & 7 & 0 & 0 & 0 & 15 \\ 5 & 5 & 14 & 0 & 5 & 5 \\ 6 & 7 & 0 & 0 & 5 & 5 \\ 7 & 8 & 1 & 1 & 13 & 7 \end{pmatrix}_{0,4}$$

using the initial region image $h_0 = (1)_{0,3}$ and input parameter $t = 3$.

5.5. Define a new region-growing algorithm REGION that acts exactly like GROW, except that the original input subimage can have a domain larger than one pixel. Apply REGION to the image f of Figure 5.9 using the input subimage

$$f_0 = \begin{pmatrix} 1 & 1 \\ 1 & 1 \end{pmatrix}_{4,4}$$

and the input parameter $t = 2$.

5.6. Design a new region-growing algorithm REGROW that acts exactly like GROW, except that the uniformity condition at each step is given by

$$|f(u, v) - z| < t$$

where z is the gray value at the single pixel in the initial subimage input. Apply REGROW to image h of Exercise 5.4 with input parameter 3.

5.7. Do a walk-through similar to that in Figure 5.11 for the application of GROW to Example 5.4. As in that figure, begin with h and h_1.

5.8. For

$$S = \begin{pmatrix} 1 & 1 & 1 & 1 & * & * & * \\ 1 & * & * & 1 & * & * & * \\ 1 & * & * & 1 & 1 & 1 & 1 \\ 1 & * & * & * & * & * & 1 \\ 1 & * & * & * & * & 1 & 1 \\ 1 & 1 & 1 & 1 & 1 & 1 & * \end{pmatrix}_{0,5}$$

find FILL(S) by performing a walk-through of the block diagram in Figure 5.17. Include the walk-throughs of TEMPPRO.

5.9. Consider the image

$$S = \begin{pmatrix} 1 & 1 & 1 & * & * & * & * \\ 1 & * & 1 & * & 1 & 1 & 1 \\ 1 & * & 1 & 1 & 1 & * & 1 \\ 1 & * & * & * & * & * & 1 \\ 1 & 1 & 1 & 1 & 1 & 1 & 1 \end{pmatrix}_{0,4}$$

Find FILL(S). (A walk-through is not necessary.) Why is the output of FILL(S) not what it should be if it were to correctly fill the curve?

5.10. Let

$$g = \begin{pmatrix} * & 0 & 0 & 0 & 1 & 2 & 2 \\ 0 & 1 & 5 & 5 & 6 & 4 & 2 \\ 2 & 1 & 6 & 1 & 2 & 6 & 2 \\ * & 1 & 5 & 0 & 0 & 5 & 5 \\ 1 & 5 & 5 & 5 & 6 & 5 & 1 \\ 2 & 2 & 5 & 3 & 2 & 5 & 0 \end{pmatrix}_{4,4}$$

and

$$g_1 = \begin{pmatrix} 5 & 5 & 5 & 5 \\ 5 & 0 & 0 & 5 \\ 5 & 0 & 0 & 5 \\ \circledS & 5 & 5 & 5 \end{pmatrix}$$

Find MATCH(g, g_1; 25).

6

TRANSFORM TECHNIQUES

6.1 Image-Processing Transform Techniques

An image-processing transform technique is an operation applied to an image which usually converts the image into a new structure. Sometimes the new structure will also be an image, but this is not essential to the discussion. Convenience, ease of handling, and ease of understanding are among the most common reasons for applying a transform technique to an image. Indeed, often a task being performed with the utilization of transform techniques can be accomplished without them by invoking other mathematical procedures.

Transform techniques are widely characterized by the way in which they are employed. Moreover, they involve not only the (forward) transform process itself, but also a corresponding inverse transform process.

Given a task to be performed on an image, a transform is applied to convert the image into another structure. This new structure can be thought of as the image in a "different world." In this new world, it might be possible to obtain the desired result by performing a simpler procedure than the one that would have been required in the original image world. Of course, the output of this simpler procedure resides in the different world. Therefore, to complete the solution of the original problem, an inverse transform is taken that maps this output back into the image world. The result of the inverse mapping provides the desired solution to the original problem.

Perhaps a simple, nontechnical example will help to illustrate the methodology. Suppose a 300-pound dumbbell is to be placed on top of a table (see Figure 6.1). The task to be performed is the placement of this heavy weight on the table in room A. Although it is a directly achievable task, it is somewhat difficult to accomplish. It would

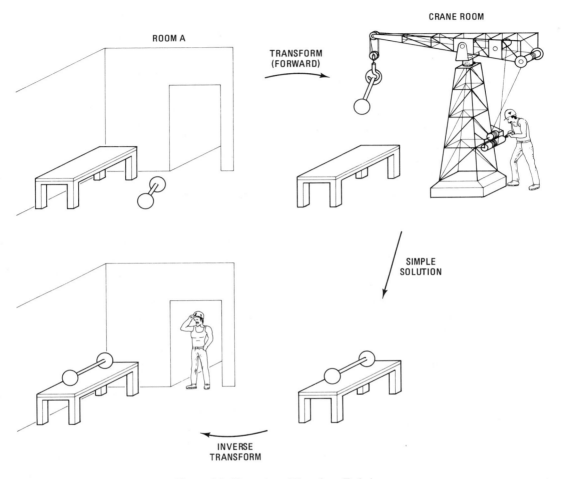

Figure 6.1 Illustration of Transform Technique

make more sense to apply a transform technique to help solve the problem. The (forward) transform for this application is the process of rolling both the dumbbell and the table into the crane room (Figure 6.1). Once these are inside the crane room, the crane can easily lift the weight and place it on the table. The problem is now solved, but in the wrong room. The inverse transform must be applied; that is, the table with the weight on it must be rolled back into room A. Once this inverse operation is completed, the original task is finished.

Those who have completed a course in differential equations are probably familiar with the Laplace transform. (If you haven't, you can skip this paragraph.) The Laplace transform allows the solution of certain types of differential equations to be accomplished by the use of elementary algebraic techniques. For instance, the transform is applied to a first-order linear differential equation with constant coefficients. The result is a new equation not involving derivatives. The transform has taken us from the differential equation world into the algebra world. Once in the algebra world, the problem is solved by elementary techniques learned in high school. But the solution so obtained is not the one ultimately desired. The final result is secured by applying an inversion technique. The output of this last inversion (inverse transform) is the desired solution of the original differential equation.

In Section 6.2, many useful transform techniques will be introduced along with their benefits. This will be followed by an in-depth investigation of numerous image-processing transform techniques.

6.2 Transform Techniques Widely Prevalent in Image Processing

The major transform techniques to be presented in this chapter operate on bound matrices. These techniques are useful for virtually all areas of image processing. For instance, in image restoration and enhancement, a transform technique such as the discrete Fourier transform might be applied to the originally observed image. The resulting structure (in the transform world) might then be multiplied by an appropriate filtering function (also see Section 2.3). This filter will allow certain frequency characteristics to be attenuated and others to be enhanced. An inverse transform procedure is then applied to the output of the filter. The purpose of all this processing might be to provide a better estimate of the actual image, this estimate being based on the observed image. The construction of an appropriate filter depends on empirical factors. As a case in point, in image-restoration methodologies it might be obtained through the utilization of mathematical models representing the imaging sensor which is being used to provide the observed image. In any event, the discrete Fourier transform and similar transform techniques will be described in subsequent sections.

Frequently, image classification and recognition are performed by correlating two images (see Section 6.13). The correlated images are variants of an observed image and a pattern image stored in the data base. This type of procedure can be performed in an expedient manner by employing transform techniques. Instead of performing the laborious correlation directly, a transform technique is applied to both images. The resulting structures are more easily combined in the transform world. For instance, in the case of the discrete Fourier transform, the combining operation corresponding to correlation involves little more than multiplication. An inverse transform of the combined structure in the transform world provides the desired result in the image world. A similar procedure is widely used in image creation. As an illustration, consider the creation of a synthetic aperture radar image. Here, instead of performing some type of correlation for determining the image directly from the output of the radar, a transform procedure similar to the one mentioned previously is exploited.

Transform procedures are among the best known and most practiced methods for performing image compression. Instead of directly storing or transmitting a given image, a transform is taken of that image. The particular type of transform employed has the property of producing a structure that contains the same amount of information as the original image, with little or no redundancy. As a consequence, the structure produced by the transform is *optimal* in the sense that it contains a maximum amount of information in as little space as possible. This is similar to the simple concept of minimal bound matrices, which was introduced earlier. In any event, depending on the purposes to be achieved, the more optimal output structure of the transform can be stored in memory or transmitted to a desired destination.

6.3 Vector Transform

A simple but important transform technique applied to images is the vector transform. This operation is very similar to the range operator RANGE defined in Section 1.11. In fact, the output of the vector transform is precisely the transpose of the output of the range operator. Given a bound matrix f, the vector transform of f, VECTRAN(f), is the column vector whose entries consist of the nonstar values of f. The gray values in VECTRAN(f) are organized from top to bottom by assuming the corresponding gray values in the original image f to be ordered lexigraphically top down and left to right. The block diagram for the vector transform is

$$f \longrightarrow \boxed{\text{VECTRAN}} \longrightarrow \vec{f} = \text{VECTRAN}(f)$$

where the notation $\vec{f}$ is often employed in place of the acronym notation.

Example 6.1

$$f = \begin{pmatrix} 4 & 5 & * \\ 3 & -1 & 7 \end{pmatrix}_{2,\,3} \longrightarrow \boxed{\text{VECTRAN}} \longrightarrow \vec{f} = \begin{pmatrix} 4 \\ 3 \\ 5 \\ -1 \\ 7 \end{pmatrix}$$

Notice that the vector $\vec{f}$ is a 5 by 1 and not a 6 by 1 vector since there is a single star among the six entries in f. Note also that the actual location of the bound matrix in the grid is irrelevant when applying VECTRAN since every translation yields the same output. Finally, note that the output of VECTRAN is exactly the transpose of the output of RANGE.

In applications involving VECTRAN, the domain extractor DOMAIN must also be employed to allow a bound matrix to be formed after the vector $\vec{f}$ = VECTRAN(f) has been processed. In other words, instead of directly processing the original image f, a VECTRAN operation is performed to yield the vector $\vec{f}$. The vector $\vec{f}$ is converted into a new vector $\vec{g}$ on which an inverse transform is then performed. The result is the bound matrix which would have been obtained by directly processing f. An illustration of the general procedure is given in Figure 6.2. In the case of VECTRAN, the inverse transform almost always involves the output of the DOMAIN operation and can be thought of as a CREATE operation.

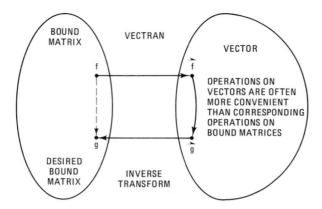

Figure 6.2 VECTRAN Procedure

Among the reasons for using the VECTRAN operator is that it is often more convenient to operate on vectors than it is to operate on general matrices. An instance of the use of VECTRAN will be given in Section 6.4 in conjunction with least-squares restoration.

6.4 Least-squares Image Restoration

Image restoration is the process of cleaning up an image that has been distorted due to errors introduced by imaging sensors. Image restoration is an estimation process. It involves the development and utilization of inverse models of imaging sensors. An elementary instance of the restoration process will now be presented.

Suppose f is an observed image of a given object and $\vec{f}$ = VECTRAN(f). Moreover, suppose the true but unknown image of the given object is g, and that $\vec{g}$ = VECTRAN(g). Suppose further that there is a matrix H, not a bound matrix, such that $\vec{f} = H\,\vec{g}$, where $H\,\vec{g}$ is the usual multiplication of a matrix times a vector. The matrix H is called the *design matrix* for the imaging sensor that obtained f. It provides a model of that sensor. Finally, suppose that H is a square matrix with nonzero determinant. If we desire the image g, the following steps can be followed:

1) Compute DOMAIN(f).
2) Let $\vec{g} = H^{-1}\,\vec{f}$, where H^{-1} is the inverse of H.
3) Perform a creation-type operation involving the gray values in $\vec{g}$ and DOMAIN(f) to produce the desired image g.

As an illustration of this process, consider Example 6.2.

Example 6.2

Let the observed image be

$$f = \begin{pmatrix} 3 & 4 \\ 2 & 1 \end{pmatrix}_{0,\,0}$$

According to step 1, we obtain

$$\text{DOMAIN}(f) = [(0, 0), (0, -1), (1, 0), (1, -1)]$$

Now let us make the assumption that the sensor is perfect except that it yields gray values which are exactly one-half the actual gray values, and that it makes this error on a pixel-for-pixel basis. Put into matrix form, this last statement gives the specification for the design matrix H. It tells us that

$$H = \begin{pmatrix} \frac{1}{2} & 0 & 0 & 0 \\ 0 & \frac{1}{2} & 0 & 0 \\ 0 & 0 & \frac{1}{2} & 0 \\ 0 & 0 & 0 & \frac{1}{2} \end{pmatrix}$$

since multiplication of a vector by H will yield a vector whose component values are one-half the original. Letting $\vec{f} = \text{VECTRAN}(f)$,

$$\vec{f} = \begin{pmatrix} 3 \\ 2 \\ 4 \\ 1 \end{pmatrix}$$

Similarly, letting the desired image

$$g = \begin{pmatrix} a & c \\ b & d \end{pmatrix}_{0, 0}$$

where a, b, c, and d are the gray values to be found, we have

$$\vec{g} = \begin{pmatrix} a \\ b \\ c \\ d \end{pmatrix}$$

By the suppositions made regarding the sensor distortion,

$$\vec{f} = H \vec{g}$$

Therefore,

$$\vec{g} = H^{-1} \vec{f}$$

or

$$\begin{pmatrix} a \\ b \\ c \\ d \end{pmatrix} = \begin{pmatrix} 2 & 0 & 0 & 0 \\ 0 & 2 & 0 & 0 \\ 0 & 0 & 2 & 0 \\ 0 & 0 & 0 & 2 \end{pmatrix} \begin{pmatrix} 3 \\ 2 \\ 4 \\ 1 \end{pmatrix} = \begin{pmatrix} 6 \\ 4 \\ 8 \\ 2 \end{pmatrix}$$

Hence the desired image is

$$g = \begin{pmatrix} 6 & 8 \\ 4 & 2 \end{pmatrix}_{0,\,0}$$

A more general situation arises when the relationship $\vec{f} = H\vec{g}$ holds true and the matrix H is not necessarily square. In the *overdetermined* situation, where H is an n by m full rank matrix with $n \geq m$, we have $\vec{g} = H^+ \vec{f}$, where H^+ is the pseudo-inverse of the matrix H. In this case, the pseudo-inverse is given by $H^+ = (H'H)^{-1} H'$, where H' denotes the transpose of H. (The pseudo-inverse is defined in the Appendix.) When H is a square matrix, $H^+ = H^{-1}$.

A *least-squares* procedure for image restoration which utilizes VECTRAN will now be given. The procedure employs both intra- and interpixel gray-level information. In the former case, observed gray levels of a given pixel are a function of only the actual gray level of that same pixel. In the latter case, the observed gray levels of a given pixel depend on the actual gray levels of other pixels. The goal in restoration is to make a best estimate of the true gray value of a pixel based on observed gray values. Sometimes more than one image of a specific object is given. For instance, this occurs when two different sensors are used to observe the same object, or when a fixed object is observed at two different times by the same sensor and from the same perspective. In any case, $n \geq 1$ observed images $f_1, f_2, \ldots, f_n$ might be given for the purpose of producing an estimate $\hat{g}$ of the image g. The procedure for finding $\hat{g}$ is as follows:

1) Find DOMAIN(g).
2) Take VECTRAN(f_i) $= \vec{f}_i$, for $i = 1, 2, \ldots, n$, and form the vector

$$\vec{f} = \begin{pmatrix} \vec{f}_1 \\ \vec{f}_2 \\ \vdots \\ \vec{f}_n \end{pmatrix}$$

3) Take VECTRAN(g) $= \vec{g}$ and form $\vec{f} = H\vec{g}$, where it is assumed that the design matrix H is an n by m matrix of full rank with $n \geq m$. (Note that $\vec{f}$ is known from the observations and H is known from our knowledge concerning the action of the sensors.)

4) Use the pseudo-inverse relation $\hat{\vec{g}} = H^+ \vec{f}$, where $H^+ = (H'H)^{-1} H'$. This yields the least-squares estimate $\hat{\vec{g}}$ of $\vec{g}$.

5) Use the DOMAIN(g) information and $\hat{\vec{g}}$ to find $\hat{g}$.

The entire five-step procedure is illustrated in Figure 6.3.

Before numerous examples are given to illustrate the steps in the aforementioned optimal restoration procedure, the criterion for optimality wil be presented. Put succinctly, the problem is this: When H is a full rank n by m matrix with $n \geq m$, the vector equation $\vec{f} = H\vec{g}$ is often a contradiction in that, given the vector $\vec{f}$ and the matrix H, there often does not exist a vector $\vec{g}$ such that $\vec{f} = H\vec{g}$. In other words, given the data of observation, $\vec{f}$, and the design matrix resulting from sensor construction, H, there likely does not exist an actual vector $\vec{g}$ which would yield the data $\vec{f}$ from the sensor H. Because of this, it is more accurate to write

$$\vec{f} = H\vec{g} + \vec{e}$$

where $\vec{e}$ is an error vector used to "take up the slack." The next best thing to finding $\vec{g}$ such that $\vec{e}$ is identically zero is to find $\vec{g}$ such that $\vec{e}$ is as small as possible in some sense. A commonly employed goodness criterion is to make small $E = \vec{e}' \cdot \vec{e}$, the sum of the squares of the tuples in the error vector $\vec{e}$. In other words, we try to minimize the quantity

$$E = e_1^2 + e_2^2 + e_3^2 + \cdots + e_k^2$$

where

$$\vec{e} = \begin{pmatrix} e_1 \\ e_2 \\ \vdots \\ e_k \end{pmatrix}$$

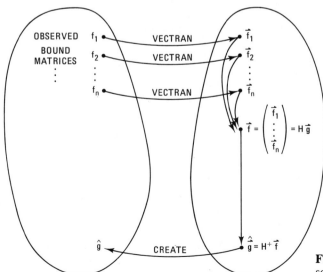

Figure 6.3 VECTRAN for Least-squares Applications

It turns out that E is minimized if we take the vector $\hat{\vec{g}}$, where $\hat{\vec{g}} = H^+ \vec{f}$. This is the reason for the previously outlined procedure.

A noncomplicated application of the least-squares technique involving redundant or excess intrapixel information will now be presented.

Example 6.3

For simplicity, images involving only two gray values will be utilized in the following presentation. Assume that the actual image of object x existing in the real world is

$$g = (a \quad b)_{0,\,0}$$

It might be that a equals 3 and b equals 3.7, but these values are hardly ever known.

Due to sensor limitations, the observed image of the object x may differ from g. Knowing this, and if time and memory constraints permit, more than one observation of the fixed object x can be taken. It will be assumed that the sensor is utilized three times and that it yields the three observed images

$$f_1 = (3 \quad 3)_{0,\,0}$$

$$f_2 = (2 \quad *)_{0,\,0}$$

$$f_3 = (4 \quad 4)_{0,\,0}$$

Notice that we deliberately did not make f_1, f_2, or f_3 equal to the actual image. The goal is to find an estimate of the actual image using only the observed images f_1, f_2, and f_3.

The procedure to employ has been sketched in Figure 6.3. The domain of interest is

$$\text{DOMAIN}(g) = \text{DOMAIN}[(a \quad b)_{0,\,0}] = [(0,\,0),\,(1,\,0)]$$

Next, notice that each observed image involves only points from the domain just found. Also, every point in the domain has at least one observed gray value, thereby allowing a gray-value estimate to be obtained for every point in the domain.

VECTRAN is applied to each observed image. We obtain

$$\vec{f}_1 = \text{VECTRAN}(f_1) = \begin{pmatrix} 3 \\ 3 \end{pmatrix}$$

$$\vec{f}_2 = \text{VECTRAN}(f_2) = (2)$$

$$\vec{f}_3 = \text{VECTRAN}(f_3) = \begin{pmatrix} 4 \\ 4 \end{pmatrix}$$

The total *observation vector* $\vec{f}$ is formed from the concatenation of these three vectors. Hence,

$$\vec{f} = \begin{pmatrix} 3 \\ 3 \\ 2 \\ 4 \\ 4 \end{pmatrix}$$

By taking

$$\vec{g} = \text{VECTRAN}(g) = \begin{pmatrix} a \\ b \end{pmatrix}$$

the *state vector* $\vec{g}$ is obtained.

We now make the assumption that the design matrix H involves only unity scale factors of gray values of identical pixels. Gray values of only identical pixels influence each other. This is the intrapixel assumption previously mentioned. The following overdetermined system is thereby obtained:

$$\begin{pmatrix} 3 \\ 3 \\ 2 \\ 4 \\ 4 \end{pmatrix} = \begin{pmatrix} 1 & 0 \\ 0 & 1 \\ 1 & 0 \\ 1 & 0 \\ 0 & 1 \end{pmatrix} \cdot \begin{pmatrix} a \\ b \end{pmatrix}$$

or $\vec{f} = H \vec{g}$. Invoking the pseudo-inverse relationship

$$\hat{\vec{g}} = [(H'H)^{-1} H'] \vec{f}$$

gives

$$\hat{\vec{g}} = \begin{pmatrix} \frac{1}{3} & 0 \\ 0 & \frac{1}{2} \end{pmatrix} \begin{pmatrix} 1 & 0 & 1 & 1 & 0 \\ 0 & 1 & 0 & 0 & 1 \end{pmatrix} \begin{pmatrix} 3 \\ 3 \\ 2 \\ 4 \\ 4 \end{pmatrix}$$

$$\text{or } \hat{\vec{g}} = \begin{pmatrix} \frac{9}{3} \\ \frac{7}{2} \end{pmatrix}$$

$$\text{or } \begin{pmatrix} \hat{a} \\ \hat{b} \end{pmatrix} = \begin{pmatrix} 3 \\ \frac{7}{2} \end{pmatrix}$$

By employing the creation operator CREATE, the best estimate, in the least-squares sense, of the actual image is produced. Indeed

$$\hat{g} = \text{CREATE}[\text{DOMAIN}(g), \text{ transpose of } \begin{pmatrix} 3 \\ \frac{7}{2} \end{pmatrix}],$$

$$= \text{CREATE}([(0, 0), (1, 0)], [3, \frac{7}{2}])$$

$$= (3 \quad 3.5)_{0, 0}$$

Put simply,

$$\hat{g} = (\hat{a} \quad \hat{b})_{0,\,0} = (3 \quad 3.5)_{0,\,0}$$

Notice that the choice of design matrix resulted in each gray value of $\hat{g}$ being the mean of the observed values for the given pixel.

Example 6.4 illustrates the manner in which interpixel information might be used in determining a least-squares best estimate of an actual image.

Example 6.4

For convenience, it will once again be assumed that the actual image possesses only two pixels with gray values. In particular, assume that an estimate of the actual image $g = (a \quad b)_{0,\,0}$ is desired. A single observed image f is given, where

$$f = \begin{pmatrix} * & 2 & * \\ 4 & 5 & 1 \\ * & * & 6 \end{pmatrix}_{-1,\,1}$$

Best estimates at only these two locations are desired

In this model it will be assumed that the gray values of neighboring pixels in the actual image influence the gray values in the observed image. In particular, it will be assumed that the observed value of gray at a given pixel equals 0.6 times the actual value of gray at that pixel, plus 0.1 times the actual gray value of each of its four strong neighboring pixels, those either directly above, below, to the right, or to the left of the pixel itself. This information is used in setting up the full-rank design matrix. The equation $\vec{f} = H\vec{g}$ is given by

$$\begin{pmatrix} 4 \\ 2 \\ 5 \\ 1 \\ 6 \end{pmatrix} = \begin{pmatrix} 0.1 & 0 \\ 0.1 & 0 \\ 0.6 & 0.1 \\ 0.1 & 0.6 \\ 0 & 0.1 \end{pmatrix} \cdot \begin{pmatrix} a \\ b \end{pmatrix}$$

where $\vec{f} = \text{VECTRAN}(f)$ and $\vec{g} = \text{VECTRAN}(g)$. The manner in which the sensor characteristics yield H should be recognized. Indeed, componentwise, the preceding vector equation can be interpreted as five equations:

$$4 = (0.1)a = (0.1) \text{ times the actual value of its right neighbor}$$

$$2 = (0.1)a = (0.1) \text{ times the actual value of its lower neighbor}$$

$$5 = (0.6)a + (0.1)b = (0.6) \text{ times its actual value, plus } (0.1)$$
$$\text{times the actual value of its right neighbor}$$

$$1 = (0.1)a + (0.6)b = (0.1) \text{ times the actual value of its left}$$
$$\text{neighbor, plus } (0.6) \text{ times its actual value}$$

$$6 = (0.1)b = (0.1) \text{ times the actual value of its upper neighbor}$$

Moreover, note that $\text{DOMAIN}(g) = [(0, 0), (1, 0)]$.

The best estimate $\hat{\bar{g}}$ of the state vector, in the least-squares sense, is again given using the pseudo-inverse H^+. We must find $\hat{\bar{g}} = H^+ \vec{f}$, where $H^+ = (H'H)^{-1} H'$. In this case,

$$H'H = \begin{pmatrix} 0.39 & 0.12 \\ 0.12 & 0.38 \end{pmatrix}$$

Therefore,

$$(H'H)^{-1} = \frac{1}{(0.38 \times 0.39) - (0.12)^2} \begin{pmatrix} 0.38 & -0.12 \\ -0.12 & 0.39 \end{pmatrix}$$

$$= \begin{pmatrix} 2.84 & -0.89 \\ -0.89 & 2.91 \end{pmatrix}$$

Consequently,

$$(H'H)^{-1} H' = \begin{pmatrix} 0.284 & 0.284 & 1.614 & -0.254 & -0.090 \\ -0.090 & -0.090 & -0.247 & 1.659 & 0.281 \end{pmatrix}$$

We obtain

$$\hat{\bar{g}} = \begin{pmatrix} \hat{a} \\ \hat{b} \end{pmatrix} = \begin{pmatrix} 8.984 \\ 1.637 \end{pmatrix}$$

Using the domain information previously extracted, the desired estimated image is found:

$$(\hat{a} \quad \hat{b})_{0,\,0} = (8.984 \quad 1.637)_{0,\,0}$$

6.5 Operations on Bound Matrices Similar to Regular Matrices

Numerous operations can be performed on bound matrices that are similar to operations done in the usual matrix algebra. These operations can be described in terms of block diagrams involving the more primitive operations given in Chapter 1. Some will be applied to a subclass of bound matrices whose members resemble regular matrices. To begin, we shall make a brief comparison between regular matrices and bound matrices.

The distinction between a bound matrix and a regular matrix is twofold. The possible inclusion of stars in the former and not in the latter is an extension-type difference. On the other hand, the fact that a bound matrix is "bound," meaning it possesses a specific location in Z × Z, while a regular matrix is "free," meaning it has no location, is a structural difference. If we consider only bound matrices with no internal stars, the first distinction between the two kinds of matrices is removed. Consequently, numerous operations defined on regular matrices can be extended to the subclass of bound matrices having information density 1. Furthermore, various matrix operations can be defined on bound matrices which can be shown to hold independently of the location of the bound matrix.

First, it is necessary to provide some preliminary definitions regarding specific types of bound matrices. An m by n bound matrix f is said to be a *square* bound matrix if $m = n$. If the m by n bound matrix f has either $m = 1$ or $n = 1$, then f is called a *bound vector*. In the former case, it is called a *bound row vector* and in the latter case it is called a *bound column vector*. The *transpose* of the m by n bound matrix $f = (a_{pq})_{uv}$ is the n by m bound matrix $f' = (a_{qp})_{uv}$. The transpose f' is obtained from f by making the rows of the former equal to the columns of the latter.

Example 6.5

Consider the bound row vector

$$f = (1 \quad 2 \quad * \quad 3)_{3, 4}$$

the 3 by 2 bound matrix

$$g = \begin{pmatrix} 3 & 4 \\ 2 & * \\ 1 & 5 \end{pmatrix}_{2, 5}$$

and the square bound matrix

$$h = \begin{pmatrix} 2 & 4 \\ 1 & * \end{pmatrix}_{5, 3}$$

The transposes of these images are respectively given by the bound column vector

$$f' = \begin{pmatrix} 1 \\ 2 \\ * \\ 3 \end{pmatrix}_{3, 4}$$

the 2 by 3 bound matrix

$$g' = \begin{pmatrix} 3 & 2 & 1 \\ 4 & * & 5 \end{pmatrix}_{2, 5}$$

and the square bound matrix

$$h' = \begin{pmatrix} 2 & 1 \\ 4 & * \end{pmatrix}_{5, 3}$$

Figure 6.4 shows that the transpose operation can be constructed from the operations given in Chapter 1. In examining the block diagram in that figure, it is important to note that the output of the operation FLIP is an image of the form $g = (b_{ij})_{u'v'}$, where $u' = -v$ and $v' = -u$. This is the reason for the translation operation.

Some square bound matrices have a transpose with entries identical to the original bound matrix. Such a bound matrix is called *symmetric*. Similarly, if f is a square bound matrix such that $f' = -f$, then f is said to be *skew symmetric*.

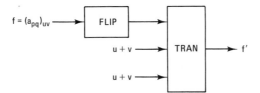

Figure 6.4 Block Diagram for TRANSPOSE Operation

At this point, we shall note the notational changes which occur in the present chapter. Previously, we have employed acronyms to represent operations on bound matrices. For instance, instead of employing the notation f' to denote the transpose of a bound matrix, we have consistently utilized a notation of the form TRANSPOSE(f). In fact, the expression $-f$ actually stands for SUB(f), the previously employed symbolism. Hence, the equation $f' = -f$ would perhaps be better written as TRANSPOSE(f) = SUB(f). Why the change at this point? The answer is quite simple. Because of the preponderance of matrix-type operations to be employed in the image-transform methodology, we believe it is appropriate to utilize the notational manner customarily associated with matrix algebra. There has not been any fundamental alteration of the operational approach taken previously throughout the text. The change is merely one of symbology. The methodology of image transforms is, in fact, still operational. This operational methodology is not simply an approach taken for reasons of style; rather, it is inherent in the mathematical nature of the structures under consideration.

Bound matrices with information density 1, are of special interest and are called *saturated*. Some types of symmetric saturated bound matrices are the following:

1) A *zero* bound matrix, which has only zero gray values.

2) A *diagonal* (square) bound matrix, which has zero entries off the main diagonal, that is, off the $-45°$ diagonal starting from the upper-left corner of the matrix.

3) A *scalar* bound matrix, a diagonal square bound matrix with all entries along the main diagonal being equal.

4) An *identity* bound matrix, a scalar bound matrix with 1's on the main diagonal. The notation $ID(n)_{ij}$ is employed to denote the identity bound matrix of dimensions n by n at location (i, j).

An n by n saturated bound matrix $f = (a_{pq})_{ij}$ is said to be *orthogonal* if $X(f', f) = ID(n)_{ij}$, where X denotes bound matrix multiplication, as defined in Section 1.12.

Example 6.6

The bound matrix

$$f = \begin{pmatrix} 2 & 0 \\ 0 & 3 \end{pmatrix}_{4,\,5}$$

is diagonal, but it is not scalar. The image

$$g = \begin{pmatrix} 4 & 0 \\ 0 & 4 \end{pmatrix}_{4,\,5}$$

is scalar, and so also is

$$ID(2)_{33} = \begin{pmatrix} 1 & 0 \\ 0 & 1 \end{pmatrix}_{3,\ 3}$$

the identity bound matrix of size 2 by 2 located at pixel (3, 3) in the grid. Furthermore,

$$h = \begin{pmatrix} \cos\theta & -\sin\theta \\ \sin\theta & \cos\theta \end{pmatrix}_{3,\ 3}$$

is a 2 by 2 orthogonal bound matrix, since $X(h', h) = ID(2)_{33}$.

It is useful to define the concept of a diagonal bound matrix for those bound matrices which are not necessarily square. For any saturated bound matrix f, f is called *diagonal* if all entries off the main diagonal (the $-45°$ diagonal starting from the upper-left entry) are equal to 0. This definition reduces to the usual definition for square bound matrices. The concept will prove useful when we study the singular-value decomposition of images.

Example 6.7

Both f and g are diagonal images:

$$f = \begin{pmatrix} 3 & 0 & 0 & 0 \\ 0 & 4 & 0 & 0 \\ 0 & 0 & 0 & 0 \end{pmatrix}_{5,\ 9} \quad , \quad g = \begin{pmatrix} 2 & 0 & 0 \\ 0 & -1 & 0 \\ 0 & 0 & 4 \\ 0 & 0 & 0 \end{pmatrix}_{8,\ 3}$$

Various functional-type operations are defined for certain bound matrices just as similar operations are defined for regular matrices. For the n by n saturated bound matrix $f = (a_{pq})_{uv}$, the determinant, symbolized $\mathrm{DET}(f)$, is the number obtained by forming

$$\sum_p (-1)^{t(p)}\, a_{1j_1} a_{2j_2} \ldots a_{nj_n}$$

just as it is for the usual matrix (a_{pq}). Here, p varies over all $n!$ permutations of 1, 2, . . ., n, $t(p)$ is the number of transpositions needed to restore the permutation p to natural order, and $j_1 j_2 \ldots j_n$ denotes one of the $n!$ permutations.

Example 6.8

If the image f is

$$f = \begin{pmatrix} 3 & 7 \\ 8 & 2 \end{pmatrix}_{4,\ 5}$$

then $\mathrm{DET}(f) = 3 \cdot 2 - 7 \cdot 8 = -50$.

Bound matrices can be partitioned into subimages or blocks just like usual matrices.

Example 6.9

The image

$$f = \begin{pmatrix} 3 & 4 & 2 & \vdots & 0 & 0 \\ 1 & 8 & 9 & \vdots & 3 & 2 \\ 2 & 1 & 0 & \vdots & 1 & 4 \\ \cdots & \cdots & \cdots & \vdots & \cdots & \cdots \\ 2 & 3 & 5 & \vdots & 7 & 8 \end{pmatrix}_{9,\,0}$$

is partitioned into four blocks. The blocks are the following subimages: the square bound matrix

$$g = \begin{pmatrix} 3 & 4 & 2 \\ 1 & 8 & 9 \\ 2 & 1 & 0 \end{pmatrix}_{9,\,0}$$

the bound matrix

$$h = \begin{pmatrix} 0 & 0 \\ 3 & 2 \\ 1 & 4 \end{pmatrix}_{12,\,0}$$

the bound row vector

$$e = (2 \quad 3 \quad 5)_{9,\,-3}$$

and the bound row vector

$$q = (7 \quad 8)_{12,\,-3}$$

In Example 6.9, the subimages of f are obtained by using the SELECT operation. Furthermore, when the EXTADD operation is employed on all of them, f is obtained.

A row or column bound vector in an image can be mapped into a true vector using VECTRAN. The vector will have the same number of tuples as the bound vector if and only if the bound vector has information density 1. When this is the case, the linear independence and linear dependence type concepts of usual vector algebra can be attributed to bound vectors. Therefore, the concept of rank for a saturated bound matrix f can be defined. Here, the rank of f, denoted RANK(f), is the greatest number of linearly independent rows or columns of f. Rows of f occur by partitioning f into bound row vectors, and columns of f arise from a partition of f into bound column vectors. The rank could alternately be defined as the dimension of the largest sized nonvanishing determinant in f.

Example 6.10

If

$$f = \begin{pmatrix} 1 & 0 & 1 & 0 \\ 2 & 1 & 3 & 0 \\ 0 & 2 & 2 & 0 \\ 1 & 1 & 2 & 0 \end{pmatrix}_{8,\,9}$$

then RANK$(f) = 2$. This is most easily seen by selecting the following bound column vectors from f:

$$e = \begin{pmatrix} 1 \\ 2 \\ 0 \\ 1 \end{pmatrix}_{8,\,9} \qquad g = \begin{pmatrix} 0 \\ 1 \\ 2 \\ 1 \end{pmatrix}_{9,\,9} \qquad a = \begin{pmatrix} 1 \\ 3 \\ 2 \\ 2 \end{pmatrix}_{10,\,9}$$

and the zero bound column vector

$$b = \begin{pmatrix} 0 \\ 0 \\ 0 \\ 0 \end{pmatrix}_{11,\,9}$$

Let $\vec{e}$, $\vec{g}$, $\vec{a}$, and $\vec{b}$ be the respective outputs of VECTRAN applied to e, g, a, and b. Since $\vec{a} = \vec{e} + \vec{g}$, where $\vec{e}$ and $\vec{g}$ are not scalar multiples of one another, and since $\vec{b}$ is a zero vector, there are only two linearly independent vectors among the four. Hence, RANK$(f) = 2$.

For square bound matrices which are saturated, it is possible to find eigenvalues and eigenvectors. The procedure is exactly the same as for regular matrices. The method is discussed when the singular-value decomposition of images is defined.

Throughout the text, bound matrices have had values a_{pq} equal to a real number or a star. When working with the discrete Fourier transform, complex quantities are employed. For this reason, it is necessary to introduce an extended definition of image by which nonreal complex gray values are also allowed in a bound matrix. The complex-valued bound matrices will only be employed in this text in conjunction with the discrete Fourier transform. While the use of complex entries in regular matrices is commonplace, care must be taken when utilizing some of the operations previously defined on bound matrices. In particular, two complex-valued bound matrices cannot be employed as inputs in the MAX and MIN operators. Nevertheless, most other operations defined for (real) bound matrices can be employed with complex-valued images as inputs.

Example 6.11

Let

$$f = \begin{pmatrix} 2i & 3 + i \\ 4 & 5 - i \end{pmatrix}_{0,\,0}$$

and
$$h = \begin{pmatrix} i & 4 - 2i \\ 5 & 0 \end{pmatrix}_{0,\,0}$$

where $i^2 = -1$. These images can be added pixelwise:

$$\text{ADD}(f, h) = \begin{pmatrix} 3i & 7 - i \\ 9 & 5 - i \end{pmatrix}_{0,\,0}$$

They can be multiplied pixelwise:

$$\text{MULT}(f, h) = \begin{pmatrix} -2 & 14 - 2i \\ 20 & 0 \end{pmatrix}_{0,\,0}$$

They can be multiplied as matrices:

$$\text{X}(f, h) = \begin{pmatrix} 13 + 5i & 4 + 8i \\ 25 - i & 16 - 8i \end{pmatrix}_{0,\,0}$$

A scalar multiplication can also be performed:

$$\text{SCALAR}(2; f) = \begin{pmatrix} 4i & 6 + 2i \\ 8 & 10 - 2i \end{pmatrix}_{0,\,0}$$

Numerous other operations can be performed. For instance,

Moreover, the conjugate $\overline{f}$ of f can be defined by conjugating each entry of f. Thus,

$$\overline{f} = \begin{pmatrix} -2i & 3 - i \\ 4 & 5 + i \end{pmatrix}_{0,\,0}$$

6.6 Matrix Image Transforms

A number of transform techniques useful in image processing can be described using a common schema. This common representation involves two types of entities, bound matrices and regular matrices, which are (matrix) multiplied together.

Given the n by m bound matrix $(b_{pq})_{rt} = b$, this structure can be premultiplied by an arbitrary k by n matrix A, possibly having complex-valued entries. It can also be postmultiplied by an m by s matrix C. In the former case, the resulting structure is the k by m *complex bound matrix* $(d_{ls})_{rt} = d$. Specifically,

$$d_{ls} = \sum_{i=1}^{n} a_{li} b_{is}$$

is the entry in row l and column s, where $1 \le l \le k$, $1 \le s \le m$, and b_{is} is the entry in B. If any of the entries b_{is} are equal to a star, then d_{ls} is a star; otherwise, it will be the real or complex number specified. This type of multiplication is denoted PREMLT(A, b) and symbolized using the block diagram

Matrix $A \longrightarrow$ [PREMLT] $\longrightarrow d$ Bound matrix

Bound matrix $b \longrightarrow$

The postmultiplication operation of b by C is an n by s bound matrix. It is represented as POSTMLT(b, C) $= e$ and symbolized by the block diagram

Bound matrix $b \longrightarrow$ [POSTMLT] $\longrightarrow e$ Bound matrix

Matrix $C \longrightarrow$

The entry e_{pq}, $1 \le p \le n$, $1 \le q \le s$, in e, is found by the summation

$$e_{pq} = \sum_{i=1}^{n} b_{pi} c_{iq}$$

If any b_{pi} is a star, so also is e_{pq}.

Example 6.12

Consider the matrix

$$A = \begin{pmatrix} 3 & 4 & 2 \\ -1 & 2 & 3 \end{pmatrix}$$

and the image

$$b = \begin{pmatrix} 3 & 2 \\ * & 4 \\ 1 & 1 \end{pmatrix}_{0,0}$$

Then a 2 by 2 bound matrix d results from the PREMLT operation:

$A \longrightarrow$ [PREMLT] $\longrightarrow \begin{pmatrix} * & 24 \\ * & 9 \end{pmatrix}_{0,0}$

$b \longrightarrow$

As a further illustration, an example is presented where A is not real valued.

Example 6.13

Consider the 3 by 2 matrix

$$A = \begin{pmatrix} i & 2+i \\ 3i & 2 \\ 0 & 1 \end{pmatrix}$$

and the 2 by 2 bound matrix

$$b = \begin{pmatrix} 2 & -1 \\ 1 & 1 \end{pmatrix}_{3,\,3}$$

Then

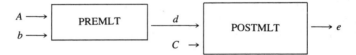

$$A \longrightarrow \boxed{\text{PREMLT}} \longrightarrow d = \begin{pmatrix} 2 + 3i & 2 \\ 2 + 6i & 2 - 3i \\ 1 & 1 \end{pmatrix}_{3,\,3}$$

where the first row, first column entry of the matrix d is $d(3, 3) = i \times 2 + (2 + i) \times 1 = 2i + 2 + i = 2 + 3i$.

The postmultiplication operation is performed similarly to the premultiplication operation, as illustrated in Example 6.14.

Example 6.14

Consider the operations

$$A \longrightarrow \boxed{\text{PREMLT}} \xrightarrow{\;d\;} \boxed{\text{POSTMLT}} \longrightarrow e$$

where

$$A = (3 \quad 4)$$

$$b = \begin{pmatrix} 1 & -1 \\ 5 & 2 \end{pmatrix}_{0,\,0}$$

and

$$C = \begin{pmatrix} 1 & 2 & 1 \\ 3 & 4 & 2 \end{pmatrix}$$

This could be written symbolically as $d = Ab$ and $e = dC$, or as $e = AbC$. Performing the indicated operations,

$$d = (23 \quad 5)_{0,\,0}$$

and

$$e = (38 \quad 66 \quad 33)_{0,\,0}$$

Many transforms specified in the following sections will involve a pre- and post-multiplication of a given image by a matrix. These transform techniques are called *matrix image transforms*. They are represented symbolically by

$$e = AbC$$

or

$$e = \text{POSTMLT}[\text{PREMLT}(A, b), C]$$

They can also be represented using block diagrams, as in Example 6.13. Figure 6.5 illustrates the transform procedure and its use in problem solving.

Referring to Figure 6.5, after the transform e is obtained, simple operations are performed on it to yield another bound matrix. An inverse matrix image transform is then taken. The situation most often encountered is where

$$e = AbC$$

with A and C being nonsingular square matrices. In this case, the inverse matrix image transform is obtained by employing the inverses of matrices A and C, A^{-1} and C^{-1}, respectively. Here, $g = A^{-1}fC^{-1}$ or equivalently $g = \text{POSTMLT[PREMLT}(A^{-1}, f), C^{-1}]$. Using block diagrams, the inverse matrix image transform is given by

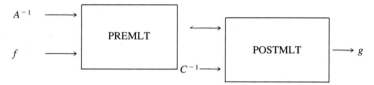

It should be noted that, when the original image b is saturated and if there exists A^{-1} and C^{-1}, then $b = A^{-1}eC^{-1}$. However, if b is not saturated, the preceding result need not hold. Example 6.15 illustrates this point.

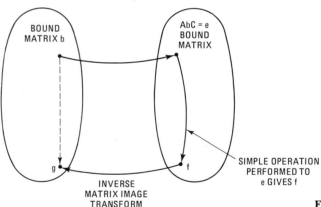

Figure 6.5 Matrix Image Transform

Example 6.15

Let

$$A = \begin{pmatrix} 1 & 2 \\ 4 & 3 \end{pmatrix}$$

Then

$$A^{-1} = \frac{\begin{pmatrix} -3 & 2 \\ 4 & -1 \end{pmatrix}}{5}$$

Let

$$C = \begin{pmatrix} 2 & 0 \\ 0 & 1 \end{pmatrix}$$

Then

$$C^{-1} = \frac{\begin{pmatrix} 1 & 0 \\ 0 & 2 \end{pmatrix}}{2}$$

If the bound matrix b is given by

$$b = \begin{pmatrix} 1 & 0 \\ * & 0 \end{pmatrix}_{0,0}$$

then

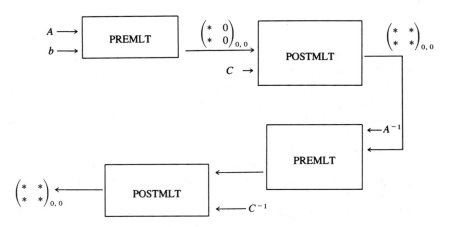

6.7 Notation When Using the Matrix Image Transform

To facilitate the applications which follow, a slight change in notation will be consistently utilized when matrix image transforms are employed. Given an m by n matrix, be it regular or bound, the first row will be labeled 0, the next row will be labeled 1, and so on. The last row will be labeled $m - 1$. Similarly, the columns will be labeled 0 through

$n - 1$ inclusive. As a result, the regular m by n matrix and the bound m by n matrix b are respectively represented in the following manner when used in matrix image transforms:

$$\begin{pmatrix} a_{00} & a_{01} & \cdots & a_{0,\,n-1} \\ a_{10} & a_{11} & \cdots & a_{1,\,n-1} \\ \vdots & \vdots & & \vdots \\ a_{m-1,\,0} & a_{m-1,\,1} & \cdots & a_{m-1,\,n-1} \end{pmatrix}$$

and

$$\begin{pmatrix} b_{00} & b_{01} & \cdots & b_{0,\,n-1} \\ b_{10} & b_{11} & \cdots & b_{1,\,n-1} \\ \vdots & \vdots & & \vdots \\ b_{m-1,\,0} & b_{m-1,\,1} & \cdots & b_{m-1,\,n-1} \end{pmatrix}_{p,\,q}$$

An additional convention regarding notation must be presented prior to the application of the matrix image transform. It will be assumed that for any m by n bound matrix f employed in the next few sections that the row and column labeling agrees with the functional labeling. In other words, $f(p, q) = f_{pq}$, where p is the row, q is the column, $0 \le p \le m - 1$ and $0 \le q \le n - 1$. Hence the bound matrix f is given by

$$\begin{pmatrix} f(0, 0) & f(0, 1) & \cdots f(0, n - 1) \\ f(1, 0) & f(1, 1) & \cdots f(1, n - 1) \\ \vdots & \vdots & \vdots \\ f(m - 1, 0) & f(m - 1, 1) \cdots f(m - 1, n - 1) \end{pmatrix}_{r,\,s}$$

It must be emphasized that in this new notation the expression $f(p, q)$ does not mean that f has the gray value $f(p, q)$ at the pixel location (p, q); rather, $f(p, q)$ indicates the gray value for the row–column position (p, q). Two points are important. First, this new notation is only employed when the matrix image transform is being utilized, and it is employed for the sake of notational convenience. All matrix image transform techniques can be implemented using the customary notation, but that would lead to excessively ornate symbolism.

A second point is that any image can be transformed into one in which its original pixel gray values appear in a manner consistent with the new matrix image transform notation. The transformation can be accomplished with translations and rotations, and therefore can be inverted by similar operations. This representation will not be given explicitly in the text because it is nothing more than a somewhat complicated notational exercise.

Example 6.16

Consider the image

$$f = \begin{pmatrix} 1 & 2 \\ * & -3 \end{pmatrix}_{2,\,1}$$

In the usual functional gray-value notation,

$$f(2, 1) = 1, \qquad f(3, 1) = 2$$
$$f(2, 0) = * \qquad f(3, 0) = -3$$

This notation simply places a gray value at the appropriate spot on the grid. In the new notation to be temporarily adopted for use with the matrix image transform,

$$f(0, 0) = 1, \qquad f(0, 1) = 2$$
$$f(1, 0) = * \qquad f(1, 1) = -3$$

In this latter notation, $f(0, 0)$ denotes the gray value at the zero row and zero column location. Even though the functional notation is not employed, the location of the bound matrix is still specified through the use of the subscript pair $(2, 1)$. To put the matter succinctly, the bound matrix is written in exactly the same format; the only difference is the interpretation of the notation $f(p, q)$. The gray-level entry in the uppermost, leftmost location is called $f(0, 0)$, instead of being called $f(2, 1)$.

With the new representation, the previously discussed pre- and postmultiplication of the m by n bound matrix f by the square matrices A and B is

$$F = AfB$$

where the p, q entry in the m by n bound matrix F is

$$F(p, q) = \sum_{r=0}^{m-1} \sum_{s=0}^{n-1} a_{pr} f(r, s) b_{sq}$$

with $0 \le p \le m - 1$ and $0 \le q \le n - 1$.

Example 6.17

Let the image

$$f = \begin{pmatrix} f(0, 0) & f(0, 1) \\ f(1, 0) & f(1, 1) \end{pmatrix}_{x, y}$$

$$A = \begin{pmatrix} a_{00} & a_{01} \\ a_{10} & a_{11} \end{pmatrix}$$

and

$$B = \begin{pmatrix} b_{00} & b_{01} \\ b_{10} & b_{11} \end{pmatrix}$$

Then, in $F = AfB$,

$$F(0, 0) = \sum_{r=0}^{1} \sum_{s=0}^{1} a_{0r} f(r, s) b_{s0}$$

that is,

$$F(0, 0) = a_{00} f(0, 0) b_{00} + a_{00} f(0, 1) b_{10} + a_{01} f(1, 0) b_{00}$$
$$+ a_{01} f(1, 1) b_{10}$$

This value of $F(0, 0)$, together with similar computations for $F(0, 1)$, $F(1, 0)$, and $F(1, 1)$, can easily be validated by actually multiplying out the matrices. Indeed,

$$Af = \begin{pmatrix} a_{00}f(0, 0) + a_{01}f(1, 0) & a_{00}f(0, 1) + a_{01}f(1, 1) \\ a_{10}f(0, 0) + a_{11}f(1, 0) & a_{10}f(0, 1) + a_{11}f(1, 1) \end{pmatrix}_{x, y}$$

and $AfB = F$ can be easily found.

6.8 Discrete Fourier Transform

Given the m by n bound matrix

$$f = \begin{pmatrix} f(0, 0) & f(0, 1) & \ldots f(0, n-1) \\ f(1, 0) & f(1, 1) & \ldots f(1, n-1) \\ \vdots & \vdots & \vdots \\ f(m-1, 0) & f(m-1, 1) & \ldots f(m-1, n-1) \end{pmatrix}_{u, v}$$

the *discrete Fourier transform* (DFT) of f is the image

$$F = \begin{pmatrix} F(0, 0) & F(0, 1) & \ldots F(0, n-1) \\ F(1, 0) & F(1, 1) & \ldots F(1, n-1) \\ \vdots & \vdots & \vdots \\ F(m-1, 0) & F(m-1, 1) & \ldots F(m-1, n-1) \end{pmatrix}_{u, v}$$

where the gray value $F(p, q)$ in F is given by

$$F(p, q) = \frac{1}{m \cdot n} \sum_{r=0}^{m-1} \sum_{s=0}^{n-1} f(r, s) e^{-2\pi i \left(\frac{r \cdot p}{m} + \frac{s \cdot q}{n} \right)}, \qquad i = \sqrt{-1}$$

As indicated in Section 6.6, the matrix image transform $F = AfB$ has a typical entry

$$F(p, q) = \sum_{r=0}^{m-1} \sum_{s=0}^{n-1} a_{pr} f(r, s) b_{sq}$$

This expression can be compared with that of the discrete Fourier transform. It follows that the a_{pr} element of the m by m matrix A would be

$$a_{pr} = \frac{e^{\frac{(-2\pi i\, rp)}{m}}}{m}, \qquad 0 \le p, r \le m - 1$$

In a similar manner, the b_{sq} entry in B must be

$$b_{sq} = \frac{e^{\frac{(-2\pi i\, sq)}{n}}}{n}, \qquad 0 \le s, q \le n - 1$$

Consequently, the discrete Fourier transform of the image f could be written as a matrix image transform where matrices A and B contain exponentials as their entries. The m by m matrix A is

$$A = \frac{1}{m} \begin{pmatrix} 1 & 1 & 1 & \cdots & 1 \\ 1 & e^{(-2\pi i)/m} & e^{(-4\pi i)/m} & \cdots & e^{[-2\pi i(m-1)]/m} \\ 1 & e^{(-4\pi i)/m} & e^{(-8\pi i)/m} & \cdots & e^{[-4\pi i(m-1)]/m} \\ \vdots & \vdots & \vdots & & \vdots \\ 1 & e^{[-2\pi i(m-1)]/m} & e^{[-4\pi i(m-1)]/m} & \cdots & e^{[-2\pi i(m-1)^2]/m} \end{pmatrix}$$

The matrix B is similarly described.

Example 6.18

Find the discrete Fourier transform F of the image

$$f = \begin{pmatrix} 1 & 0 \\ 2 & 0 \\ 0 & 1 \\ -1 & 0 \end{pmatrix}_{4,\,5}$$

Since f is a 4 by 2 bound matrix,

$$F = AfB$$

where A is a 4 by 4 matrix of exponentials and B is a 2 by 2 matrix of exponentials as described previously. The matrix image transform gives

$$F = \frac{1}{8} \begin{pmatrix} 1 & 1 & 1 & 1 \\ 1 & e^{(-2\pi i)/4} & e^{(-4\pi i)/4} & e^{(-6\pi i)/4} \\ 1 & e^{(-4\pi i)/4} & e^{(-8\pi i)/4} & e^{(-12\pi i)/4} \\ 1 & e^{(-6\pi i)/4} & e^{(-12\pi i)/4} & e^{(-18\pi i)/4} \end{pmatrix} \begin{pmatrix} 1 & 0 \\ 2 & 0 \\ 0 & 1 \\ -1 & 0 \end{pmatrix}_{4,\,5} \begin{pmatrix} 1 & 1 \\ 1 & e^{(-2\pi i)/2} \end{pmatrix}$$

Simplification of the entries in the A and B matrices gives

$$e^{(-\pi i)/2} = -i = e^{(-5\pi i)/2} = e^{(-9\pi i)/2}$$

$$e^{-\pi i} = -1 = e^{-3\pi i}$$

$$e^{(-3\pi i)/2} = i$$

$$e^{-2\pi i} = 1 = e^0$$

Hence

$$F = \frac{1}{8} \begin{pmatrix} 1 & 1 & 1 & 1 \\ 1 & -i & -1 & i \\ 1 & -1 & 1 & -1 \\ 1 & i & -1 & -i \end{pmatrix} \begin{pmatrix} 1 & 0 \\ 2 & 0 \\ 0 & 1 \\ -1 & 0 \end{pmatrix}_{4,\,5} \begin{pmatrix} 1 & 1 \\ 1 & -1 \end{pmatrix}$$

One multiplication yields

$$F = \frac{1}{8} \begin{pmatrix} 1 & 1 & 1 & 1 \\ 1 & -i & -1 & i \\ 1 & -1 & 1 & -1 \\ 1 & i & -1 & -i \end{pmatrix} \begin{pmatrix} 1 & 1 \\ 2 & 2 \\ 1 & -1 \\ -1 & -1 \end{pmatrix}_{4,\,5}$$

while a second gives

$$F = \frac{1}{8} \begin{pmatrix} 3 & 1 \\ -3i & 2 - 3i \\ 1 & -1 \\ 3i & 2 + 3i \end{pmatrix}_{4,\,5}$$

It should be emphasized that, in general, the image F has complex entries.

Applications involving the discrete Fourier transform simply modify the transformed image F. An inverse transform is applied to this result. The inverse Fourier transform is defined in Section 6.9.

6.9 Inverse Discrete Fourier Transform

The m by m matrix A and the n by n matrix B employed in the discrete Fourier transform (DFT) of f are both nonsingular. As a consequence, the inverse matrix image transform exists. It is called the *inverse discrete Fourier transform*. If it happens that f is saturated, the (forward) DFT, which is given by $F = AfB$, is directly invertible with $f = A^{-1}FB^{-1}$. If f is not saturated (if there are stars in the minimal bound matrix for f), the preceding inverse relation might not hold. In any event, for any complex image G, the new image $A^{-1}GB^{-1} = g$ will be called the *inverse discrete Fourier transform* (IDFT) of G.

The inverses of the matrices A and B are very easy to find since it can be shown that $A^{-1} = m\,\overline{A}$ and $B^{-1} = n\,\overline{B}$, where $\overline{A}$ and $\overline{B}$ are the respective conjugates of A and B.

Example 6.19

Referring to Example 6.18, the *Fourier matrix A* was given by

$$A = \frac{1}{4} \begin{pmatrix} 1 & 1 & 1 & 1 \\ 1 & -i & -1 & i \\ 1 & -1 & 1 & -1 \\ 1 & i & -1 & -i \end{pmatrix}$$

Therefore,

$$A^{-1} = 4\overline{A} = \begin{pmatrix} 1 & 1 & 1 & 1 \\ 1 & i & -1 & -i \\ 1 & -1 & 1 & -1 \\ 1 & -i & -1 & i \end{pmatrix}$$

A simple multiplication shows the correctness of this relation; indeed, $AA^{-1} = I$, where I is the identity matrix.

In the general case, the matrix A^{-1} has the general element $a_{pq} = e^{(2\pi i pq)/m}$. Consequently,

$$A^{-1} = \begin{pmatrix} 1 & 1 & 1 & \cdots & 1 \\ 1 & e^{(2\pi i)/m} & e^{(4\pi i)/m} & \cdots & e^{[2\pi i(m-1)]/m} \\ 1 & e^{(4\pi i)/m} & e^{(8\pi i)/m} & \cdots & e^{[4\pi i(m-1)]/m} \\ \vdots & \vdots & \vdots & & \vdots \\ 1 & e^{[2\pi i(m-1)]/m} & e^{[4\pi i(m-1)]/m} & \cdots & e^{[2\pi i(m-1)^2]/m} \end{pmatrix}$$

Note that $(A^{-1})' = A^{-1}$.

Example 6.20 illustrates the use of the inverse discrete Fourier transform in retrieving a saturated image.

Example 6.20

Refer to Example 6.18, where the discrete Fourier transform of f is

$$F = AfB = \frac{1}{8} \begin{pmatrix} 3 & 1 \\ -3i & 2-3i \\ 1 & -1 \\ 3i & 2+3i \end{pmatrix}_{4,\ 5}$$

The inverse transform is $g = nm \, \overline{A} F \overline{B}$, and so

$$g = \frac{1}{8} \begin{pmatrix} 1 & 1 & 1 & 1 \\ 1 & i & -1 & -i \\ 1 & -1 & 1 & -1 \\ 1 & -i & -1 & i \end{pmatrix} \begin{pmatrix} 3 & 1 \\ -3i & 2-3i \\ 1 & -1 \\ 3i & 2+3i \end{pmatrix}_{4,\ 5} \begin{pmatrix} 1 & 1 \\ 1 & -1 \end{pmatrix}$$

$$= \frac{1}{8} \begin{pmatrix} 4 & 4 \\ 8 & 8 \\ 4 & -4 \\ -4 & -4 \end{pmatrix}_{4,\ 5} \begin{pmatrix} 1 & 1 \\ 1 & -1 \end{pmatrix}$$

$$= \frac{1}{8} \begin{pmatrix} 8 & 0 \\ 16 & 0 \\ 0 & 8 \\ -8 & 0 \end{pmatrix}_{4,\ 5} = f$$

6.10 Cyclic Convolutions

Let f and h be m by n saturated bound matrices at the same location (u, v) in the pixel plane. The *cyclic* (or *circular*) convolution of f with h is the m by n bound matrix g, also located at (u, v), with gray values

$$g(p, q) = \frac{1}{mn} \sum_{r=0}^{m-1} \sum_{s=0}^{n-1} f(r, s) h(p-r, q-s)$$

It is assumed that the values of h not defined in the sum are obtained by a periodic extension:

$$h(am + j, bn + k) = h(j, k)$$

for all integers a and b. Example 6.21 illustrates the methodology for taking cyclic convolutions. The cyclic convolution of f and h is denoted by CCONV(f, g). The block diagram is

$$
\begin{array}{ccc}
f \longrightarrow & \\
 & \boxed{\text{CCONV}} \longrightarrow & \text{CCONV}(f, g) \\
h \longrightarrow &
\end{array}
$$

Example 6.21

Let

$$
f = \begin{pmatrix} 1 & 0 \\ 2 & 0 \\ 0 & 1 \\ -1 & 0 \end{pmatrix}_{4,\ 5}
$$

as in Example 6.18. Let

$$
h = \begin{pmatrix} 2 & 3 \\ 0 & 0 \\ 4 & 1 \\ -1 & 0 \end{pmatrix}_{4,\ 5}
$$

Letting $g = \text{CCONV}(f, h)$, the summation formula for cyclic convolution yields

$$
g(3, 1) = \frac{1}{8} \sum_{r=0}^{3} \sum_{s=0}^{1} f(r, s)\, h(3 - r, 1 - s)
$$

$$
= \frac{1}{8} [f(0, 0) \times h(3, 1) + f(0, 1) \times h(3, 0) + f(1, 0) \times h(2, 1)
$$

$$
+ f(2, 0) \times h(1, 1) + f(1, 1) \times h(2, 0) + f(3, 0) \times h(0, 1)
$$

$$
+ f(3, 1) \times h(0, 0) + f(2, 1) \times h(1, 0)]
$$

$$
= \frac{-1}{8}
$$

Also,

$$
g(3, 0) = \frac{1}{8} \sum_{r=0}^{3} \sum_{s=0}^{1} f(r, s)\, h(3 - r, -s)
$$

To compute $g(3, 0)$, we must employ the ($s = 1$) terms $h(3, -1)$, $h(2, -1)$, $h(1, -1)$, and $h(0, -1)$. These are obtained from h by periodic extension. In other words, these terms refer to the $s = -1$ column of h, which is the same as the $s = 1$ column of h. Hence $h(3, -1) = 0$, $h(2, -1) = 1$, $h(1, -1) = 0$, and $h(0, -1) = 3$. In any event, $g(3, 0) = \frac{5}{8}$. Proceeding through the remaining entries of g, we obtain

$$
g = \frac{1}{8} \begin{pmatrix} 1 & 7 \\ 0 & 4 \\ 8 & 3 \\ 5 & -1 \end{pmatrix}_{4,\ 5}
$$

The steps involved in finding $g = \text{CCONV}(f, h)$ from f and h can be rigorously specified by utilizing operators previously introduced; indeed, the cyclic convolution is actually a type of moving-average filter. However, because of the changes introduced to facilitate the use of the matrix image transform, it cannot be constructed directly from the FILTER operation introduced in Chapter 2. Nevertheless, it can be constructed in a similar manner by using 180° rotation, translation, addition, multiplication, and extension. An intuitive description of the template specification of CCONV is now presented.

Take the 180° rotation of h, $\text{NINETY}^2(h)$. Then extend that rotation periodically by filling the plane with copies of $\text{NINETY}^2(h)$ (see Figure 6.6). Once this has been done, translate f so that its uppermost, leftmost pixel is treated as the center of the *mask* f, and so that this center sits in turn over each pixel of the first copy of $\text{NINETY}^2(h)$. Proceed lexigraphically top down and left to right with this "center," each time performing a dot product operation DOT. Record each dot product output in the corresponding pixel location of a new image, to be temporarily called g_0. Finally, rotate g_0 180° and multiply by $1/mn$ to obtain $g = \text{CCONV}(f, h)$. Example 6.22 illustrates this template methodology.

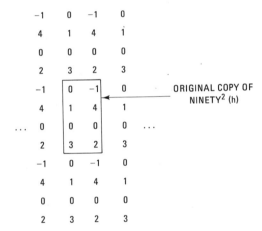

Figure 6.6 Periodic Representation of Circular Convolution

Example 6.22

The result of Example 6.21 will be obtained by the template technique. Referring to Figure 6.6, the image f is translated so that its $(0, 0)$ pixel (matrix image transform notation) is placed over the $(0, 0)$ pixel of the original copy of $\text{NINETY}^2(h)$. A dot product operation is performed on the periodically extended image to obtain

$$g_0(0, 0) = \text{DOT}\left[\begin{pmatrix} 0 & -1 \\ 1 & 4 \\ 0 & 0 \\ 3 & 2 \end{pmatrix}, \begin{pmatrix} 1 & 0 \\ 2 & 0 \\ 0 & 1 \\ -1 & 0 \end{pmatrix}\right] = -1$$

Now f is translated so that its $(0, 0)$ pixel is placed over the $(1, 0)$ pixel of the original copy of $\text{NINETY}^2(h)$. Once again a dot product is performed to obtain

$$g_0(1, 0) = \text{DOT}\left[\begin{pmatrix} 1 & 4 \\ 0 & 0 \\ 3 & 2 \\ 0 & -1 \end{pmatrix}, \begin{pmatrix} 1 & 0 \\ 2 & 0 \\ 0 & 1 \\ -1 & 0 \end{pmatrix}\right] = 3$$

Continuing with the translations and dot products, we obtain

$$g_0 = \begin{pmatrix} -1 & 5 \\ 3 & 8 \\ 4 & 0 \\ 7 & 1 \end{pmatrix}$$

A rotation of g_0 through $180°$ and scalar multiplication by $\frac{1}{8}$ gives $g = \frac{1}{8}\text{ NINETY}^2(g_0)$, which agrees with the output of Example 6.21.

Example 6.22 motivates the use of circulant matrices in conjunction with the VEC-TRAN operation in determining circular convolutions.

6.11 Vector Transformation Method for Finding Circular Convolutions

Given two m by n images f and h located at the same pixel, if $g = \text{CCONV}(f, h)$ is desired using the VECTRAN technique, then the following steps should be employed.

Step 1: Let $\vec{f} = \text{VECTRAN}(f)$ and determine $\text{DOMAIN}(f)$.
Step 2: Let $K = \text{NINETY}^2(h)$. Then

$$K = \begin{pmatrix} h(m - 1, n - 1) & \cdots & h(m - 1, 0) \\ \vdots & & \vdots \\ h(0, n - 1) & \cdots & h(0, 0) \end{pmatrix}_{p, q}$$

Let $\vec{t} = \text{VECTRAN}(K)$ and $\vec{t}\,'$ be the transpose of $\vec{t}$. Form the bound matrix K_1, which is a cyclic shift of the rows of K:

$$K_1 = \begin{pmatrix} h(m - 2, n - 1) & \cdots & h(m - 2, 0) \\ \vdots & & \vdots \\ h(0, n - 1) & \cdots & h(0, 0) \\ h(m - 1, n - 1) & \cdots & h(m - 1, 0) \end{pmatrix}_{p, q}$$

Let $\vec{t}_1 = \text{VECTRAN}(K_1)$ and form $\vec{t}\,'_1$. The bound matrix K_1 could be found by selecting the last row from K, followed by using the extension and translation operations. In a similar fashion, an additional cyclic shift of the rows, this time from K_1, should be performed to obtain

$$K_2 = \begin{pmatrix} h(m - 3, n - 1) & \cdots & h(m - 3, 0) \\ \vdots & & \vdots \\ h(0, n - 1) & \cdots & h(0, 0) \\ h(m - 1, n - 1) & \cdots & h(m - 1, 0) \\ h(m - 2, n - 1) & \cdots & h(m - 2, 0) \end{pmatrix}_{p, q}$$

Then let $\vec{t}_2 = \text{VECTRAN}(K_2)$ and form $\vec{t}_2'$. Continue this process until K_{m-1} is found along with $\vec{t}_{m-1}'$, where

$$K_{m-1} = \begin{pmatrix} h(0, n-1) & \cdots & h(0, 0) \\ \vdots & & \vdots \\ h(1, n-1) & \cdots & h(1, 0) \end{pmatrix}_{p, q}$$

$\vec{t}_{m-1} = \text{VECTRAN}(K_{m-1})$ and $\vec{t}_{m-1}'$ is the transpose of $\vec{t}_{m-1}$. Next go back to K and perform a cyclic shift of the first column to obtain

$$K_m = \begin{pmatrix} h(m-1, n-2) & \cdots & h(m-1, 0) & h(m-1, n-1) \\ \vdots & & \vdots & \vdots \\ h(0, n-2) & \cdots & h(0, 0) & h(0, n-1) \end{pmatrix}_{p, q}$$

Let $\vec{t}_m = \text{VECTRAN}(K_m)$ and find $\vec{t}_m'$. All the cyclic row shifts must be applied to K_m just as they were applied to K. The corresponding VECTRAN operations should also be taken. We obtain

$$K_{m+1} = \begin{pmatrix} h(m-2, n-2) & \cdots & h(m-2, 0) & h(m-2, n-1) \\ \vdots & & \vdots & \vdots \\ h(0, n-2) & \cdots & h(0, 0) & h(0, n-1) \\ h(m-1, n-2) & \cdots & h(m-1, 0) & h(m-1, n-1) \end{pmatrix}_{p, q}$$

$\vec{t}_{m+1} = \text{VECTRAN}(K_{m+1})$, and the transpose $\vec{t}_{m+1}'$. Then we find K_{m+2}, $\vec{t}_{m+2}$, $\vec{t}_{m+2}'$, $\ldots$,

$$K_{2m-1} = \begin{pmatrix} h(0, n-2) & \cdots & h(0, 0) & h(0, n-1) \\ \vdots & & \vdots & \vdots \\ h(1, n-2) & \cdots & h(1, 0) & h(1, n-1) \end{pmatrix}_{p, q}$$

$\vec{t}_{2m-1} = \text{VECTRAN}(K_{2m-1})$, and $\vec{t}_{2m-1}'$. Now we go back to K_m and give a cyclic shift to the first column to obtain K_{2m}. The process of cyclically shifting the rows is continued, thereby giving K_{2m}, K_{2m+1}, $\ldots$, K_{3m-1} and the vectors $\vec{t}_{2m}$, $\ldots$, $\vec{t}_{3m-1}'$. This is repeated until all the $m-1$ row cyclic shifts are applied to the $n-1$ column shift matrices and the corresponding vectors found. Consequently, the final vector, $\vec{t}_{nm-1}'$, is the transpose of $\vec{t}_{nm-1} = \text{VECTRAN}(K_{nm-1})$, where

$$K_{nm-1} = \begin{pmatrix} h(0, 0) & \cdots & h(0, 1) \\ \vdots & & \vdots \\ h(1, 0) & \cdots & h(1, 1) \end{pmatrix}_{p, q}$$

Step 3: Next, the following vector equation, in matrix partitioned form, should be written:

$$
\vec{g} = \begin{pmatrix}
\vec{t}\,'_{nm\,-\,1} \\
\vdots \\
\vec{t}\,'_{(n\,-\,1)m\,-\,1} \\
\hline
\vdots \\
\hline
\vec{t}\,'_{2m\,-\,1} \\
\vdots \\
\vec{t}\,'_{m} \\
\hline
\vec{t}\,'_{m\,-\,1} \\
\vdots \\
\vec{t}\,'_{1} \\
\vec{t}\,'
\end{pmatrix}
$$

In each of the n partitioned submatrices (indicated by dashed lines), there will be n submatrices, which are *circulant* submatrices. Circulant matrices have rows that are cyclic shifts of each other. They are also Toeplitz matrices; that is, all $-45°$ diagonal terms are the same.

    Step 4: The final step is to use $\vec{g}$ and DOMAIN(f), and to divide by mn, to find g.

Example 6.23

    Suppose

$$
f = \begin{pmatrix} 2 & 0 \\ 0 & 3 \\ 1 & -1 \end{pmatrix}_{0,\,0} , \qquad
h = \begin{pmatrix} 0 & 3 \\ 1 & 1 \\ -1 & 0 \end{pmatrix}_{0,\,0}
$$

and $g = \text{CCONV}(f, h)$ is desired. The steps outlined give the following result:

    Step 1: Form

$$
\vec{f} = \text{VECTRAN}(f) = \begin{pmatrix} 2 \\ 0 \\ 1 \\ 0 \\ 3 \\ -1 \end{pmatrix}
$$

Note that DOMAIN(f) = $[(0, 0), (0, -1), (0, -2), (1, 0), (1, -1), (1, -2)]$.

Step 2: Form

$$K = \text{NINETY}^2(h) = \begin{pmatrix} 0 & -1 \\ 1 & 1 \\ 3 & 0 \end{pmatrix}_{-1,\ 2}$$

Then

$$\vec{t} = \text{VECTRAN}(K) = \begin{pmatrix} 0 \\ 1 \\ 3 \\ -1 \\ 1 \\ 0 \end{pmatrix}$$

and

$$\vec{t}\,' = (0 \quad 1 \quad 3 \quad -1 \quad 1 \quad 0)$$

A cyclic shift of K is performed to obtain

$$K_1 = \begin{pmatrix} 1 & 1 \\ 3 & 0 \\ 0 & -1 \end{pmatrix}_{-1,\ 2}$$

Then

$$\vec{t}_1 = \text{VECTRAN}(K_1) = \begin{pmatrix} 1 \\ 3 \\ 0 \\ 1 \\ 0 \\ -1 \end{pmatrix}$$

and

$$\vec{t}_1' = (1 \quad 3 \quad 0 \quad 1 \quad 0 \quad -1)$$

All told, there are two distinct cyclic shifts of K and its column shift matrix K_3. Therefore, there arises $\vec{t}\,'$ and five other transposes resulting from the five cyclic shifts. Other than $\vec{t}\,'$ and $\vec{t}_1'$, the others are

$$\vec{t}_2' = (3 \quad 0 \quad 1 \quad 0 \quad -1 \quad 1)$$

$$\vec{t}_3' = (-1 \quad 1 \quad 0 \quad 0 \quad 1 \quad 3)$$

$$\vec{t}_4' = (1 \quad 0 \quad -1 \quad 1 \quad 3 \quad 0)$$

$$\vec{t}_5' = (0 \quad -1 \quad 1 \quad 3 \quad 0 \quad 1)$$

Step 3: Form the vector equation in matrix partition form:

$$\vec{g} = \begin{pmatrix} \vec{t}\,'_5 \\ \vec{t}\,'_4 \\ \vec{t}\,'_3 \\ \vec{t}\,'_2 \\ \vec{t}\,'_1 \\ \vec{t}\,' \end{pmatrix} \vec{f}$$

$$= \left(\begin{array}{rrr:rrr} 0 & -1 & 1 & 3 & 0 & 1 \\ 1 & 0 & -1 & 1 & 3 & 0 \\ -1 & 1 & 0 & 0 & 1 & 3 \\ \hdashline 3 & 0 & 1 & 0 & -1 & 1 \\ 1 & 3 & 0 & 1 & 0 & -1 \\ 0 & 1 & 3 & -1 & 1 & 0 \end{array} \right) \begin{pmatrix} 2 \\ 0 \\ 1 \\ 0 \\ 3 \\ -1 \end{pmatrix}$$

Notice that the submatrices indicated by dashed lines are circulant matrices. Multiplication gives

$$\vec{g} = \begin{pmatrix} 0 \\ 10 \\ -2 \\ 3 \\ 3 \\ 6 \end{pmatrix}$$

Step 4: Using the domain information along with $\vec{g}$ gives

$$g = \frac{1}{6} \begin{pmatrix} 0 & 3 \\ 10 & 3 \\ -2 & 6 \end{pmatrix}_{0,\,0}$$

6.12 Discrete Fourier Transform for Determining Cyclic Convolutions

Cyclic convolutions are easily found using the discrete Fourier transform. We use the following procedure to find $g = \text{CCONV}(f, h)$:

1) Take the discrete Fourier transform F of f and the discrete Fourier transform H of h.
2) Let $G = \text{MULT}(F, H)$.
3) The image g is found by taking the inverse discrete Fourier tranform of G.

The procedure is outlined in Figure 6.7.

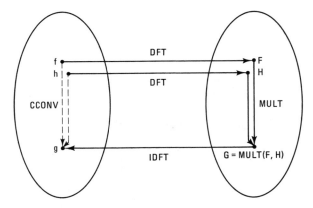

Figure 6.7 Use of DFT To Find CCONV

Example 6.24

Refer to Example 6.21, where f and h were cyclically convolved. In Example 6.18, the discrete Fourier transform of F was found to be

$$F = \frac{1}{8} \begin{pmatrix} 3 & 1 \\ -3i & 2-3i \\ 1 & -1 \\ 3i & 2+3i \end{pmatrix}_{4,\,5}$$

In a similar manner, the discrete Fourier transform of h is

$$H = \frac{1}{8} \begin{pmatrix} 9 & 1 \\ -i & -4-i \\ 11 & 3 \\ -i & -4+i \end{pmatrix}_{4,\,5}$$

A simple multiplication gives

$$G = \text{MULT}(F, H) = \frac{1}{64} \begin{pmatrix} 27 & 1 \\ -3 & -11+10i \\ 11 & -3 \\ -3 & -11-10i \end{pmatrix}_{4,\,5}$$

The inverse discrete Fourier transform of G is

$$g = \frac{1}{64} \begin{pmatrix} 1 & 1 & 1 & 1 \\ 1 & i & -1 & -i \\ 1 & -1 & 1 & -1 \\ 1 & -i & -1 & i \end{pmatrix} \begin{pmatrix} 27 & 1 \\ -3 & -11+10i \\ 11 & -3 \\ -3 & -11-10i \end{pmatrix}_{4,\,5} \begin{pmatrix} 1 & 1 \\ 1 & -1 \end{pmatrix}$$

$$= \frac{1}{64} \begin{pmatrix} 1 & 1 & 1 & 1 \\ 1 & i & -1 & -i \\ 1 & -1 & 1 & -1 \\ 1 & -i & -1 & i \end{pmatrix} \begin{pmatrix} 28 & 26 \\ -14+10i & 8-10i \\ 8 & 14 \\ -14-10i & 8+10i \end{pmatrix}_{4,\,5}$$

$$= \frac{1}{64} \begin{pmatrix} 8 & 56 \\ 0 & 32 \\ 64 & 24 \\ 40 & -8 \end{pmatrix}_{4,\ 5} = \frac{1}{8} \begin{pmatrix} 1 & 7 \\ 0 & 4 \\ 8 & 3 \\ 5 & -1 \end{pmatrix}_{4,\ 5}$$

This agrees with the result of Example 6.21.

6.13 Cyclic Correlation and the Discrete Fourier Transform

An operation similar to the cyclic convolution is the cyclic correlation of two m by n saturated bound matrices located at (u, v) in the pixel plane. The result of correlating f and h is the m by n bound matrix g, also located at (u, v), with gray values

$$g(p,\ q) = \frac{1}{mn} \sum_{r\ =\ 0}^{m\ -\ 1} \sum_{s\ =\ 0}^{n\ -\ 1} f(r,\ s)\ h(p\ +\ r,\ q\ +\ s)$$

The values of h not defined in the sum are obtained by periodic extension, by assuming that $h(am + j, bn + k) = h(j, k)$ for all integers a and b. The result of circularly correlating images f and h is denoted by CCOR(f, h). It has the block diagram

$$f \longrightarrow \boxed{\quad\text{CCOR}\quad} \longrightarrow \quad \text{CCOR}(f,\ h)$$
$$h \longrightarrow$$

Since the gray values of g are found from summing the product of the gray values of f and translates of the gray values of h, this operation (as is the case with circular convolution) can be represented in terms of more primitive block operations. Indeed, in a manner similar to the template implementation of the cyclic convolution, let f_1 be the image obtained from placing copies of f directly to the left, to the right, above, below, and at the corners of the original image f. (Note that we do not rotate f.) Let h_1 be h translated so that its uppermost, leftmost pixel is situated at the origin. Then

$$\text{CCOR}(f,\ h) = \text{SCALAR}\left[\frac{1}{mn};\ \text{FILTER}(f_1;\ h_1) \right]$$

In other words, the cyclic correlation is nothing but the scalar multiple of a moving-average filter of an image which has been extended periodically one frame in each direction of the grid.

Like cyclic convolution, cyclic correlation can be easily performed using the DFT. We use the following procedure to find $g = \text{CCOR}(f, h)$:

1) Take the DFT F of f and the DFT H of h.
2) Form the conjugate $\overline{H}$ of the complex image H.
3) Let $G = \text{MULT}(F, \overline{H})$.

4) $g = \text{CCOR}(f, h)$ is found by taking the inverse discrete Fourier transform (IDFT) of G.

A simple example will be given to illustrate these relationships.

Example 6.25

Given the images

$$f = \begin{pmatrix} 2 \\ 3 \end{pmatrix}_{0,\,0} \qquad \text{and} \qquad h = \begin{pmatrix} 1 \\ -1 \end{pmatrix}_{0,\,0}$$

$$g = \text{CCOR}(f, h) = \begin{pmatrix} g(0,0) \\ g(1,0) \end{pmatrix}_{0,\,0} = \begin{pmatrix} \dfrac{2-3}{2} \\ \dfrac{3-2}{2} \end{pmatrix}_{0,\,0} = \begin{pmatrix} -\dfrac{1}{2} \\ \dfrac{1}{2} \end{pmatrix}_{0,\,0}$$

This result could also be found using the transform technique indicated previously:

1) $F = \text{DFT}(f) = AfB = \dfrac{1}{2} \begin{pmatrix} 1 & 1 \\ 1 & -1 \end{pmatrix} \begin{pmatrix} 2 \\ 3 \end{pmatrix}_{0,\,0}$ (1)

$$= \begin{pmatrix} \dfrac{5}{2} \\ -\dfrac{1}{2} \end{pmatrix}_{0,\,0}$$

Similarly, $H = \text{DFT}(h) = \dfrac{1}{2} \begin{pmatrix} 1 & 1 \\ 1 & -1 \end{pmatrix} \begin{pmatrix} 1 \\ -1 \end{pmatrix}_{0,\,0}$ (1)

$$= \begin{pmatrix} 0 \\ 1 \end{pmatrix}_{0,\,0}$$

2) In this example, H is a bound matrix in the true sense; there are no non-real-valued complex entries, so $\overline{H} = H$.

3) $G = \text{MULT}(F, H) = \begin{pmatrix} 0 \\ -\dfrac{1}{2} \end{pmatrix}_{0,\,0}$

4) $g = \text{IDFT}(G) = A^{-1}GB^{-1}$

$$= \begin{pmatrix} 1 & 1 \\ 1 & -1 \end{pmatrix} \begin{pmatrix} 0 \\ -\dfrac{1}{2} \end{pmatrix}_{0,\,0}$$ (1)

$$= \begin{pmatrix} -\dfrac{1}{2} \\ \dfrac{1}{2} \end{pmatrix}_{0,\,0}$$

6.14 Discrete Cosine Transform

The *discrete cosine transform* is also a matrix image transform. As the name suggests, the elements of the transform matrices involve cosines evaluated at certain points. Part of the motivation behind utilizing cosines in the form given relates to the Chebyshev polynomials. The Chebyshev polynomials, when evaluated at the cosine entries in the matrices subsequently to be given, exhibit certain orthonormal properties. For the n by n bound matrix f, the discrete cosine transform of f is given by

$$g = AfA'$$

This transform is denoted by $g = \text{DCT}(f)$. The block diagram illustrating the transform is

$$f \longrightarrow \boxed{\text{DCT}} \longrightarrow g$$

The matrix A has entries

$$a_{jk} = \begin{cases} \dfrac{1}{\sqrt{n}}, & \text{for all } k = 0 \\[2em] \sqrt{\dfrac{2}{n}} \cos\left[\dfrac{(2j + 1)\,k\pi}{2n}\right], & \text{for } k = 1, 2, \dots, n - 1 \\ & \qquad j = 0, 1, \dots, n - 1 \end{cases}$$

A' is the transpose of the matrix A. The inverse discrete cosine transform of g is given by

$$h = A'gA$$

The block diagram illustrating this transform is

$$g \longrightarrow \boxed{\text{IDCT}} \longrightarrow h$$

When f is saturated,

$$f \longrightarrow \boxed{\text{DCT}} \longrightarrow \boxed{\text{IDCT}} \longrightarrow h = f$$

Example 6.26

Let

$$f = \begin{pmatrix} 3 & 2 \\ 4 & -2 \end{pmatrix}_{0,\,0}$$

Then $g = \mathrm{DCT}(f)$ is given by

$$
g = \begin{pmatrix} \dfrac{1}{\sqrt{2}} & \cos\dfrac{\pi}{4} \\[2mm] \dfrac{1}{\sqrt{2}} & \cos\dfrac{3\pi}{4} \end{pmatrix} \begin{pmatrix} 3 & 2 \\ 4 & -2 \end{pmatrix}_{0,\,0} \begin{pmatrix} \dfrac{1}{\sqrt{2}} & \dfrac{1}{\sqrt{2}} \\[2mm] \cos\dfrac{\pi}{4} & \cos\dfrac{3\pi}{4} \end{pmatrix}
$$

$$
= \begin{pmatrix} \dfrac{7}{2} & \dfrac{7}{2} \\[2mm] \dfrac{3}{2} & -\dfrac{5}{2} \end{pmatrix}_{0,\,0}
$$

Furthermore, since f is saturated, $h = \mathrm{IDCT}(g) = f$. The discrete cosine transform is used in a manner similar to the discrete Fourier transform.

6.15 Hadamard Transform

Let f be an m by n bound matrix where m and n are both powers of 2. The *Hadamard transform* g of f is a matrix image transform with $g = H_{mm} f H_{nn}$, where H_{mm} and H_{nn} are Hadamard matrices. This transform is also represented by

$$
g = \mathrm{HADTR}(f)
$$

and in block diagram form as

$$
f \;\longrightarrow\; \boxed{\quad \mathrm{HADTR} \quad} \;\longrightarrow\; g
$$

The Hadamard matrix $H_{2,\,2}$ is defined by

$$
H_{2,\,2} = \begin{pmatrix} 1 & 1 \\ 1 & -1 \end{pmatrix}
$$

All other Hadamard matrices $H_{2q,\,2q}$ are defined recursively, in matrix partitioned form, by

$$
H_{2q,\,2q} = \begin{pmatrix} H_{q,\,q} & H_{q,\,q} \\ H_{q,\,q} & -H_{q,\,q} \end{pmatrix}
$$

For instance,

$$
H_{4,\,4} = \begin{pmatrix} 1 & 1 & 1 & 1 \\ 1 & -1 & 1 & -1 \\ 1 & 1 & -1 & -1 \\ 1 & -1 & -1 & 1 \end{pmatrix}
$$

which is the Kronecker product of $H_{2, 2}$ with itself:

$$H_{4, 4} = H_{2, 2} \; \textcircled{K} \; H_{2, 2}$$

In general, if q is any nonnegative, integral power of 2, then

$$H_{2q, 2q} = H_{2, 2} \; \textcircled{K} \; H_{2, 2} \; \textcircled{K} \; \ldots \; \textcircled{K} \; H_{2, 2}$$

Moreover, the Hadamard matrix is symmetric,

$$H'_{q, q} = H_{q, q}$$

and the matrix $q^{-\frac{1}{2}} H_{q, q}$ is orthogonal,

$$\frac{1}{q} H_{q, q} \cdot H'_{q, q} = I$$

Consequently,

$$H_{q, q}^{-1} = \frac{1}{q} H_{q, q} \quad .$$

and the inverse Hadamard transform is given by

$$\text{IHADTR}(g) = \frac{1}{m \cdot n} H_{m, m} g H_{n, n}$$

The inverse Hadamard transform has the block diagram

$$g \quad \longrightarrow \quad \boxed{\text{IHADTR}} \quad \longrightarrow \quad \text{IHADTR}(g)$$

If f is saturated, then

$$f \quad \longrightarrow \quad \boxed{\text{HADTR}} \quad \longrightarrow \quad \boxed{\text{IHADTR}} \quad \longrightarrow \quad f$$

and the inverse transform exactly inverts the forward transform. The Hadamard transform is used in a manner similar to the DFT.

Example 6.27

Let

$$f = \begin{array}{cc} 2 & 4 \\ 1 & 0 \\ 0 & 0 \\ 3 & 1 \\ 4 & 2 \\ 0 & 2 \\ 2 & 3 \\ 1 & 1 \end{array}_{3, 4}$$

Then $g = \text{HADTR}(f) = H_{8,\,8}\, f\, H_{2,\,2}$, where

$$
H_{8,\,8} = \left(\begin{array}{cccc:cccc}
1 & 1 & 1 & 1 & 1 & 1 & 1 & 1 \\
1 & -1 & 1 & -1 & 1 & -1 & 1 & -1 \\
1 & 1 & -1 & -1 & 1 & 1 & -1 & -1 \\
1 & -1 & -1 & 1 & 1 & -1 & -1 & 1 \\
\hdashline
1 & 1 & 1 & 1 & -1 & -1 & -1 & -1 \\
1 & -1 & 1 & -1 & -1 & 1 & -1 & 1 \\
1 & 1 & -1 & -1 & -1 & -1 & 1 & 1 \\
1 & -1 & -1 & 1 & -1 & 1 & 1 & -1
\end{array}\right)
$$

Since

$$
fH_{2,\,2} = \left(\begin{array}{cc}
6 & -2 \\
1 & 1 \\
0 & 0 \\
4 & 2 \\
6 & 2 \\
2 & -2 \\
5 & -1 \\
2 & 0
\end{array}\right)_{3,\,4}
$$

it follows that

$$
g = \left(\begin{array}{cc}
26 & 0 \\
8 & -2 \\
4 & -2 \\
10 & 4 \\
-4 & 2 \\
-6 & -8 \\
2 & -4 \\
8 & -6
\end{array}\right)_{3,\,4}
$$

6.16 *Singular-value Decomposition Transform*

The singular-value decomposition transform is another matrix-type transform. When applied to an m by n bound matrix of information density 1, that is, a saturated bound matrix, it yields another m by n bound matrix g of simpler form than f. It is denoted by $g = \text{SVDT}(f)$. The block diagram is

$$
f \longrightarrow \boxed{\text{SVDT}} \longrightarrow g
$$

The resulting image will be in a *diagonal form*; it will have pixels consisting of all zero gray values, with the possible exception of positive values along the $-45°$ diagonal starting at the $g(0,\,0)$ entry. The number of positive entries along the $-45°$ diagonal equals the rank of the bound matrix.

Example 6.28

If

$$f = \begin{pmatrix} 1 & 2 \\ 4 & 3 \end{pmatrix}_{0,\,0}$$

then f has rank 2, since the determinant of f equals $-5 \neq 0$. It follows that

$$g = \text{SVDT}(f) = \begin{pmatrix} \sigma_1 & 0 \\ 0 & \sigma_2 \end{pmatrix}_{0,\,0}$$

where the values σ_1 and σ_2 are positive and will be found later.

Example 6.29

If

$$f = \begin{pmatrix} 1 & 2 & 0 \\ 2 & 4 & 0 \\ 3 & 6 & 0 \\ 4 & 8 & 0 \end{pmatrix}_{4,\,7}$$

then f has rank 1 and consequently

$$\text{SVDT}(f) = \begin{pmatrix} \sigma_1 & 0 & 0 \\ 0 & 0 & 0 \\ 0 & 0 & 0 \\ 0 & 0 & 0 \end{pmatrix}_{4,\,7}$$

with $\sigma_1 > 0$.

Example 6.30

If

$$f = \begin{pmatrix} 1 & 2 & 0 & 0 \\ 4 & 3 & 0 & 0 \\ 0 & 0 & 1 & 2 \end{pmatrix}_{7,\,3}$$

then f has rank 3. Consequently,

$$\text{SVDT}(f) = \begin{pmatrix} \sigma_1 & 0 & 0 & 0 \\ 0 & \sigma_2 & 0 & 0 \\ 0 & 0 & \sigma_3 & 0 \end{pmatrix}_{7,\,3}$$

with $\sigma_1,\,\sigma_2,\,\sigma_3 > 0$.

The singular-value decomposition transform is useful in image restoration, compression, and numerous other areas of image processing.

It will be seen that $g = \text{SVDT}(f)$ can be written as $g = AfC$, where A and C are orthogonal matrices. It is customary to order the values σ_i in g such that $\sigma_1 \geqslant \sigma_2 \geqslant \cdots$

$\geq \sigma_r > 0$. Just what the values σ_i are and how to compute them along with matrices A and C will be demonstrated.

Given the saturated bound matrix f of rank r, we use the following steps to find A, C, and g:

Step 1: Form the image $h = X(f', f)$, where f' is the transpose of the bound matrix f, and X denotes the matrix multiplication operation for bound matrices.

Step 2: Since the n by n matrix h is symmetric and positive semidefinite, the eigenvalues of h are all nonnegative. Furthermore, h has rank r, and therefore there are r nonzero eigenvalues. Find these eigenvalues, denote them by σ_i^2, and order them such that $\sigma_1^2 \geq \sigma_2^2 \geq \cdots \geq \sigma_r^2 > 0$. From this, g can be found by stringing the values σ_i along the $-45°$ diagonal.

Step 3: Find all the eigenvectors $\vec{v}_i$ associated with the eigenvalues of h. The eigenvectors associated with distinct eigenvalues will be orthogonal and should be normalized. The eigenvectors (if more than one) associated with the same eigenvalue will be linearly independent and therefore should be orthonormalized. Note that $n - r$ of the eigenvalues are zero and the eigenvector(s) corresponding to this eigenvalue must also be found.

Step 4: Let $C = (\vec{v}_1 \ \vec{v}_2 \ldots \vec{v}_n)$.

Step 5: Define the r by n matrix B whose rows consist of the transposes of the eigenvectors corresponding to nonzero eigenvalues:

$$B = \begin{pmatrix} \vec{v}'_1 \\ \vec{v}'_2 \\ \vdots \\ \vec{v}'_r \end{pmatrix}$$

Let D be the r by r diagonal matrix with entries $1/\sigma_i$:

$$D = \begin{pmatrix} \dfrac{1}{\sigma_1} & 0 & 0 & \ldots & 0 \\ 0 & \dfrac{1}{\sigma_2} & 0 & \ldots & 0 \\ \vdots & \vdots & \vdots & & \vdots \\ 0 & 0 & 0 & \ldots & \dfrac{1}{\sigma_r} \end{pmatrix}$$

Set $U = DBf'$. U is an r by m matrix. Define

$$A = \begin{pmatrix} U \\ L \end{pmatrix}$$

where L is any $m - r$ by m matrix such that A is orthogonal. This will give $g = \text{SVDT}(f) = AfC$. This ends the construction.

The inverse singular-value decomposition transform of g is given by

$$h = A'gC'$$

It is denoted $h = \mathrm{ISVDT}(g)$. In block diagram form,

$$g \quad \longrightarrow \quad \boxed{\quad \mathrm{ISVDT} \quad} \quad \longrightarrow \quad h$$

Furthermore, under the conditions set forth herein it is always true that

$$f \longrightarrow \boxed{\quad \mathrm{SVDT} \quad} \stackrel{g}{\longrightarrow} \boxed{\quad \mathrm{ISVDT} \quad} \longrightarrow h = f$$

Example 6.31

Let

$$f = \begin{pmatrix} 1 & 2 \\ 4 & 3 \end{pmatrix}_{0,\,0}$$

as in Example 6.28. The bound matrix $g = \mathrm{SVDT}(f) = AfC$ will be found using the steps just outlined.

Step 1: Notice that

$$f' = \begin{pmatrix} 1 & 4 \\ 2 & 3 \end{pmatrix}_{0,\,0}$$

and

$$h = X(f', f) = \begin{pmatrix} 17 & 14 \\ 14 & 13 \end{pmatrix}_{0,\,0}$$

Step 2: The eigenvalues of h are found by solving the characteristic equation

$$\det\begin{pmatrix} 17 - \tau & 14 \\ 14 & 13 - \tau \end{pmatrix} = 0$$

That is, $\tau^2 - 30\tau + 25 = 0$. Hence the eigenvalues of h are $\sigma_1^2 = 15 + 10\sqrt{2}$ and $\sigma_2^2 = 15 - 10\sqrt{2}$.
Consequently,

$$g = \begin{pmatrix} \sqrt{15 + 10\sqrt{2}} & 0 \\ 0 & \sqrt{15 - 10\sqrt{2}} \end{pmatrix}_{0,0}$$

and all that remains to be found are the matrices A and C.

Step 3: For eigenvalue σ_1^2, the eigenvector $\begin{pmatrix} x \\ y \end{pmatrix}$ is found from

$$\begin{pmatrix} 2 - 10\sqrt{2} & 14 \\ 14 & -2 - 10\sqrt{2} \end{pmatrix} \begin{pmatrix} x \\ y \end{pmatrix} = 0$$

Therefore, the normalized eigenvector is

$$\vec{v}_1 = \frac{\begin{pmatrix} 2 + 10\sqrt{2} \\ 14 \end{pmatrix}}{\sqrt{400 + 40\sqrt{2}}}$$

The second normalized eigenvector is

$$\vec{v}_2 = \frac{\begin{pmatrix} 2 - 10\sqrt{2} \\ 14 \end{pmatrix}}{\sqrt{400 - 40\sqrt{2}}}$$

Step 4: The orthogonal matrix C is therefore

$$C = \begin{pmatrix} \dfrac{2 + 10\sqrt{2}}{\sqrt{400 + 4\sqrt{2}}} & \dfrac{2 - 10\sqrt{2}}{\sqrt{400 - 4\sqrt{2}}} \\ \dfrac{14}{\sqrt{400 + 4\sqrt{2}}} & \dfrac{14}{\sqrt{400 - 4\sqrt{2}}} \end{pmatrix}$$

Step 5: In this case, since $r = n$, the matrix

$$B = \begin{pmatrix} \dfrac{2 + 10\sqrt{2}}{\sqrt{400 + 40\sqrt{2}}} & \dfrac{14}{\sqrt{400 + 40\sqrt{2}}} \\ \dfrac{2 - 10\sqrt{2}}{\sqrt{400 - 40\sqrt{2}}} & \dfrac{14}{\sqrt{400 - 40\sqrt{2}}} \end{pmatrix}$$

and the matrix

$$D = \begin{pmatrix} \dfrac{1}{\sqrt{15 + 10\sqrt{2}}} & 0 \\ 0 & \dfrac{1}{\sqrt{15 - 10\sqrt{2}}} \end{pmatrix}$$

Consequently, $U = D B f'$ is a 2 by 2 matrix and L is not needed. $A = D B f'$ is easily found, thus providing all the unknowns in $g = A f C$.

Before the example is concluded, it should be mentioned that the eigenvalues of the bound matrix f itself are $\tau_1 = 5$ and $\tau_2 = -1$. Therefore, the spectral decomposition of f is not easily related to SVDT(f). However, it is interesting that for any symmetric positive semi-definite bound matrix f, SVDT(f) and the spectral decomposition do coincide.

6.17 Singular-value Decomposition for Least-squares Problems

The singular-value decomposition procedure given in Section 6.16 can be employed when least-squares solutions are needed in regular or bound matrix problems.

Consider the m by n matrix f of rank r, where $m \geqslant n = r$. If the solution to the matrix equation $f \vec{v} = \vec{b}$ is desired, then, as discussed in Section 6.4, $\vec{v} = f^+ \vec{b}$ is the least-squares solution, where f^+ is the pseudo-inverse of f.

If g is the singular-value decomposition of f, $g = $ SVDT(f), then g is representable as $g = A f C$, where A and C are orthogonal matrices and g is an all-zero matrix with the exception of positive entries along the main diagonal. Forming the inverse transform gives

$$f = A' \, g \, C'$$

Therefore,

$$f' = C \, g' \, A$$

and

$$(f'f)^{-1} = (C \, g' \, g \, C')^{-1}$$
$$= C(g'g)^{-1} \, C'$$

Thus,

$$f^+ = (f'f)^{-1} f' = C(g'g)^{-1} \, g' \, A = C \, g^+ \, A$$

In other words, the pseudo-inverse of a matrix f can be obtained from the pseudo-inverse of the singular-value decomposition matrix. The latter matrix is trivial to work with since it has nonzero entries only along the main diagonal. The procedure outlined is illustrated in Figure 6.8.

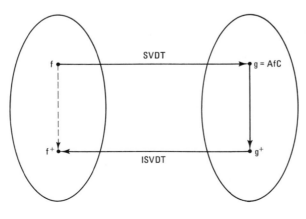

Figure 6.8 Singular-value Decomposition for Pseudo-Inverse Composition

Example 6.32

Assume that the sum of the gray values of a pixel p_1 and another pixel p_2 is observed to be equal to 3. However, the gray value of each pixel is independently observed to be equal to 1. Find the best estimate $(\hat{x}, \hat{y})$ in the least-squares sense for the gray value x of pixel p_1 and the gray value y of pixel p_2.

The preceding assumptions lead to a matrix equation of the form $f\,\vec{v} = \vec{b}$, where

$$f = \begin{pmatrix} 1 & 1 \\ 0 & 1 \\ 1 & 0 \end{pmatrix}$$

$$\vec{v} = \begin{pmatrix} x \\ y \end{pmatrix}$$

and

$$\vec{b} = \begin{pmatrix} 3 \\ 1 \\ 1 \end{pmatrix}$$

The singular-value decomposition of the rank 2 matrix f will be found next:

1) Letting $h = f'f$ gives

$$h = \begin{pmatrix} 2 & 1 \\ 1 & 2 \end{pmatrix}$$

2) The eigenvalues of h are found from the characteristic equation $\tau^2 - 4\tau + 3 = 0$, and so the eigenvalues are $\tau_1 = 3$ and $\tau_2 = 1$. It follows that

$$g = \begin{pmatrix} \sqrt{3} & 0 \\ 0 & 1 \\ 0 & 0 \end{pmatrix}$$

3) The normalized eigenvectors are

$$\vec{v}_1 = \frac{\begin{pmatrix} 1 \\ 1 \end{pmatrix}}{\sqrt{2}} \quad \text{and} \quad \vec{v}_2 = \frac{\begin{pmatrix} 1 \\ -1 \end{pmatrix}}{\sqrt{2}}$$

4) The matrix

$$C = \begin{pmatrix} \dfrac{1}{\sqrt{2}} & \dfrac{1}{\sqrt{2}} \\ \dfrac{1}{\sqrt{2}} & -\dfrac{1}{\sqrt{2}} \end{pmatrix}$$

5) Form the matrix

$$B = \begin{pmatrix} \dfrac{1}{\sqrt{2}} & \dfrac{1}{\sqrt{2}} \\ \dfrac{1}{\sqrt{2}} & -\dfrac{1}{\sqrt{2}} \end{pmatrix}$$

and let

$$D = \begin{pmatrix} \dfrac{1}{\sqrt{3}} & 0 \\ 0 & 1 \end{pmatrix}$$

$U = DBf'$ is easily found:

$$U = \begin{pmatrix} \dfrac{1}{\sqrt{3}} & 0 \\ 0 & 1 \end{pmatrix} \begin{pmatrix} \dfrac{1}{\sqrt{2}} & \dfrac{1}{\sqrt{2}} \\ \dfrac{1}{\sqrt{2}} & -\dfrac{1}{\sqrt{2}} \end{pmatrix} \begin{pmatrix} 1 & 0 & 1 \\ 1 & 1 & 0 \end{pmatrix}$$

$$= \begin{pmatrix} \dfrac{1}{\sqrt{6}} & \dfrac{1}{\sqrt{6}} \\ \dfrac{1}{\sqrt{2}} & -\dfrac{1}{\sqrt{2}} \end{pmatrix} \begin{pmatrix} 1 & 0 & 1 \\ 1 & 1 & 0 \end{pmatrix}$$

$$= \begin{pmatrix} \dfrac{2}{\sqrt{6}} & \dfrac{1}{\sqrt{6}} & \dfrac{1}{\sqrt{6}} \\ 0 & -\dfrac{1}{\sqrt{2}} & \dfrac{1}{\sqrt{2}} \end{pmatrix}$$

Since $A = \begin{pmatrix} U \\ L \end{pmatrix}$ must be a 3 by 3 matrix, the matrix L, which is a 1 by 3, must be found. The fact that A must be orthogonal implies that the bottom row of A is the cross product of the two top rows. Forming the cross product

$$\begin{array}{ccc|cc} \vec{i} & \vec{j} & \vec{k} & \vec{i} & \vec{j} \\[2mm] \dfrac{2}{\sqrt{6}} & \dfrac{1}{\sqrt{6}} & \dfrac{1}{\sqrt{6}} & \dfrac{2}{\sqrt{6}} & \dfrac{1}{\sqrt{6}} \\[2mm] 0 & -\dfrac{1}{\sqrt{2}} & \dfrac{1}{\sqrt{2}} & 0 & -\dfrac{1}{\sqrt{2}} \end{array}$$

gives

$$\dfrac{2}{\sqrt{12}}\vec{i} - \dfrac{2}{\sqrt{12}}\vec{j} - \dfrac{2}{\sqrt{12}}\vec{k}.$$

Consequently,

$$
A = \begin{pmatrix} \dfrac{2}{\sqrt{6}} & \dfrac{1}{\sqrt{6}} & \dfrac{1}{\sqrt{6}} \\[2ex] 0 & -\dfrac{1}{\sqrt{2}} & \dfrac{1}{\sqrt{2}} \\[2ex] \dfrac{2}{\sqrt{12}} & -\dfrac{2}{\sqrt{12}} & -\dfrac{2}{\sqrt{12}} \end{pmatrix}
$$

A check that $AfC = g$ follows.

$$
AfC = \begin{pmatrix} \dfrac{2}{\sqrt{6}} & \dfrac{1}{\sqrt{6}} & \dfrac{1}{\sqrt{6}} \\[2ex] 0 & -\dfrac{1}{\sqrt{2}} & \dfrac{1}{\sqrt{2}} \\[2ex] \dfrac{2}{\sqrt{12}} & -\dfrac{2}{\sqrt{12}} & -\dfrac{2}{\sqrt{12}} \end{pmatrix} \begin{pmatrix} 1 & 1 \\ 0 & 1 \\ 1 & 0 \end{pmatrix} \begin{pmatrix} \dfrac{1}{\sqrt{2}} & \dfrac{1}{\sqrt{2}} \\[2ex] \dfrac{1}{\sqrt{2}} & -\dfrac{1}{\sqrt{2}} \end{pmatrix}
$$

$$
= \begin{pmatrix} \dfrac{3}{\sqrt{6}} & \dfrac{3}{\sqrt{6}} \\[2ex] \dfrac{1}{\sqrt{2}} & -\dfrac{1}{\sqrt{2}} \\[2ex] 0 & 0 \end{pmatrix} \begin{pmatrix} \dfrac{1}{\sqrt{2}} & \dfrac{1}{\sqrt{2}} \\[2ex] \dfrac{1}{\sqrt{2}} & -\dfrac{1}{\sqrt{2}} \end{pmatrix}
$$

$$
= \begin{pmatrix} \dfrac{6}{\sqrt{12}} & 0 \\[2ex] 0 & \dfrac{2}{2} \\[2ex] 0 & 0 \end{pmatrix}
$$

$$
= \begin{pmatrix} \sqrt{3} & 0 \\ 0 & 1 \\ 0 & 0 \end{pmatrix} = g
$$

The pseudo-inverse of g is very easy to find.

$$
g^{+} = (g'g)^{-1}g' = \begin{pmatrix} \dfrac{1}{3} & 0 \\[2ex] 0 & 1 \end{pmatrix} \begin{pmatrix} \sqrt{3} & 0 & 0 \\ 0 & 1 & 0 \end{pmatrix} = \begin{pmatrix} \dfrac{\sqrt{3}}{3} & 0 & 0 \\[2ex] 0 & 1 & 0 \end{pmatrix}
$$

The pseudo-inverse of f is found from

$$
f^{+} = Cg^{+}A
$$

We obtain

$$f^+ = \begin{pmatrix} \frac{1}{\sqrt{2}} & \frac{1}{\sqrt{2}} \\ \frac{1}{\sqrt{2}} & -\frac{1}{\sqrt{2}} \end{pmatrix} \begin{pmatrix} \frac{\sqrt{3}}{3} & 0 & 0 \\ 0 & 1 & 0 \end{pmatrix} \begin{pmatrix} \frac{2}{\sqrt{6}} & \frac{1}{\sqrt{6}} & \frac{1}{\sqrt{6}} \\ 0 & -\frac{1}{\sqrt{2}} & \frac{1}{\sqrt{2}} \\ \frac{2}{\sqrt{12}} & -\frac{2}{\sqrt{12}} & -\frac{2}{\sqrt{12}} \end{pmatrix}$$

$$= \begin{pmatrix} \frac{1}{\sqrt{6}} & \frac{1}{\sqrt{2}} & 0 \\ \frac{1}{\sqrt{6}} & -\frac{1}{\sqrt{2}} & 0 \end{pmatrix} \begin{pmatrix} \frac{2}{\sqrt{6}} & \frac{1}{\sqrt{6}} & \frac{1}{\sqrt{6}} \\ 0 & -\frac{1}{\sqrt{2}} & \frac{1}{\sqrt{2}} \\ \frac{2}{\sqrt{12}} & -\frac{2}{\sqrt{12}} & -\frac{2}{\sqrt{12}} \end{pmatrix}$$

$$= \begin{pmatrix} \frac{1}{3} & -\frac{1}{3} & \frac{2}{3} \\ \frac{1}{3} & \frac{2}{3} & -\frac{1}{3} \end{pmatrix}$$

The solution in the least-squares sense to the original problem is

$$\hat{\vec{v}} = f^+ \vec{b} = \begin{pmatrix} \frac{4}{3} \\ \frac{4}{3} \end{pmatrix}$$

and the best estimate as to the value of gray for both pixels is $\frac{4}{3}$.

6.18 Outer Product Representation of the Singular-value Decomposition

The outer product representation of the singular-value decomposition is easily found using matrix partitioning. Given the matrix f of rank r,

$$g = \text{SVDT}(f) = AfC$$

where the matrices A and C are orthogonal. Furthermore, the columns of C consist of all the orthonormal eigenvectors of $f'f$; that is, $C = (\vec{v}_1 \quad \vec{v}_2 \dots \vec{v}_n)$. For convenience, let $\vec{c}_i = \vec{v}_i$.

The orthogonality of A and C gives

$$f = A'gC'$$

where

$$C' = \begin{pmatrix} \vec{c}\,'_1 \\ \vec{c}\,'_2 \\ \vdots \\ \vec{c}\,'_n \end{pmatrix}$$

Write the A' matrix as $(\vec{a}_1 \quad \vec{a}_2 \ldots \vec{a}_m)$, where each $\vec{a}_i$ is an m by 1 column vector in A'. Then, for an m by n matrix f with $m \geq n \geq r$, the equation $f = A'gC'$ becomes

$$f = (\vec{a}_1 \quad \vec{a}_2 \ldots \vec{a}_m) \begin{pmatrix} \sigma_1 & 0 & \ldots & 0 & 0 & \ldots & 0 \\ 0 & \sigma_2 & \ldots & 0 & 0 & \ldots & 0 \\ \vdots & \vdots & \ddots & \vdots & \vdots & & \vdots \\ 0 & 0 & \ldots & \sigma_r & 0 & \ldots & 0 \\ 0 & 0 & \ldots & 0 & 0 & \ldots & 0 \\ \vdots & \vdots & & \vdots & \vdots & & \vdots \\ 0 & 0 & \ldots & 0 & 0 & \ldots & 0 \end{pmatrix} \begin{pmatrix} \vec{c}\,'_1 \\ \vec{c}\,'_2 \\ \vdots \\ \vec{c}\,'_n \end{pmatrix}$$

As a result,

$$f = (\vec{a}_1 \quad \vec{a}_2 \ldots \vec{a}_m) \begin{pmatrix} \sigma_1 \vec{c}\,'_1 \\ \sigma_2 \vec{c}\,'_2 \\ \vdots \\ \sigma_r \vec{c}\,'_r \\ 0 \\ \vdots \\ 0 \end{pmatrix}$$

Therefore,

$$f = \sigma_1 \vec{a}_1 \vec{c}\,'_1 + \sigma_2 \vec{a}_2 \vec{c}\,'_2 + \cdots + \sigma_r \vec{a}_r \vec{c}\,'_r$$

gives the desired outer product representation of f.

When f is an m by n matrix of rank r with $n \geq m \geq r$, a similar discussion gives precisely the same conclusion.

Example 6.33

Refer to Example 6.32, where

$$f = \begin{pmatrix} \dfrac{2}{\sqrt{6}} & 0 & \dfrac{2}{\sqrt{12}} \\ \dfrac{1}{\sqrt{6}} & -\dfrac{1}{\sqrt{2}} & -\dfrac{2}{\sqrt{12}} \\ \dfrac{1}{\sqrt{6}} & \dfrac{1}{\sqrt{2}} & -\dfrac{2}{\sqrt{12}} \end{pmatrix} \begin{pmatrix} \sqrt{3} & 0 \\ 0 & 1 \\ 0 & 0 \end{pmatrix} \begin{pmatrix} \dfrac{1}{\sqrt{2}} & \dfrac{1}{\sqrt{2}} \\ \dfrac{1}{\sqrt{2}} & -\dfrac{1}{\sqrt{2}} \end{pmatrix}$$

By employing the outer product representation, it follows that

$$f = \sqrt{3} \begin{pmatrix} \frac{2}{\sqrt{6}} \\ \frac{1}{\sqrt{6}} \\ \frac{1}{\sqrt{6}} \end{pmatrix} \begin{pmatrix} \frac{1}{\sqrt{2}} & \frac{1}{\sqrt{2}} \end{pmatrix} + \begin{pmatrix} 0 \\ -\frac{1}{\sqrt{2}} \\ \frac{1}{\sqrt{2}} \end{pmatrix} \begin{pmatrix} \frac{1}{\sqrt{2}} & -\frac{1}{\sqrt{2}} \end{pmatrix}$$

$$= \begin{pmatrix} 1 & 1 \\ \frac{1}{2} & \frac{1}{2} \\ \frac{1}{2} & \frac{1}{2} \end{pmatrix} + \begin{pmatrix} 0 & 0 \\ -\frac{1}{2} & \frac{1}{2} \\ \frac{1}{2} & -\frac{1}{2} \end{pmatrix} = \begin{pmatrix} 1 & 1 \\ 0 & 1 \\ 1 & 0 \end{pmatrix}$$

This is the desired result.

EXERCISES

6.1. We are given three observations f_1, f_2, and f_3 of the image $g = (a \quad b)_{0, 0}$, where

$$f_1 = (2 \quad 2)_{0, 0}$$

$$f_2 = (* \quad 1)_{0, 0}$$

$$f_3 = (2 \quad *)_{0, 0}$$

Utilize the VECTRAN operation in conjunction with the pseudo-inverse procedure to find a least-squares intrapixel best estimate $\hat{g}$ of g.

6.2. Employ the least-squares estimation technique discussed in Example 6.4 for interpixel information. Use this model and the single observed image

$$f = \begin{pmatrix} 2 & 1 & 0 & 3 \\ 0 & 1 & 2 & 2 \\ 0 & 0 & 1 & 1 \end{pmatrix}_{-1, 1}$$

to determine the estimate $\hat{g}$ of $g = (a \quad b)_{0, 0}$.

6.3. Use the operation NINETY and TRAN in block diagram form to find the transpose of

$$f = \begin{pmatrix} 3 & 7 \\ 2 & 1 \\ 4 & 2 \end{pmatrix}_{7, 3}$$

Provide a trace of each operational step.

6.4. Show that the following bound matrix h is orthogonal; that is, $X(h', h) = ID(2)_{3, 3}$.

$$h = \begin{pmatrix} \cos \theta & -\sin \theta \\ \sin \theta & \cos \theta \end{pmatrix}_{3, 3}$$

Is h skew symmetric?

6.5. Let

$$f = \begin{pmatrix} 1 & 2 & 4 \\ 2 & 4 & 3 \\ 2 & 4 & 5 \end{pmatrix}_{3, 0}$$

(a) Find DET(f).
(b) What is RANK(f)?

6.6. Let

$$f = \begin{pmatrix} 3i & 2i \\ 4 - i & 5 \end{pmatrix}_{0, 3}$$

and

$$g = \begin{pmatrix} 2 & -i \\ 1 + i & 3 \end{pmatrix}_{0, 3}$$

Find the following complex-valued bound matrices:

(a) ADD(f, g)   (d) SCALAR($3; f$)
(b) MULT(f, g)   (e) EXTMULT[f, TRAN(f; 1, 1)]
(c) X(f, g)

6.7. Consider the image

$$f = \begin{pmatrix} 1 & 4 \\ 2 & 3 \end{pmatrix}_{3, 4}$$

Using the functional notation defined in Chapter 1, we have $f(3, 4) = 1$, $f(3, 3) = 2$, $f(4, 4) = 4$, and $f(4, 3) = 3$. What is $f(0, 0)$, $f(0, 1)$, $f(1, 0)$, and $f(1, 1)$ using the following?

(a) The functional notation of Chapter 1.
(b) The notation adapted in Section 6.7 for matrix image transforms.

6.8. Find the discrete Fourier transform G of the image

$$g = \begin{pmatrix} 1 & 0 \\ 2 & 1 \\ 0 & 2 \\ -1 & 0 \end{pmatrix}_{5, 6}$$

6.9. Find IDFT(G), where $G = $ DFT(g) and g is given in Exercise 6.8. Show all work.

6.10. Consider the image g of Exercise 6.8 and the image

$$f = \begin{pmatrix} 1 & 2 \\ 3 & 4 \\ 0 & 0 \\ 2 & 1 \end{pmatrix}_{5,\,6}$$

(a) Find CCONV(f, g) directly from the definition given in Section 6.10.
(b) Find CCONV(f, g) using VECTRAN and the circulant matrix approach shown in Section 6.11.
(c) Find CCONV(f, g) using the discrete Fourier transform approach outlined in Section 6.12.

6.11. Using the images f and g as given in Exercises 6.10 and 6.8, respectively, find CCOR(f, g).

6.12. Find $H_{8,\,8}$; also, set this up using $H_{8,\,8} = H_{2,\,2} \circledK H_{2,\,2} \circledK H_{2,\,2}$.

6.13. Let f be the image

$$\begin{pmatrix} 1 & 3 \\ 4 & 2 \end{pmatrix}_{2,\,2}$$

Find $g = \text{SVDT}(f)$.

6.14. Express f given in Exercise 6.13 using the outer product representation given in Section 6.18.

7

IMAGING ARCHITECTURE

This chapter has a multiple purpose: First, several state-of-the-art concurrent computer architectures are briefly described. The different computer organizations discussed are used in handling the difficult computational bound matrix operations found in digital image processing. Second, various examples are provided to illustrate how different computer designs can implement the same mathematical operations. These examples illustrate the importance of structuring data and equations in judicious ways, as well as the importance of algorithm development for multi-processing. Finally, the block diagram language developed in the text, along with the bound matrix representation, is employed in rigorously specifying the manner in which the distinct architectures perform their operations. A one-to-one correspondence exists between the bound matrix block diagram representations and output patterns as determined by the respective architectures. The architectures presented here are compatible with VLSI design and development philosophy. Systolic, wavefront array, and data-flow architectures are described.

7.1 Data-flow Systems

Data-flow is a method for connecting functions using flows of data. Data-flow architectures utilize graphical languages similar to the block diagram notation employed throughout this text. Unlike most conventional computers, which have program counters and utilize control flow, data-flow computers execute their instructions as soon as all the operands have arrived. After an instruction has been executed (or has fired), the result of the execution is transmitted to all other instructions which need this result as an input. Instructions fire in an asynchronous manner. Counters are employed for each instruction to keep count of the number of operands which have arrived and how many more operands are needed for instruction execution.

Information in a data-flow system is often organized utilizing *activity packets* (or *activity templates*). At the top of the activity template (depicted in Figure 7.1), the operation to be performed, the opcode, is specified. The number of operands needed for execution of the instruction is also given in the template. As operands arrive, this number is decremented in a special counter until it reaches zero, in which case execution of the instruction occurs. There is room in the template to store each of the operands as they arrive. Finally, the lower positions in the activity template contain the address of all other activity templates which need the result of this operation. As soon as an operation fires, the result is transmitted to all addresses specified and stored as operands in the destination activity templates. As an elementary illustration of how these activity packets are used, consider Example 7.1.

OPCODE	N
OPERAND 1	
OPERAND 2	
$\vdots$	
OPERAND N	
ADDRESS OF DESTINATION ACTIVITY TEMPLATE 1	
ADDRESS OF DESTINATION ACTIVITY TEMPLATE 2	
$\vdots$	
ADDRESS OF DESTINATION ACTIVITY TEMPLATE M	

Figure 7.1 Data Flow Activity Packet

Example 7.1

We wish to find the real part and the length L of the product of two complex numbers $z = x + iy$ and $w = u + iv$ using a data-flow architecture. We obtain $R = xu - yv$ as the real part of the product and $I = xv + yu$ as the imaginary part. Then

$$L = \sqrt{R^2 + I^2}$$

The result, using activity packets, is given in Figure 7.2.

In Example 7.1, the four multiply operations to the extreme left could all fire concurrently. The minus operation can only be executed after the product of y and v is formed, and the add operation on top can only fire after minus yv is formed and the product of x and u is created. As soon as this addition $[xu + (-yv)]$ is performed, the result is shipped to three places, one to R and the other two as inputs to a multiply activity packet which will form $(xu - yv)^2$.

Images could appear as operands in activity packets, and the opcodes could be the operations described in this text. As an illustration, consider Example 7.2.

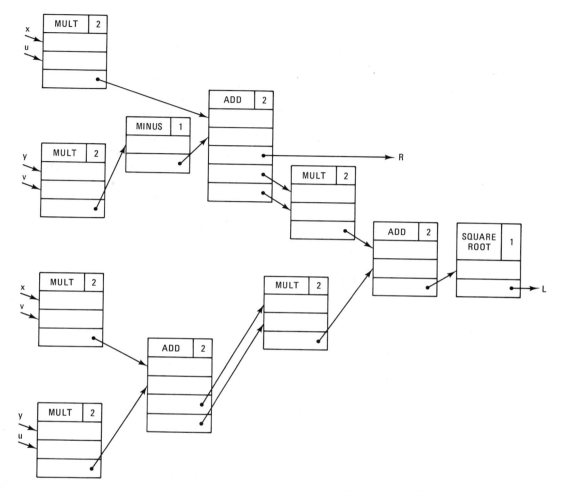

Figure 7.2 Data Flow Program for Length and Real Part of Complex Number

Example 7.2

Refer to Section 3.4, where a discussion of the Roberts gradient was given using various norms. In particular, the Roberts gradient using maxima criteria is illustrated in Figure 7.3. Thus, $g = \max(|G_1|, |G_2|)$, where $G_1 = x_0 - x_2$, $G_2 = x_1 - x_3$, and x_0, x_1, x_2 and x_3 are pixel gray values in the image f, located as follows:

x_2	x_1
x_3	x_0

This same operation is described using activity templates. Note that the only difference between the block diagrams of Figure 7.3 and the activity template approach given in

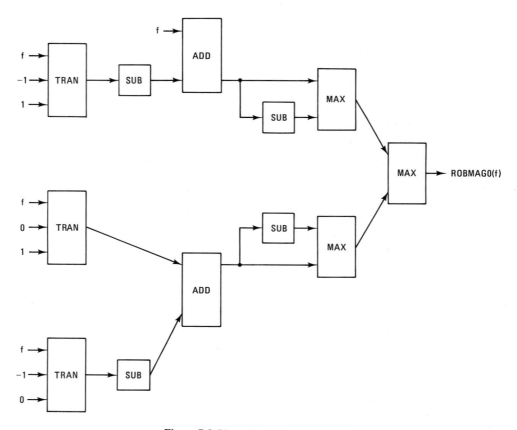

Figure 7.3 Block Diagram Of ROBMAG

Figure 7.4 is the slight difference in notation. The diagrams correspond in a one-to-one manner.

In Figure 7.3, the upper addition can be performed only after all the pixels in the image f have been translated one unit to the left and up one unit, and the gray values have been multiplied by -1. The bottom addition can be performed only after both TRAN $(f; 0, 1)$ and SUB[TRAN$(f; -1, 0)$] have been formed.

7.2 Systolic Processors

A systolic system consists of a set of interconnected cells, each capable of performing a simple operation. Information in such a system flows in a pipelined fashion and communication with the outside world only occurs at *boundary cells*. Systolic architectures

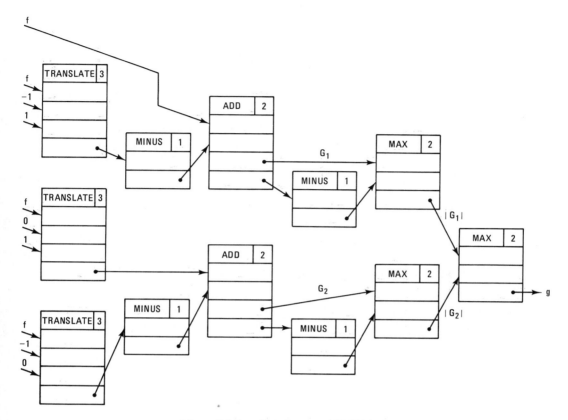

Figure 7.4 Data Flow Program Of ROBMAG

were designed to handle *compute-bound* types of applications. Here, the number of operations in a computation is large compared to the amount of input–output instructions. Ordinary matrix multiplication represents a compute-bound task.

An array of systolic cells will be implemented in this section to illustrate the ordinary matrix multiplication application. In this, as well as in any other application using systolic architectures, data are used effectively at each cell while being *pumped* from cell to cell along the structure. The synchronous pulsing of data is ensured at the algorithmic level by using an external clock.

A systolic array usually has a simple (geometric) structure involving local connections. Each cell performs simple identical tasks.

Each systolic cell in the following discussion operates in identical fashion. There are two inputs to each cell: an upper input x_i and a left input y_i:

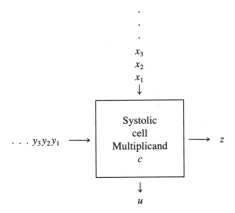

Outputs for each cell appear to the right (z) and below (u). The lower output equals the upper input unchanged, but delayed by one unit of time. The right output equals the sum of the left input with the product of c and the upper input. An execution trace follows.

After clock pulse 1 occurs, we have

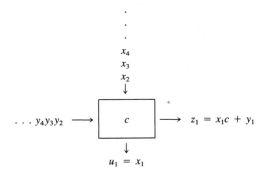

Upon the conclusion of the second clock pulse,

$$x_4$$
$$x_3$$
$$\downarrow$$

$$\ldots y_5 y_4 y_3 \longrightarrow \boxed{\quad c \quad} \longrightarrow z_2 = x_2 c + y_2$$

$$\downarrow$$
$$u_2 = x_2$$

and so on.

These cells are connected to perform various specialized operations. If this is done, each cell operates independently from one another in a synchronous fashion. An external clock is employed to ensure rhythmic operation of the systolic array with all processor operations in unison.

A cell can be connected in various ways, but usually the right (bottom) output of a cell is connected to the left (upper) input of another cell. To illustrate this horizontal connection, consider the following diagram:

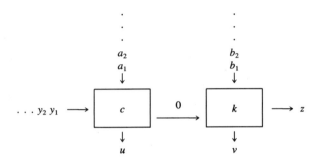

After the first clock pulse, we obtain

After the second clock pulse,

In general, after the nth clock pulse, $u_n = a_n$, $v_n = b_n$ and $z_n = y_{n-1} + a_{n-1}c + kb_n$. To reinforce these ideas, consider Example 7.3.

Example 7.3

We wish to form the product of two 2 by 2 matrices,

$$\begin{pmatrix} a_{11} & a_{12} \\ a_{21} & a_{22} \end{pmatrix} \begin{pmatrix} b_{11} & b_{12} \\ b_{21} & b_{22} \end{pmatrix} = \begin{pmatrix} c_{11} & c_{12} \\ c_{21} & c_{22} \end{pmatrix}$$

using a systolic array. Generalization to n by n matrices is immediate. First, we describe the way the input should be set up. This is followed by how the desired output is obtained. Finally, an execution trace is provided giving a step-by-step account of the input, the output, and each processor's status after every clock pulse.

The initial configuration is depicted in Figure 7.5. Only four inputs are illustrated in this diagram since four clock pulses would be needed to obtain the desired result. The output of the array will be as follows:

After clock pulse	4	3	2	1
Upper channel output	0	c_{12}	c_{11}	0
Lower channel output	c_{22}	c_{21}	0	0

This is seen in detail in Figures 7.6 through 7.9.

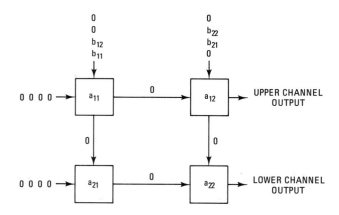

Figure 7.5 Initial Systolic Configuration

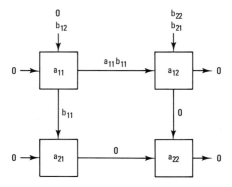

Figure 7.6 Systolic Configuration after 1st Clock Pulse

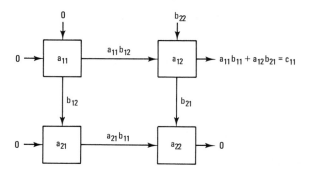

Figure 7.7 Systolic Configuration after 2nd Clock Pulse

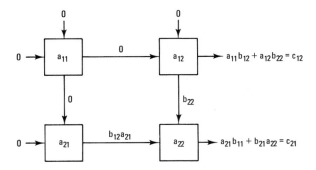

Figure 7.8 Systolic Configuration after 3rd Clock Pulse

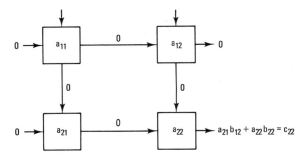

Figure 7.9 Systolic Configuration after 4th Clock Pulse

During the first clock pulse, b_{11} is utilized from the top in the upper-left systolic processor, and there is a zero input into all the other processors, thus giving the configuration of Figure 7.6 at the completion of the pulse. After the second clock pulse, the array is as given in Figure 7.7. We notice that the first desired output c_{11} appears from the upper channel. It has resulted from summing $a_{11}b_{11}$ (the left input) with the product of the multiplication of the upper input and a_{12}. After the third clock pulse, two more desired outputs are provided (Figure 7.8). When the fourth clock pulse is completed, we are left with the result in Figure 7.9.

7.3 Systolic Matrix Multiplication Using Block Diagrams

Block diagrams will now be utilized to rigorously specify the systolic matrix multiplication scheme described in Section 7.2. The input, or the set-up phase, is discussed first. Recall that the matrix

$$a = \begin{pmatrix} \textcircled{a_{11}} & a_{12} \\ a_{21} & a_{22} \end{pmatrix}$$

is to be postmultiplied by the matrix

$$b = \begin{pmatrix} \textcircled{b_{11}} & b_{12} \\ b_{21} & b_{22} \end{pmatrix}$$

to obtain the matrix

$$c = \begin{pmatrix} \textcircled{c_{11}} & c_{12} \\ c_{21} & c_{22} \end{pmatrix}$$

As can be seen, it is assumed that these matrices are bound, and the $(1, 1)$ elements of these matrices are located at the origin. Referring to Figure 7.5, it is seen that the matrix a is in the appropriate form for computation, but the matrix b is not. Thus, a $90°$ counterclockwise rotation of the matrix b is performed and the matrix f is obtained:

$$b \longrightarrow \boxed{\text{NINETY}} \longrightarrow f = \begin{pmatrix} b_{12} & b_{22} \\ \textcircled{b_{11}} & b_{21} \end{pmatrix}$$

The top inputs to the systolic processor are now in the proper form. The timing is taken care of by staggering the two columns of f. To do this, first use the selection operation to remove the first column from f:

$$f \longrightarrow \begin{array}{l} 2\rightarrow \\ 1\rightarrow \\ 0\rightarrow \\ 1\rightarrow \end{array} \boxed{\text{SELECT}} \longrightarrow g = \begin{pmatrix} b_{12} \\ \textcircled{b_{11}} \end{pmatrix}$$

Next, use the selection operator again to extract the second column of f:

$$f \longrightarrow \begin{array}{l} 2\rightarrow \\ 1\rightarrow \\ 1\rightarrow \\ 1\rightarrow \end{array} \boxed{\text{SELECT}} \longrightarrow q = \begin{pmatrix} * & b_{22} \\ \textcircled{$*$} & b_{21} \end{pmatrix}$$

Then translate q one pixel up:

$$q \longrightarrow \boxed{\text{TRAN}} \longrightarrow \text{TRAN}(q; 0, 1) = \begin{pmatrix} * & b_{22} \\ * & b_{21} \\ \circledast & * \end{pmatrix}$$

with inputs q, 0, 1 to the TRAN box.

Finally, using the extension operator on g and $\text{TRAN}(q; 0, 1)$ yields the top input to the systolic processor:

$$\begin{array}{c} g \longrightarrow \\ \text{TRAN}(q; 0, 1) \longrightarrow \end{array} \boxed{\text{EXTEND}} \longrightarrow l = \begin{pmatrix} * & * \\ * & b_{22} \\ b_{12} & b_{21} \\ \circled{b_{11}} & * \end{pmatrix}$$

In order to simplify notation, in the sequel we will write $f_{i,\,j}$ to denote the translation $\text{TRAN}(f; i, j)$. For instance, $\text{TRAN}(q; 0, 1)$ will be written as $q_{0,\,1}$.

The actual upper input to the systolic processor has zeros where there are stars inside l. An additional use of the extension operator provides zeros at the star locations in l and at locations $(0, -1)$ and $(1, -1)$.

$$\begin{array}{c} l \longrightarrow \\ \begin{pmatrix} 0 & 0 \\ 0 & 0 \\ 0 & 0 \\ \circledcirc & 0 \\ 0 & 0 \end{pmatrix} \longrightarrow \end{array} \boxed{\text{EXTEND}} \longrightarrow t = \begin{pmatrix} 0 & 0 \\ 0 & b_{22} \\ b_{12} & b_{21} \\ \circled{b_{11}} & 0 \\ 0 & 0 \end{pmatrix}$$

The multiplications for the systolic array occur at each clock pulse and involve the matrix a and translates of the matrix t. At the first clock pulse, we obtain

$$\begin{array}{c} a \longrightarrow \\ t \longrightarrow \end{array} \boxed{\text{MULT}} \longrightarrow i = \begin{pmatrix} a_{11}b_{11} & 0 \\ 0 & 0 \end{pmatrix}_{0,\,0}$$

Then lower the image t one pixel down:

$$\begin{array}{c} t \longrightarrow \\ 0 \longrightarrow \\ -1 \longrightarrow \end{array} \boxed{\text{TRAN}} \longrightarrow t_{0,\,-1} = \begin{pmatrix} 0 & 0 \\ 0 & b_{22} \\ \circled{b_{12}} & b_{21} \\ b_{11} & 0 \\ 0 & 0 \end{pmatrix}$$

The second clock pulse yields

$$\begin{array}{c} a \longrightarrow \\ t_{0,\,-1} \longrightarrow \end{array} \boxed{\text{MULT}} \longrightarrow j = \begin{pmatrix} a_{11}b_{12} & a_{12}b_{21} \\ a_{21}b_{11} & 0 \end{pmatrix}_{0,\,0}$$

Lowering the upper input to the systolic processors another pixel down gives

$$t_{0,-1} \longrightarrow \atop 0 \longrightarrow \atop -1 \longrightarrow \quad \boxed{\text{TRAN}} \quad \longrightarrow \quad t_{0,-2} = \begin{pmatrix} 0 & 0 \\ ⓪ & b_{22} \\ b_{12} & b_{21} \\ b_{11} & 0 \\ 0 & 0 \end{pmatrix}$$

Multiplying when the third clock pulse occurs provides

$$\begin{matrix} a \longrightarrow \\ t_{0,-2} \longrightarrow \end{matrix} \quad \boxed{\text{MULT}} \quad \longrightarrow \quad k = \begin{pmatrix} ⓪ & a_{12}b_{22} \\ a_{21}b_{12} & a_{22}b_{21} \end{pmatrix}$$

Translating $t_{0,-2}$ an additional unit down gives

$$\begin{matrix} t_{0,-2} \longrightarrow \\ 0 \longrightarrow \\ -1 \longrightarrow \end{matrix} \quad \boxed{\text{TRAN}} \quad \longrightarrow \quad t_{0,-3} = \begin{pmatrix} ⓪ & 0 \\ 0 & b_{22} \\ b_{12} & b_{21} \\ b_{11} & 0 \\ 0 & 0 \end{pmatrix}$$

A final multiplication provides the matrix

$$\begin{matrix} a \longrightarrow \\ t_{0,-3} \longrightarrow \end{matrix} \quad \boxed{\text{MULT}} \quad \longrightarrow \quad m = \begin{pmatrix} ⓪ & 0 \\ 0 & a_{22}b_{22} \end{pmatrix}$$

The output for the systolic array is obtained by translating and adding, using the matrices i, j, k, and m, followed by the EXTADD operation.

$$\begin{matrix} i \rightarrow \\ 3 \rightarrow \\ 0 \rightarrow \end{matrix} \quad \boxed{\text{TRAN}} \quad \rightarrow \begin{pmatrix} ⊛ & * & * & a_{11}b_{11} & 0 \\ * & * & * & 0 & 0 \end{pmatrix} = i_{3,0}$$

$j_{2,0}$ is the translate of j two units to the right:

$$\begin{matrix} j \rightarrow \\ 2 \rightarrow \\ 0 \rightarrow \end{matrix} \quad \boxed{\text{TRAN}} \quad \rightarrow \begin{pmatrix} ⊛ & * & a_{11}b_{12} & a_{12}b_{21} & * \\ * & * & a_{21}b_{11} & 0 & * \end{pmatrix} = j_{2,0}$$

$k_{1,0}$ is the one-pixel translate of k to the right:

$$\begin{matrix} k \rightarrow \\ 1 \rightarrow \\ 0 \rightarrow \end{matrix} \quad \boxed{\text{TRAN}} \quad \rightarrow \begin{pmatrix} ⊛ & 0 & a_{12}b_{22} & * & * \\ * & a_{21}b_{12} & a_{22}b_{21} & * & * \end{pmatrix} = k_{1,0}$$

The desired result is obtained by adding (see Section 1.10):

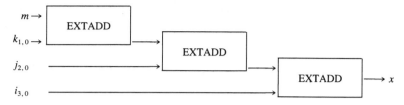

where

$$x = \begin{pmatrix} \textcircled{0} & 0 & a_{11}b_{12} + a_{12}b_{22} & a_{11}b_{11} + a_{12}b_{21} & 0 \\ 0 & a_{21}b_{12} + a_{22}b_{22} & a_{21}b_{11} + a_{22}b_{21} & 0 & 0 \end{pmatrix}$$

7.4 Wavefront Array Processors

Wavefront array processors fit right into the VLSI revolution. Once again, emphasis is placed on massive parallelism, simple connections, modular design, and regularity. Similar to the systolic array, a repetitive modular structure is insisted upon with localized communications. However, unlike systolic processors, there is no external clock, and, in fact, wavefront array processors perform their task in an asynchronous manner. Information is transmitted whenever it has been computed, and computing begins once all the operands are present. Thus, a wavefront array processor is also a data-flow processor. Wavefront array processors are a cross between a systolic processor and a data-flow processor; they make use of the best points of each.

The main objective of this section is to show how a wavefront processor processes information and to illustrate this on matrix multiplication, as was done using the systolic processors. It will be assumed that each cell is programmed to perform the same repetitive simple operation described next.

A wavefront array cell has two input channels, a left and a top. When both inputs are present, the processor multiplies the inputs together and adds the result onto the contents of an internal memory within the cell. The top input is shipped out to the bottom output, and the left input is transmitted out to the right output:

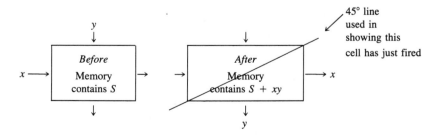

A powerful special-purpose data-flow computer results by connecting numerous cells together. A cell can fire only when both inputs are present. A 2 by 2 matrix multiplication is performed in Example 7.4; generalization to n by n matrices is immediate.

Example 7.4

If we want to use a wavefront array to perform the matrix multiplication

$$\begin{pmatrix} a_{11} & a_{12} \\ a_{21} & a_{22} \end{pmatrix} \begin{pmatrix} b_{11} & b_{12} \\ b_{21} & b_{22} \end{pmatrix}$$

and obtain the matrix

$$\begin{pmatrix} c_{11} & c_{12} \\ c_{21} & c_{22} \end{pmatrix}$$

the appropriate input scheme is illustrated in Figure 7.10. Note that the initial contents of each cell's internal memory is set equal to zero.

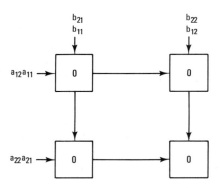

Figure 7.10 Initial Wave Front Array Process Conditions

The desired output for this processor appears inside each cell after all the inputs are used up, that is, after each cell has executed twice. Cells execute at different times from one another; there is no external clock. At the outset, only the leftmost, uppermost cell executes, since only it has both operands available (see Figure 7.11). Then all cells except the right-bottommost cell execute, as illustrated in Figure 7.12, which shows two waves of

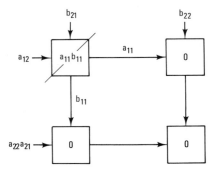

Figure 7.11 Upper-Left Cell Fired

information. Then all but the leftmost, uppermost cell executes, as depicted in Figure 7.13, and the waves move forward and down. Finally, the bottom-right cell executes for the second time. Now all the cells can be read and the results obtained (see Figure 7.14).

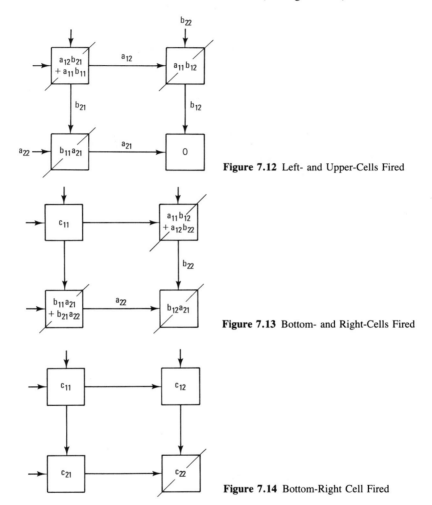

Figure 7.12 Left- and Upper-Cells Fired

Figure 7.13 Bottom- and Right-Cells Fired

Figure 7.14 Bottom-Right Cell Fired

7.5 Describing Wavefront Array Matrix Multiplication Using Block Diagrams

Again it is assumed that matrix

$$a = \begin{pmatrix} a_{11} & a_{12} \\ a_{21} & a_{22} \end{pmatrix}$$

and matrix

$$b = \begin{pmatrix} \textcircled{b_{11}} & b_{12} \\ b_{21} & b_{22} \end{pmatrix}$$

are to be multiplied to form matrix

$$c = \begin{pmatrix} \textcircled{c_{11}} & c_{12} \\ c_{21} & c_{22} \end{pmatrix}$$

using block diagrams and bound matrices. This is to be done in the same way as the wavefront array processor carries out the operations, as described in Section 7.4.

First, setting up the input occurs by using the rotation and flip operations in succession. Specifically, the top input f is found from the formula $f = \text{NINETY}[\text{FLIP}(b)]$: in detail, we have

$$b \quad \rightarrow \quad \boxed{\text{FLIP}} \quad \rightarrow \quad \begin{pmatrix} \textcircled{b_{11}} & b_{21} \\ b_{12} & b_{22} \end{pmatrix} \quad \rightarrow \quad \boxed{\text{NINETY}} \quad \rightarrow \quad \begin{pmatrix} b_{21} & b_{22} \\ \textcircled{b_{11}} & b_{12} \end{pmatrix} = f$$

Similarly, the left input to the systolic array is $g = \text{FLIP}[\text{NINETY}(a)]$:

$$a \quad \rightarrow \quad \boxed{\text{NINETY}} \quad \rightarrow \quad \begin{pmatrix} a_{12} & a_{22} \\ \textcircled{a_{11}} & a_{21} \end{pmatrix} \quad \rightarrow \quad \boxed{\text{FLIP}} \quad \rightarrow \quad \begin{pmatrix} a_{12} & \textcircled{a_{11}} \\ a_{22} & a_{21} \end{pmatrix} = g$$

Each cell executes twice, starting with the upper-left cell (see Figure 7.10). The result of the first execution is found by multiplying f and g; the result is $\alpha = \text{MULT}(f, g)$.

$$\begin{matrix} f & \longrightarrow \\ g & \longrightarrow \end{matrix} \quad \boxed{\text{MULT}} \quad \longrightarrow \quad \begin{pmatrix} a_{11}b_{11} & * \\ * & * \end{pmatrix}_{0,\,0} = \alpha$$

Now all but the bottom-right cell can execute. To describe this action, which we shall call β, using block diagrams, it will be necessary to flip the last column of f and the last row in g. If we let

$$u = \begin{pmatrix} b_{21} & b_{12} \\ \textcircled{b_{11}} & b_{22} \end{pmatrix}$$

and $\quad v = \begin{pmatrix} a_{12} & \textcircled{a_{11}} \\ a_{21} & a_{22} \end{pmatrix}$

then u can be obtained from b and f as follows:

$$b = \begin{pmatrix} \boxed{b_{11}} & b_{12} \\ b_{21} & b_{22} \end{pmatrix} \quad \begin{matrix} 2\to \\ 1\to \\ 1\to \\ 0\to \end{matrix} \boxed{\text{SELECT}} \longrightarrow \begin{pmatrix} \circledast & b_{12} \\ \ast & b_{22} \end{pmatrix}$$

$$\begin{matrix} 0 & \to \\ 1 & \to \end{matrix} \boxed{\text{TRAN}} \to \begin{pmatrix} \ast & b_{12} \\ \circledast & b_{22} \end{pmatrix} \longrightarrow \boxed{\text{EXTEND}} \to \begin{pmatrix} b_{21} & b_{12} \\ \boxed{b_{11}} & b_{22} \end{pmatrix} = u$$

$$f = \begin{pmatrix} b_{21} & b_{22} \\ \boxed{b_{11}} & b_{12} \end{pmatrix}$$

Similarly, v can be obtained from a and g:

$$a = \begin{pmatrix} \boxed{a_{11}} & a_{12} \\ a_{21} & a_{22} \end{pmatrix} \quad \begin{matrix} 1\to \\ 2\to \\ 0\to \\ -1\to \end{matrix} \boxed{\text{SELECT}} \longrightarrow \begin{pmatrix} \circledast & \ast \\ a_{21} & a_{22} \end{pmatrix}$$

$$\begin{matrix} -1 & \to \\ 0 & \to \end{matrix} \boxed{\text{TRAN}} \to \begin{pmatrix} \ast & \circledast \\ a_{21} & a_{22} \end{pmatrix} \to \boxed{\text{EXTEND}} \to \begin{pmatrix} a_{12} & \boxed{a_{11}} \\ a_{21} & a_{22} \end{pmatrix} = v$$

$$g = \begin{pmatrix} a_{12} & \boxed{a_{11}} \\ a_{22} & a_{21} \end{pmatrix} \to$$

Let β denote the output of the following block diagram:

$$\begin{matrix} u & \to \\ 0 & \to \\ -1 & \to \end{matrix} \boxed{\text{TRAN}} \to u_{0,-1} = \begin{pmatrix} \boxed{b_{21}} & b_{12} \\ b_{11} & b_{22} \end{pmatrix} \to \boxed{\text{MULT}}$$

$$\begin{matrix} v & \to \\ 1 & \to \\ 0 & \to \end{matrix} \boxed{\text{TRAN}} \to v_{1,0} = \begin{pmatrix} \boxed{a_{12}} & a_{11} \\ a_{21} & a_{22} \end{pmatrix} \to$$

$$\begin{pmatrix} a_{12}b_{21} & a_{11}b_{12} \\ a_{21}b_{11} & a_{22}b_{22} \end{pmatrix}_{0,\,0} \longrightarrow$$

$$[(0, 0), (0, -1), (1, 0)] \longrightarrow$$
$$[1, 1, 1] \longrightarrow \boxed{\text{CREATE}} \longrightarrow \boxed{\text{MULT}} \longrightarrow$$

$$\alpha = \begin{pmatrix} a_{11}b_{11} & \ast \\ \ast & \ast \end{pmatrix}_{0,\,0} \longrightarrow \boxed{\text{EXTADD}} \to \beta = \begin{pmatrix} \boxed{c_{11}} & a_{11}b_{12} \\ a_{21}b_{11} & \ast \end{pmatrix}$$

Now all cells except the top left cell can execute, and the result, γ, will be described using block diagrams. Before this is done, it will again be necessary to alter the matrices f and g for convenience. This time the first column of f will be flipped, as well as the first row of g. Let

$$x = \begin{pmatrix} b_{11} & b_{22} \\ b_{21} & b_{12} \end{pmatrix}$$

and

$$y = \begin{pmatrix} a_{11} & a_{12} \\ a_{22} & a_{21} \end{pmatrix}$$

Images x and y can be obtained from b and f, and a and g, respectively:

Now, let γ denote the output from the diagram:

$$
\begin{array}{l}
\begin{array}{c} x \rightarrow \\ 0 \rightarrow \\ -1 \rightarrow \end{array}
\boxed{\text{TRAN}} \rightarrow x_{0,\,-1} = \begin{pmatrix} \circled{b_{11}} & b_{22} \\ b_{21} & b_{12} \end{pmatrix} \rightarrow
\boxed{\text{MULT}} \rightarrow \begin{pmatrix} a_{11}b_{11} & a_{12}b_{22} \\ a_{22}b_{21} & a_{21}b_{12} \end{pmatrix}_{0,\,0}
\\[2em]
\begin{array}{c} y \rightarrow \\ 1 \rightarrow \\ 0 \rightarrow \end{array}
\boxed{\text{TRAN}} \rightarrow y_{1,\,0} = \begin{pmatrix} \circled{a_{11}} & a_{12} \\ a_{22} & a_{21} \end{pmatrix} \rightarrow
\end{array}
$$

$$
\begin{array}{c}
[(1,\,0),\,(0,\,-1),\,(1,\,-1)] \rightarrow \\
[1,\,1,\,1] \longrightarrow
\end{array}
\boxed{\text{CREATE}} \rightarrow
\boxed{\text{MULT}} \rightarrow
\boxed{\text{EXTADD}} \rightarrow \begin{pmatrix} \circled{c_{11}} & c_{12} \\ c_{21} & a_{21}b_{12} \end{pmatrix} = \gamma
$$

$$
\beta = \begin{pmatrix} \circled{c_{11}} & a_{11}b_{12} \\ a_{21}b_{11} & * \end{pmatrix} \rightarrow
$$

Finally, the right bottom cell can execute again. If this is done we obtain the desired output, δ. In block form:

$$
\begin{array}{l}
\begin{array}{c} f \rightarrow \\ -1 \rightarrow \\ -1 \rightarrow \end{array}
\boxed{\text{TRAN}} \rightarrow f_{-1,\,-1} = \begin{pmatrix} b_{21} & \circled{b_{22}} \\ b_{11} & b_{12} \end{pmatrix} \rightarrow
\boxed{\text{MULT}} \rightarrow \begin{pmatrix} a_{22}b_{22} & * \\ * & * \end{pmatrix}_{0,\,0}
\\[2em]
\begin{array}{c} g \rightarrow \\ 1 \rightarrow \\ 1 \rightarrow \end{array}
\boxed{\text{TRAN}} \rightarrow g_{1,\,1} = \begin{pmatrix} a_{12} & a_{11} \\ \circled{a_{22}} & a_{21} \end{pmatrix} \rightarrow
\end{array}
$$

$$
\begin{array}{c} 1 \rightarrow \\ -1 \rightarrow \end{array}
\boxed{\text{TRAN}} \rightarrow \begin{pmatrix} \circled{*} & * \\ * & a_{22}b_{22} \end{pmatrix} \rightarrow
\boxed{\text{EXTADD}} \rightarrow \begin{pmatrix} \circled{c_{11}} & c_{12} \\ c_{21} & c_{22} \end{pmatrix} = \delta
$$

$$
\gamma = \begin{pmatrix} \circled{c_{11}} & c_{12} \\ c_{21} & a_{21}b_{12} \end{pmatrix} \rightarrow
$$

Done!

The wavefront array matrix multiplication description just provided is one of the many rigorous operational specifications that could be realized using bound matrices and block diagrams. A type of data-transfer language is thus provided by the bound matrix and block diagram operations defined herein.

EXERCISES

7.1. Provide a data-flow description of the cross-product calculation of two vectors found in Section 6.17. Use activity packets as described in Figure 7.1 and illustrated in Figure 7.2.

7.2. Refer to the block diagrams of erosion, opening, and closing given in Figure 4.5. Give analogous data-flow diagrams using activity packets for each of these operations.

7.3. Generalize the systolic processing architecture given in Section 7.2 to handle 3 by 3 matrix multiplication.

7.4. As in Section 7.4, provide an in-depth block diagram representation for the 3 by 3 systolic matrix multiplication developed in Exercise 7.3.

7.5. A typical cell in the systolic architecture as described for matrix multiplication has a multiply add unit, along with internal memory. Furthermore, there are delay registers on the input and output to allow cells to function independently of their neighbors. How would a systolic cell design differ from the preceding if morphological operations were to be performed?

7.6. Provide a step-by-step block diagram description of the multiplication of the bound matrices

$$f = \begin{pmatrix} 1 & 2 \\ 3 & 4 \end{pmatrix}_{0,0}$$

and

$$g = \begin{pmatrix} 4 & 5 \\ 6 & 7 \end{pmatrix}_{0,0}$$

using the wavefront architecture approach. Set up the initial input bound matrices detailed in Section 7.5 and propagate the waves of information as described therein.

OPERATORS

Name	Section	Name	Section
ABS	2.4	HADTR	6.15
ADD	1.6	HIST	2.5
AREA	2.6	HISTEQUAL	2.6
AV	2.4	HOREDGE	3.2
AVERAG	5.2		
		IDCT	6.14
BETWEEN	2.1	IDFT	6.13
BOUND	5.3	IHADTR	6.15
		IMAGE	1.5
CARD	4.6	INSERT	1.11
CCONV	6.10	ISVDT	6.16
CCOR	6.13		
CLOSE	4.4	LAMBDA	4.7
COMPLEMENT	4.5	LESS	2.7
CONST	2.1	LOCALSM	2.7
COPY	5.4	LOCNOISE	2.7
CREATE	1.11	LOCSMOOTH	2.4
DCT	6.14	MATCH	5.4
DET	6.5	MAX	1.6
DFT	6.9	MAXDISK	4.9
DILATE	4.3	MAXNORM	3.4
DIV	1.7	MIN	1.6
DOMAIN	1.11	MINBOUND	1.5
DOT	2.2	MULT	1.6
DX	3.2		
DY	3.2	NINETY	1.9
		NINETY^2	1.9
EQUAL	2.1	NINETY^3	1.9
ERODE	4.3	NOISE	2.4
EXTADD	1.10	NORM	3.4
EXTEND	1.10		
EXTMAX	1.10	ONENORM	3.4
EXTMIN	1.10	OPEN	4.4
EXTMULT	1.10		
		PHI	4.6
FILL	5.3	PIXMAX	5.1
FILTER	2.3	PIXSUM	1.11
FLIP	1.9	POSTMLT	6.6
		PREMLT	6.6
GRADEDGE0	3.3	PREWEDGE0	3.4
GRADEDGE1	3.3	PREWEDGE1	3.4
GRADEDGE2	3.3	PREWEDGE2	3.4
GRADMAG0	3.3	PREWMAG0	3.4
GRADMAG1	3.3	PREWMAG1	3.4
GRADMAG2	3.3	PREWMAG2	3.4
GREATER	2.1	PRO	5.1
GROW	5.1	PSI	4.6

OPERATORS (continued)

Name	Section	Name	Section
RANGE	1.11	TEMPPRO	5.3
RANK	6.5	THREELEVEL	3.5
REST	2.2	THRESH	2.1
ROBMAG2	3.4	TRAN	1.8
		TRANSPOSE	6.5
SCALAR	1.6	TRUNC	2.1
SELECT	1.10	TWONORM	3.4
SKEL	4.9		
SMOOTH	2.2	VECTRAN	6.3
SQROOT	3.3	VERTEDGE	3.2
SQUARE	2.2	VERTRACK	5.1
SUB	1.7		
SUMSQ	5.4		
SVDT	6.16	X	1.12

APPENDIX

Numerous definitions and theorems from matrix theory are employed in Chapter 6. The purpose of this brief appendix is to summarize some of that theory's basic concepts.

A rectangular array of complex numbers consisting of m rows and n columns is called an m by n matrix over C, where C denotes the field of complex numbers. Though in most instances all entries in the matrix will be real, general definitions need to be given over C. An m by n matrix A will be denoted by

$$A = \begin{pmatrix} a_{11} & a_{12} & \cdots & a_{1n} \\ a_{21} & a_{22} & \cdots & a_{2n} \\ \vdots & \vdots & & \vdots \\ a_{m1} & a_{m2} & \cdots & a_{mn} \end{pmatrix}$$

For simplicity, we often write $A = (a_{ij})$.

If $A = (a_{ij})$ and $B = (b_{ij})$ are two m by n matrices, then the sum $A + B$ is the m by n matrix $C = (c_{ij})$, where $c_{ij} = a_{ij} + b_{ij}$. If t is any complex number (scalar), then the scalar multiple of A by t is the m by n matrix $D = (d_{ij})$, where $d_{ij} = ta_{ij}$. Both summation and scalar multiplication are defined componentwise.

Now suppose $A = (a_{ik})$ is an m by n matrix and $B = (b_{kj})$ is an n by p matrix. Then the product AB (also denoted $A \cdot B$) is the m by p matrix $C = (c_{ij})$, where for $i = 1, 2, \ldots, m$ and $j = 1, 2, \ldots, p$,

$$c_{ij} = \sum_{k=1}^{n} a_{ik} b_{kj} = a_{i1} b_{1j} + a_{i2} b_{2j} + \cdots + a_{in} b_{nj}.$$

The product of A and B can be formed if, and only if, the number of columns of A equals the number of rows of B.

Some fundamental properties pertaining to the above operations are:

1) $A + B = B + A$ (commutativity of $+$)
2) $(A + B) + C = A + (B + C)$ (associativity of $+$)
3) $(AB)C = A(BC)$ (associativity of $\cdot$)
   (assuming the products exist)
4) $t(A + B) = tA + tB$ (distributivity)
5) $(t + s)A = tA + sA$ (distributivity)

It should be noted that matrix multiplication is not commutative even if both products exist; in other words, it is not true in general that $AB = BA$.

Example A.1

Let

$$A = \begin{pmatrix} 2 & 4 & 0 \\ 3 & -2 & 1 \end{pmatrix}, \quad B = \begin{pmatrix} -1 & 5 & 3 \\ 0 & 2 & 1 \end{pmatrix}, \quad C = \begin{pmatrix} 3 & 4 \\ 1 & 2 \\ 2 & 0 \end{pmatrix}$$

Then

$$A + B = \begin{pmatrix} 1 & 9 & 3 \\ 3 & 0 & 2 \end{pmatrix} \quad \text{and} \quad BC = \begin{pmatrix} 8 & 6 \\ 4 & 4 \end{pmatrix}.$$

Moreover,

$$3A = \begin{pmatrix} 6 & 12 & 0 \\ 9 & -6 & 3 \end{pmatrix}.$$

There are many special types of matrices. A square matrix has an equal number of rows and columns. If A is square with n rows and columns, A is said to be of dimension n. A diagonal matrix is a square matrix that has nonzero entries only on the main diagonal. These are the entries a_{ij} where $i = j$. The *identity* matrix of dimension n is the n by n diagonal matrix such that $a_{ii} = 1$ for $i = 1, 2, \ldots, n$. It is denoted by I. For any square matrix A of dimension n, $AI = IA = A$. Matrix B is *scalar* if it is a scalar multiple of I: $B = tI$ for some complex number t. A triangular matrix is a square matrix that has all zeros either above the main diagonal or below the main diagonal. In the first case it is called *lower diagonal* and in the second case *upper diagonal*. For an upper diagonal matrix, $a_{ij} = 0$ for $i > j$.

Given a square matrix A, we define A^k (the kth power of A) to be the product $AA \cdots A$, where there are k terms in the product. The matrix A is said to be *idempotent* if $A^2 = A$. It is *nilpotent of index* q if $A^q = \bar{0}$, but $A^{q-1} \neq \bar{0}$, where $\bar{0}$ is the matrix consisting of all 0 entries.

The *transpose* of a square matrix $A = (a_{ij})$ is defined by $A' = (b_{ij})$, where $b_{ij} = a_{ji}$; in other words, the rows of A' are the columns of B and the columns of A' are the rows of B. Fundamental properties of the transpose are $(A')' = A$, $(A + B)' = A' + B'$ and $(AB)' = B'A'$. The square matrix A is said to be symmetric if $A' = A$. It is *skew-symmetric* if $A' = -A$.

Before proceeding, we need to understand when a collection of vectors are linearly independent. Let $V_1, V_2, \ldots, V_r$ be a set of r vectors, each of them having n components. The collection is *linearly dependent* if there exists scalars $t_1, t_2, \ldots, t_n$, not all zero, such that

$$t_1 V_1 + t_2 V_2 + \cdots + t_n V_n = 0,$$

where 0 denotes the zero vector. The vector sum to the left of the equality sign is called a *linear combination*. If there does not exist a linear combination, not all scalars zero, which equals the zero vector, then $V_1, V_2, \ldots, V_n$ are said to be *linearly independent*.

Example A.2

The 3-vectors $V_1 = (2, 3, 4)$, $V_2 = (-1, 6, 3)$ and $V_3 = (4, 21, 18)$ are linearly dependent since

$$3V_1 + 2V_2 + (-1)V_3 = 0.$$

The collection V_1, V_2, and $V_4 = (1, 1, 1)$ is linearly independent. To see this, suppose there exist constants a, b, and c such that $aV_1 + bV_2 + cV_4 = (0, 0, 0)$. Then a, b, and c satisfy the three simultaneous equations:

$$2a - b + c = 0$$

$$3a + 6b + c = 0$$

$$4a + 3b + c = 0$$

The only solution of this system is given by $a = b = c = 0$. Hence, the vectors are linearly independent.

Let A be an m by n matrix. Then the *rank* of A is the maximal number of linearly independent row (or column) vectors of A. The rank of A is denoted by $r(A)$, and A is said to be of full rank whenever $A = n$ or m.

Now suppose A is a square matrix of dimension n. A is said to be *nonsingular* if there exists square matrix B of dimension n such that $AB = I$. A is said to be *singular* if such a matrix B does not exist. If $AB = I$, then it must be true that $BA = I$. Moreover, the following conditions are equivalent for an n by n matrix A:

1) A is nonsingular
2) $r(A) = n$
3) The rows of A are linearly independent.

If A is nonsingular and B is also square of dimension n, then $r(AB) = r(BA) = r(B)$. A consequence of this last point is that AB is nonsingular if, and only if, A and B are *both* nonsingular. Suppose A is nonsingular and $AC = CA = I$. Then C is called the *inverse* of A and it is denoted by A^{-1}. If A and B are both nonsingular, then $(AB)^{-1} = B^{-1}A^{-1}$. If $A' = A^{-1}$, then A is called an *orthogonal* matrix.

In order to avoid undue theoretical difficulties, the *determinant* of an n by n square matrix A can be introduced inductively by *cofactors*. If A is 1 by 1, $A = (a_{11})$, then the determinant of A is given by $\det(A) = a_{11}$. Now suppose $A = (a_{ij})$ is n by n, where $n \geq 2$. Then for any i and j between 1 and n, the cofactor of a_{ij} is defined by

$$\vdots \, A_{ij} \, \vdots \, = (-1)^{i+j} \det(A_{\langle i, j \rangle}),$$

where $A_{\langle i, j \rangle}$ is the $n - 1$ by $n - 1$ matrix obtained from A by deleting the ith row and the jth column. Inductively define the determinant of A by

$$\det(A) = \sum_{j=1}^{n} a_{ij} \, \vdots \, A_{ij} \, \vdots$$

for fixed i. This is a cofactor expansion using the ith row and it is well defined since every row cofactor expansion gives the same value. We also use column cofactor expansions:

$$\det(A) = \sum_{i=1}^{n} a_{ij} \, \vdots \, A_{ij} \, \vdots$$

for fixed j. Note that for the 2 by 2 matrix

$$A = \begin{pmatrix} a_{11} & a_{12} \\ a_{21} & a_{22} \end{pmatrix},$$

cofactor expansion by the first row yields

$$\det(A) = a_{11} \mid A_{11} \mid + a_{12} \mid A_{12} \mid$$

$$= a_{11}(-1)^{1+1} \det((a_{22})) + a_{12}(-1)^{1+2} \det((a_{21}))$$

$$= a_{11}a_{22} - a_{12}a_{21},$$

which is exactly what we should get for a 2 by 2 determinant.

Example A.3

Find the determinant of

$$A = \begin{pmatrix} 2 & 3 & 1 \\ 1 & 4 & -3 \\ 1 & 3 & -1 \end{pmatrix}$$

A cofactor expansion by the second row yields

$$\det(A) = a_{21} \mid A_{21} \mid + a_{22} \mid A_{22} \mid + a_{23} \mid A_{23} \mid$$

$$= 1\,(-1)^{2+1} \det \begin{pmatrix} 3 & 1 \\ 3 & -1 \end{pmatrix} + 4\,(-1)^{2+2} \det \begin{pmatrix} 2 & 1 \\ 1 & -1 \end{pmatrix}$$

$$+ (-3)\,(-1)^{2+3} \det \begin{pmatrix} 2 & 3 \\ 1 & 3 \end{pmatrix}$$

$$= 1\,(-1)\,(-6) + 4\,(1)\,(-3) + (-3)\,(-1)\,3 = 3.$$

Some important properties of determinants follow:

1) $\det(A') = \det(A)$.
2) $\det(AB) = \det(A)\det(B)$.
3) If $A^\wedge$ is obtained from A by interchanging two columns, then $\det(A^\wedge) = -\det(A)$.
4) A is nonsingular if, and only if, $\det(A) \neq 0$.
5) If A is nonsingular, then $\det(A^{-1}) = 1/\det(A)$.

The determinant is useful for finding the inverse of a nonsingular matrix. First, define the *adjoint* of an n by n matrix $A = (a_{ij})$ to be the n by n matrix $A^* = (a_{ij}^*)$, where $a_{ij}^* = \mid A_{ji} \mid$, the cofactor of a_{ji}. Now, if A is nonsingular, then its inverse is given by

$$A^{-1} = \frac{1}{\det(A)} A^*.$$

Example A.4

Let A be the matrix of Example A.3. Then

$$A^{-1} = \frac{1}{3}\begin{pmatrix} 5 & 6 & -13 \\ -2 & -3 & 7 \\ -1 & -3 & 5 \end{pmatrix} = \begin{pmatrix} \frac{5}{3} & 2 & -\frac{13}{3} \\ -\frac{2}{3} & -1 & \frac{7}{3} \\ -\frac{1}{3} & -1 & \frac{5}{3} \end{pmatrix}$$

Any nonzero vector V that is a solution of the matrix equation $AV = tV$, where t is some scalar and A is n by n, is called an *eigenvector* of A. To keep the dimensions correct in AV, V is written in column iorm. The scalar t is called the *eigenvalue* of A associated with V. This equation reduces to $AV - tV = 0$, and then to

$$(A - tI)V = 0.$$

But the equation has nonzero solutions if, and only if, $A - tI$ is singular. It is now equivalent to

$$\det(A - tI) = 0,$$

and is now the characteristic equation of A. Expanding as a determinant, $\det(A - tI)$ is a polynomial in t. Consequently, $\det(A - tI)$ is called the *characteristic polynomial* of the matrix A.

Example A.5

Let

$$A = \begin{pmatrix} 2 & 3 \\ 1 & 4 \end{pmatrix}$$

The characteristic equation, $\det(A - tI) = 0$, is given by

$$\det\begin{pmatrix} 2 - t & 3 \\ 1 & 4 - t \end{pmatrix} = 0,$$

which reduces to

$$t^2 - 6t + 5 = 0.$$

Solving for t gives two eigenvalues, $t_1 = 1$ and $t_2 = 5$. To find corresponding eigenvectors, let

$$V = \begin{pmatrix} u \\ v \end{pmatrix}$$

and solve $AV - tV = 0$ for both values of t. For t_1, solve

$$\begin{pmatrix} 2 & 3 \\ 1 & 4 \end{pmatrix}\begin{pmatrix} u \\ v \end{pmatrix} - \begin{pmatrix} u \\ v \end{pmatrix} = \begin{pmatrix} 0 \\ 0 \end{pmatrix}$$

This matrix equation produces two simultaneous equations:

$$u + 3v = 0$$

$$u + 3v = 0$$

Many solutions to these simultaneous equations exist; however, each solution vector is a scalar multiple of any other. An eigenvector for $t_1 = 1$ is given by

$$V_1 = \begin{pmatrix} -3 \\ 1 \end{pmatrix}$$

An eigenvector for $t_2 = 5$ is given by

$$V_2 = \begin{pmatrix} 1 \\ 1 \end{pmatrix}$$

In the preceding example it was shown that any scalar multiple of V_1 is also an eigenvector for t_1. This applies to V_2 and t_2 since the eigenvectors associated with a given eigenvalue, together with the zero vector, form a subspace. In other words, if V and W are eigenvectors with eigenvalue t, and r and s are scalars, then $rV + sW$ is also an eigenvector with eigenvalue t.

If the m by n matrix A, the m by p matrix B, the k by n matrix C and the k by p matrix D are written as an array

$$E = \begin{pmatrix} A & B \\ C & D \end{pmatrix}$$

then E is interpreted as an $m + k$ by $n + p$ matrix whose entries are the elements of A, B, C, and D in the positions symbolized above.

Example A.6

Let

$$A = \begin{pmatrix} 3 \\ -1 \end{pmatrix}, \quad B = \begin{pmatrix} 3 & -1 \\ 4 & 5 \end{pmatrix},$$

$$C = (7), \quad D = (2 \quad 3)$$

then

$$E = \left(\begin{array}{c|cc} 3 & 3 & -1 \\ -1 & 4 & 5 \\ \hline 7 & 2 & 3 \end{array} \right)$$

The matrices A, B, C, and D are often called the blocks of E, and the array itself is referred to as a partition of E. Moreover, the matrices A, B, C, and D may consist of other blocks.

The *direct* or *Kronecker product* $A \circledR B$ of a n by m matrix A with a p by q matrix B is denoted as

$$
A \ \textcircled{K} \ B = \begin{pmatrix} a_{11}B & a_{12}B & \ldots & a_{1m}B \\ a_{21}B & a_{22}B & \ldots & a_{2m}B \\ \vdots & \vdots & & \vdots \\ a_{n1}B & a_{n2}B & \ldots & a_{nm}B \end{pmatrix}
$$

Example A.7

Let

$$
A = \begin{pmatrix} 2 & 1 \\ 3 & 4 \end{pmatrix} \quad \text{and} \quad B = \begin{pmatrix} -1 & 4 \\ 2 & 5 \end{pmatrix}
$$

then

$$
A \ \textcircled{K} \ B = \left(\begin{array}{cc:cc} -2 & 8 & -1 & 4 \\ 4 & 10 & 2 & 5 \\ \hdashline -3 & 12 & -4 & 16 \\ 6 & 15 & 8 & 20 \end{array} \right)
$$

Some simple properties of the Kronecker product are given next. In the following discussion, α is a scalar and all matrices are square.

1) $(\alpha A) \ \textcircled{K} \ B = A \ \textcircled{K} \ (\alpha B) = \alpha A \ \textcircled{K} \ B$
2) $(A \ \textcircled{K} \ B) \ \textcircled{K} \ C = A \ \textcircled{K} \ (B \ \textcircled{K} \ C)$
3) $(A + B) \ \textcircled{K} \ C = A \ \textcircled{K} \ C + B \ \textcircled{K} \ C$
4) $A \ \textcircled{K} \ (B + C) = A \ \textcircled{K} \ B + A \ \textcircled{K} \ C$
5) $(A \ \textcircled{K} \ B)' = A' \ \textcircled{K} \ B'$
6) $(A \ \textcircled{K} \ B)(C \ \textcircled{K} \ D) = (AC) \ \textcircled{K} \ (BD)$

A *pseudo-inverse* of a (real) matrix A is a matrix A^+, which satisfies a, b, c, and d, given next:

a) $A \ A^+ \ A = A$
b) $A^+ \ A \ A^+ = A^+$
c) $(A^+ A)' = A^+ A$
d) $(A \ A^+)' = A \ A^+$

The pseudo-inverse of a given matrix A is always unique and is found by a simple factorization procedure. If $A = 0$, then $A^+ = 0$. If A is an m by n matrix of rank r greater than zero, then A can be written as $A = B \cdot C$, where B is an m by r matrix and C is an r by n matrix, both of rank r. The matrix B is often chosen as the r linearly independent columns of A. The matrix C is determined by satisfying the factorization relation $A = B \cdot C$ previously given. The pseudo-inverse is

$$A^+ = C'(C\,C')^{-1}\,(B'\,B)^{-1}\,B'$$

Of particular importance is the situation where $m \geq n$ and A is of full rank. In this case, $r = n$, and B can be made equal to A; therefore, $C = I$. Consequently,

$$A^+ = (B'\,B)^{-1}\,B'.$$

In any case, the system of equations corresponding to the matrix equation $Ax = y$ always has a least squares solution given by $\hat{x} = A^+y$. It is a least squares solution since if we let $\varepsilon = y - Ax$, then $\hat{x}$ minimizes the scalar quantity $\varepsilon'\varepsilon$. When A is of full rank and $m \geq n$, then $\hat{x} = A^+y = (A'\,A)^{-1}\,A'\,y$ is the unique least squares solution. Finally, if $m = n$ and A is of full rank, then

$$A^+ = A^{-1}$$

INDEX